Stream Based Design of Distributed Systems through Refinement

Dissertation

zur Erlangung des akademischen Grades
Doktorin der Naturwissenschaften
der Technisch-Naturwissenschaftlichen Fakultät
der Universität zu Lübeck

vorgelegt von

Annette Stümpel

geboren in Hildesheim

Lübeck
2003

Bibliografische Information Der Deutschen Bibliothek

Die Deutsche Bibliothek verzeichnet diese Publikation in der Deutschen
Nationalbibliografie; detaillierte bibliografische Daten sind im Internet über
http://dnb.ddb.de abrufbar.

ISBN 3-8325-0462-1

Logos Verlag Berlin
Comeniushof, Gubener Str. 47,
10243 Berlin
Tel.: +49 030 42 85 10 90
Fax: +49 030 42 85 10 92
INTERNET: http://www.logos-verlag.de

Abstract

The objective of this thesis is to develop a stream based framework for the design of components in distributed systems by stepwise refinement. We view a distributed system as a network of asynchronously communicating components connected by unidirectional channels. In our setting, the communication history on a channel is modelled by a stream of messages. A component is described by a stream processing function mapping input histories to output histories. We present five different notions of refinement, viz. state refinement, property refinement, interface refinement, architecture refinement, and communication refinement. Our main focus lies on the systematic introduction of states. The other notions of refinement are investigated with particular attention to their cooperation with state refinement.

The first part of the thesis deals with *state refinement* which conducts the systematic transition from the functional input / output behaviour of a component to a finer state oriented description based on internal state transitions. As a state-based computational model for communicating components we introduce state transition machines with input and output, which are Mealy machines liberated from the finite state space and the restriction of producing exactly one datum with each transition.

Each component whose behaviour is specified by a stream processing function can canonically be implemented as a state transition machine which records the previous input history in its state. We present concepts how to obtain state transition machines with a more compact state space by identifying input histories which have the same effect on the future behaviour of a component. The key for the introduction of states are history abstractions. With the choice of the history abstraction, the operations of the state transition machine are uniquely determined on the set of reachable states. Besides the formal foundations, we present a methodology for state refinement. In particular, the proposed technique is also applicable to components which asynchronously process input from different channels.

Property refinement narrows the set of possible behaviours of a component which arise from underspecification or nondeterminism. Underspecification on erroneous input streams can well be resolved after the introduction of states. Components which operate properly only after an initialization phase are refined by state transition machines without a determined initial state. The extension of a behaviour which is only specified for infinite input histories to finite input histories is realized by an order-theoretic method.

Interface refinement changes the representation of the input and output histories of a component using representation and abstraction functions, respectively. We show how the refinement of the input interface and of the output interface cooperates with state refinements.

The thesis completes with a survey on *architecture refinement* adapting the structure of networks built from communicating components. We obtain *communication refinement*, which changes the communication mode for a connection between two components, as an application of architecture refinement steps.

The applicability of the introduced concepts is demonstrated by the systematic development of a bounded buffer. The introduced refinement steps are powerful enough to realize a complete development of an interactive component guided by design decisions.

The thesis shows that the stream based framework supports the formal development process of distributed systems. Stream processing can bridge several views of the system under design. In particular, the state refinements introduced in this thesis close the gap between extensional system specifications based on the input / output behaviour and state oriented specification formalisms.

Acknowledgement

I wish to thank all those people who have directly or indirectly helped me in developing this thesis.

First of all, I have to thank my supervisor Prof. Walter Dosch for guiding me through my research. From him I learned much more than how to do scientific research in computer science. Furthermore, I would like to thank Prof. Dieter Hogrefe for co-refereeing the thesis.

I am indebted to my colleagues from the Institute of Software Technology and Programming Languages at the University of Lübeck, Bastian Dölle, Clemens Grelck, Sönke Magnussen, Andreas Vox, and Bernd Wiedemann for fruitful discussions. The quality of the thesis benefitted from their comments on parts of draft versions. Special thanks go to Dietmar Wolf for reliably keeping my technical working environment running. All my colleagues, including Magnus Bornemann and the secretaries Hedwig Hellkamp and Kathrin Janfeld, contributed to the warm and friendly atmosphere in the group, not only by supplying cake, chocolate, gummi bears, liquorice, and other sweets.

Finally, I thank my parents and my sister for continuous motivation and encouragement. In particular, my dear friend Christoph patiently supported me through every single month which was supposed to be the "last month before the submission of the thesis".

v

Contents

List of Examples

Chapter 1

Introduction

The design of distributed systems is a challenging and error prone task. Malfunctions and failures do not only cause annoyance, but also economical damage, and may even endanger human lives. The high complexity of the development task in connection with limited time, tight budgets and a shortage of excellently trained developers requires a well-structured development process supported by sound concepts, effective methods, and reliable tools.

During the development process, a system is stepwisely refined from a problem oriented specification towards a distributed implementation. This procedure interleaves design decisions, transformations, and routine coding. We aim at liberating developers from some routine work so that they can concentrate on the design decisions. For that purpose, we need to explicate the design decisions which underlie an implementation. With this basis, we develop refinement rules which preserve the correctness of development steps. Such a rule distils the design decision which initiates the respective refinement step, and it determines the specification resulting from the design decision. We classify the development steps according to the view of the system under design. In particular, we investigate concepts for a systematic introduction of states. Furthermore, we investigate property refinement and interface refinement steps, and finally, we introduce architecture and communication refinement. The suggested formalism for the description of behaviours supporting different views of the system is stream processing.

In the following, we place the contents of the thesis in the context of established concepts, methodologies, terminology, and formalisms.

1

1.1   Distributed Systems

A *system* combines cooperating components which continuously exchange information by communication. A component may not only receive messages from and deliver messages to other components, but also from and to the environment.

A system is structured *hierarchically*, if its components are again composed of interacting components and become subsystems that way. *Compositionality* allows for hierarchical system design, and supports the analysis and reuse of subsystems. Compositionality is indispensable, because, in general, a system cannot be modelled together with its complete environment as the environment itself is often a complex system.

According to [LL90], "In the term distributed computing, the word distributed means spread out across space". In such a spatially *distributed system* the processing units may, for example, be spread on a chip, on different continents, or in outer space. The processing units work unsynchronized and independently of each other, that means they run *concurrently* [WN95] and can only synchronize by communication.

Fundamental for a systematic development is a *specification*, that is a description of the expected behaviour, which helps developers and customers understand the system under design. Moreover, it is easier to validate a specification than an implementation, because the former carries no complicating implementation overhead. An idealistic specification method allows to design a system employing different levels of abstraction, and to address different aspects, such as correctness, reliability, liveness, security, timing, performance, in separated, yet related formalisms. An adequate specification technique should only incorporate aspects which are considered to be observable in the respective view.

For an action-based view, process algebras are used. Among the state-based specification techniques, the hierarchical statecharts [Har87] including its derivatives such as UML state diagrams, and SDL [EHS97] are outstanding. One of the most prominent specification techniques for distributed systems are classical Petri nets [Rei98], which do not allow for compositional system design. A compositional extension of Petri nets [BFH+98, BL99] labels arrows with CCS-actions.

Our Approach to Specifying and Developing Distributed Systems

Our approach to the specification of distributed systems concentrates on the components, cf. Figure 1.1, and their communication. Therefore, we

Figure 1.1: Interactive component

provide a formalism for the description of the input / output behaviour of a component and a composition technique for the static network, cf. Figure 1.2.

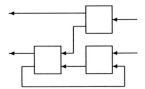

Figure 1.2: Distributed system

Our interpretation of components is wider than the idea of a component in a spatially distributed system. We see a component as a conceptual unit taking over a designated task of a system. So, processes executing several components could run on the same processing unit.

Unlike classical programs, an *interactive component* does not receive its complete input before starting to operate. The environment can permanently interact with the component in the sense that the environment can deliver more input in reaction to output from the component, as in a *reactive system*. Moreover, the component can request further input from the environment. Interaction in the classical sense is more than man-machine interaction. The impact of interaction is a widely discussed topic, see for example [Weg97], which is opposed by [PR98] and defended in [Weg98].

In our model the components communicate asynchronously via unidirectional channels. Synchronous systems are asynchronous systems with assumptions about relative process execution speeds and / or message delivery delays. [Sch93] takes the same line: "Postulating that a system is asynchronous is a non-assumption. Every system is asynchronous". *Synchronization* of components can only be achieved by (asynchronous) communication.

Our level of abstraction makes it possible, for example, to model the functional aspects of communication protocols, hardware components, routing, load balancing. It leaves aside aspects and requirements such as performance, physical transmission media, mobility, and user interfaces.

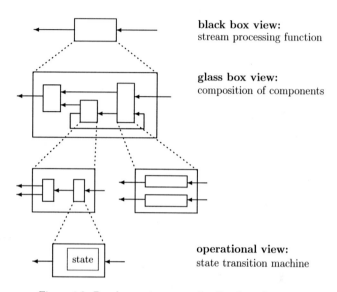

black box view:
stream processing function

glass box view:
composition of components

operational view:
state transition machine

Figure 1.3: Development process of a distributed system

The idealistic *top down development* process, cf. Figure 1.3, starts with a high-level description of the input / output behaviour of the system under development. This description neither fixes the composition structure nor does it impose an internal state. Such an external view of the system is therefore called a *black box* view. In subsequent development steps the system is decomposed into communicating subsystems. This view discloses the internal structure of the system and leads to a *glass box* view. Since our formalism is compositional, the subsystems can be developed independently. When the behaviour of a component is simple enough for a direct implementation, then the component is equipped with an internal state and state transitions which constitute an *operational* view.

1.2   Refinement

In a top down development of a complex system, its description is step by step enriched by more and more properties, details, and requirements until the description is suitable for a direct implementation. The systematic stepwise conversion of a system is called *refinement*.

A refinement step is the transformation of a representation of a system into a finer, that is more concrete related representation. The correctness of a refinement step can be established by construction through formal transformation [Fea87, Par90] or by an a posteriori verification. The notion of correctness depends on the view of the system. Refinement is closely related to a notion of observability, for example total / partial correctness [Dij76], internal events [Mil89], or stuttering equivalences [NV95].

Traditionally, refinement was restricted to pure *data refinement* [Hoa72, BD00]. Later on, [BvW90, Bac90, BvW98] introduce a refinement calculus for specifications based on state updates through commands and actions. [AL91, SL90] investigate refinement for specifications which are sequences of states. In process algebras, an action is refined into a process with an *action refinement* step [AH93, Huh97]. Refinement notions for distributed systems specified in the setting of stream processing were first introduced in [Bro93b].

A specification can be refined with regard to several aspects of a system.

Property refinement Property refinement, often also called *behavioural refinement*, may restrict the set of observable behaviours of a system.

Interface refinement A property refinement step relates system descriptions with the same interface, whereas an interface refinement step allows to change the system's interface towards the environment.

Communication refinement The communication between components can be considered from different levels of abstraction ranging from the abstract application layer to the physical layer considering bits. Communication refinement changes the granularity of interaction and thus supports the transition from abstract layers to more concrete layers.

State refinement The introduction of a state space and of transitions associated with actions between these states is a crucial step for transforming a specification into an implementation. The introduction and improvement of a state-based description is captured by state refinement.

Architecture refinement The decomposition of a system into subsystems or the restructuring of a system are conducted by architecture refinement.

Property, interface, and communication refinement modify the external view of the system. State and architecture refinement leave the input / output behaviour unchanged and increase the granularity instead. They change the internal structure of the component which is generally not observable in the external view.

Contribution of the Thesis to the Field of Refinement

We analyse refinement concepts for distributed systems based on their components in the setting of stream processing. The observability criterion for correctness is the input / output behaviour. Our refinement techniques are compositional: the local refinement of a component effects a refinement of the entire system.

A refinement step is initiated by a design decision. The refined specification is obtained by transformation and derivation instead of formal verification or systematic testing.

For each notion of refinement, viz. state, property, interface, communication, and architecture refinement, we give a definition, analyse its algebraic and compositional properties, highlight its significance during the development process and investigate some characteristic fields of application heading towards a formal design methodology based on refinement. Thereby we focus on state refinement, because the largely unexplored transition from a functional to a state-based view is crucial for an efficient implementation. Furthermore, state refinement is often the key to other refinements. For the remaining notions of refinement, we investigate their cooperation with state refinement.

1.3   Stream Processing

According to [Lan65] streams are lists with "special properties related to the sequencing of evaluation", later called lazy lists. [Bur75] investigates lists, streams and examples for functions operating on streams. Networks of communicating components were first described with functions on streams by [Kah74]. The subsequent paper [KM77] focusses on the underlying language. [Bro86] is the origin of system modelling with relations on streams.

These approaches laid the basis for mathematical semantics in the field of dataflow [Den85], for example for the functional dataflow language Lucid [WA85] which exploits the capabilities of the architecture of dataflow machines, or the applicative single assignment language Sisal [FCO90].

Streams are not only used for system modelling. For example, [Rut01] gives a coalgebraic definition of streams and investigates proof methods for streams. Runs and traces can be considered as streams of actions or states. In that context, some properties of streams can be described with temporal logics [Eme90]. An overview on the history of stream processing can be found in [Ste97]. [BS01b] gives a survey of the state of the art about system modelling with streams.

Our Application of Stream Processing

We apply stream processing for modelling the behaviour of a system by recording the communication between the system's components in the style of [Kah74]. We employ streams to sum up the communication histories on unidirectional channels in distributed systems. Communication modelling with streams abstracts from the point of time of messages and records only the temporal succession of messages on each communication line.

The functional behaviour of continuously communicating components is described by stream processing functions mapping input histories to output histories. Specifying systems with stream processing functions is compositional and thus supports modularity in a bottom up construction as well as a top down development.

Primarily, stream processing functions describe the black box view of a system. The stream processing framework also supports specifications with different degrees of abstraction, for example, the state transition view disclosing the internal state of the component, and the event-based view recording the sequence of input events, output events and possibly internal events such as state changes. The transition from a state-based to a stream-based specification is introduced in [BP00a, Bro00]. However, for a top down development the transition from a stream processing function to a state-based description seems more relevant.

The stream processing framework can serve as a semantic basis for the specification of distributed systems. We build such a formal semantic basis and develop refinement concepts on top of it.

1.4 Outline

The thesis is structured as follows. Chapter 2 surveys the foundations for streams modelling communication histories, stream processing functions modelling components, and the composition of stream processing functions modelling networks.

The focus of the thesis lies on state refinement which is treated in Chapters 3 to 8. Chapters 3 and 4 present the formal foundation and the concepts for a systematic state introduction for stream processing functions. In Chapter 3 we introduce state transition machines with input and output as a computational model for continuously processing state-based components. Chapter 4 gives a definition for state refinement guaranteeing that each stream processing function possesses a canonical state refinement which accumulates the complete previous input history in its states. We propose a construction technique for state refinements based on history abstractions recording the information of an input history which may have an effect on the future behaviour of a component.

Chapters 5 to 7 deal with a methodology for state refinement. Chapter 5 contains some characteristic applications of state refinement driven by various history abstractions. In Chapter 6, state refinement for stream processing functions validating a decomposition property is investigated. Chapter 7 specializes on control states and proposes methods how to introduce them. In Chapter 8, the presented concepts are generalized to infinite input and output streams and to stream processing functions with several input streams and several output streams.

The second part treats further notions of refinement. Chapter 9 introduces techniques for the description and resolution of underspecification, and for the specification and reduction of nondeterminism. In particular, we show how property refinement and state refinement commute. In Chapter 10, the definition and methodology for interface refinement is presented. We investigate input interface refinement and output interface refinement with respect to their cooperation with state refinement. Chapter 11 discusses architecture refinement and communication refinement. We analyse how communication refinement can be realized by architecture refinement steps.

Chapter 12 illustrates the presented refinement techniques with a case study.

We conclude the thesis with a summary emphasizing its contribution to the field of refinement of distributed systems, survey related work and give prospects of future work.

Chapter 2

Foundations

In this chapter, we introduce a formal basis for stream processing. First we collect some order theory underlying the concept of streams as communication histories. Then we define and investigate streams, stream processing functions, history abstractions comprising the information of an input history, and the composition of stream processing functions.

New contributions of the thesis include a syntactic criterion for monotonicity (cf. Subsection 2.3.1) and the introduction of history abstractions (cf. Section 2.4).

2.1 Ideals

Order theoretic concepts are fundamental for semantics. We briefly summarize definitions and results on ideals which underlie the semantic domain for stream processing. These definitions are based on complete partial orders and functions on (complete) partial orders [DP90], cf. Appendix A.

Ideal completion provides a systematic step from finite to infinite semantic objects.

Definition 2.1 (ideal, principal ideal, ideal completion)
An *ideal* I over a partial order $(M, \leq)$ is a downward closed directed subset of M. We denote the set of all ideals over M by $Idl(M)$.
The ideal $\downarrow \{x\}$ is called the *principal ideal* generated by $x \in M$.
$(Idl(M), \subseteq)$ is called the *ideal completion* of the partial order $(M, \leq)$. □

The ideals which we consider to represent streams are non-empty downward closed chains. In this case, any two elements of an ideal are comparable.

Infinite objects arise as limit points of the ideal completion on finite objects.

Definition 2.2 (finite element, limit point)
An element x of a cpo M is called *finite*, if for all directed sets $N \subseteq M$ with $x \leq \bigsqcup N$ there exists $y \in N$ such that $x \leq y$. Non-finite elements are called *limit points*. □

The next definition and the proposition characterize our semantic domain.

Definition 2.3 (algebraic cpo)
A cpo $(M, \leq)$ is called *algebraic* iff every element is the least upper bound of its finite approximations, which means that for every $x \in M$, the set $N = \{y \in M \mid y \text{ is finite and } y \leq x\}$ is directed and $x = \bigsqcup N$. □

Proposition 2.4
The ideal completion $(Idl(M), \subseteq)$ of a partial order M with a least element forms an algebraic cpo. Its finite elements are the principal ideals of the partial order.

If furthermore each pair of elements of M which has an upper bound in M also has a least upper bound in M, then the ideal completion forms a consistently complete algebraic cpo [SHLG94]. □

[Gun93] proves the first part of the proposition not only for partial orders, but also for a more general kind of orders, pre-orders, which are partial orders without antisymmetry.

Ideals are only necessary when considering infinite objects.

Lemma 2.5
An algebraic cpo $(M, \leq)$ and the set of the ideals of the finite elements of the cpo with the subset order $\subseteq$ are isomorphic. □

The following proposition [Gue81, Möl98] allows us to uniquely extend a monotonic function defined on finite streams to infinite streams.

Proposition 2.6
Every monotonic function $f : A \to D$ from a partial order A into a cpo D possesses a unique continuous extension $\widehat{f} : Idl(A) \to D$ meeting $\widehat{f}(\downarrow \{x\}) = f(x)$ by setting

$$\widehat{f}(I) \;=\; \bigsqcup{}_D f(I).$$

The above equation makes use of the shorthand notation $g(M) = \{g(m) \mid m \in M\}$ for a function $g : \mathcal{M} \to \mathcal{N}$ applied to a subset $M \subseteq \mathcal{M}$. □

2.2 Streams

Streams model the communication history of a channel, that is the temporal succession of data such as signals, messages, commands. Streams abstract from the duration and the points of time of messages and record only their succession.

2.2.1 Finite Streams

A finite stream is a finite sequence of messages.

Definition 2.7 (finite streams, empty stream, non-empty streams)
Given a non-empty set $\mathcal{A}$ of data, the set $\mathcal{A}^\star$ of *finite streams* over $\mathcal{A}$ is the least set with respect to subset inclusion defined by

$$\mathcal{A}^\star = \{\langle\rangle\} \cup \mathcal{A} \times \mathcal{A}^\star.$$

A stream is either the *empty stream* $\langle\rangle$ or is constructed by attaching ($\triangleleft$) an element to the front of a stream. $\mathcal{A}^+$ denotes the set of *non-empty streams* over $\mathcal{A}$.   □

We denote streams by capital letters and elements of streams by small letters. A stream $X = x_1 \triangleleft \ldots \triangleleft x_n \triangleleft \langle\rangle$ $(n \geq 0)$ with length $|X| = n$ is denoted by $\langle x_1, \ldots, x_n \rangle$ for short.

Definition 2.8 (concatenation)
The *concatenation* $X \& Y$ of a stream $X = \langle x_1, x_2, \ldots, x_k \rangle$ over $\mathcal{A}$ with a stream $Y = \langle y_1, y_2, \ldots, y_l \rangle$ over $\mathcal{A}$ yields the stream $\langle x_1, x_2, \ldots, x_k, y_1, y_2, \ldots, y_l \rangle$ of length $k + l$.   □

Operational progress in time is modelled by the prefix order. The longer stream is an extension of the shorter history, and, vice versa, the shorter stream is an initial history of the longer stream.

Definition 2.9 (prefix)
A stream X is called a *prefix* of a stream Y, denoted $X \sqsubseteq Y$, iff a stream R exists with $X \& R = Y$.   □

The set of finite streams together with the prefix relation forms a partial order with the empty stream as the least element. Non-empty chains of streams are directed sets and vice versa. As usual, the partial order on streams is extended point-wisely to tuples of streams.

2.2.2   Infinite Streams

Continuously processing components perpetually consume and produce data. Therefore we need infinite streams to describe infinite communication histories.

Formally, infinite streams arise as limit points of the semantic domain for stream processing. The partial order $(\mathcal{A}^\star, \sqsubseteq)$ of finite streams does not constitute a complete partial order, because infinite directed subsets have no upper bounds in $\mathcal{A}^\star$. By Proposition 2.4 these missing limit points are added by forming the ideal completion of the partial order of finite streams [Möl99]. In the resulting consistently complete algebraic cpo, finite streams are represented by finite ideals, whereas infinite streams are represented by infinite ideals.

For example, the finite ideal $\{\langle\rangle, \langle 1\rangle, \langle 1,1\rangle, \langle 1,1,1\rangle\}$ represents the finite stream $\langle 1,1,1\rangle$ whereas the infinite ideal $\{\langle\rangle, \langle 1\rangle, \langle 1,1\rangle, \langle 1,1,1\rangle, \ldots\}$ represents the infinite stream $\langle 1,1,1,\ldots\rangle$. The least element is $\langle\rangle$, or $\{\langle\rangle\}$ respectively.

An infinite stream is uniquely characterized by the (infinite) set of all its finite prefixes which approximate it. The set of finite streams $\mathcal{A}^\star$ and the finite ideals over $\mathcal{A}^\star$ are isomorphic. The isomorphism identifies a finite stream with its principal ideal and identifies a finite ideal with its greatest element, respectively.

Definition 2.10 (infinite streams)
We denote the cpo of finite and infinite streams over $\mathcal{A}$ by $\mathcal{A}^\infty := Idl(\mathcal{A}^\star)$. The set $\mathcal{A}^\infty$ of streams can be split into the set $\mathcal{A}^\star$ of *finite streams* and the set $\mathcal{A}^\omega$ of *infinite streams*:

$$\mathcal{A}^\infty \;=\; \mathcal{A}^\star \cup \mathcal{A}^\omega \qquad\qquad \square$$

In the following, the term *stream* denotes a finite stream, an infinite stream, or a finite or infinite stream depending on the respective context.

2.2.3   Basic Operations on Streams

We need basic operations on streams to manipulate communication histories.

Definition 2.11 (prefixing, postfixing)
The *prefixing* operation $\triangleleft : \mathcal{A} \times \mathcal{A}^\star \to \mathcal{A}^\star$ attaches an element to the front of a stream:

$$x \triangleleft X \;=\; \langle x\rangle \,\&\, X$$

The *postfixing* operation $\triangleright : \mathcal{A}^\star \times \mathcal{A} \to \mathcal{A}^\star$ appends an element to the rear of a stream:

$$X \triangleright x \;=\; X \,\&\, \langle x \rangle \hspace{4cm} \Box$$

The prefixing and postfixing operations bind tighter than concatenation.

Definition 2.12 (first, last, rest, lead)
The operation *first* : $\mathcal{A}^+ \to \mathcal{A}$ yields the first element of a non-empty stream:

$$\mathit{first}(x \triangleleft X) \;=\; x$$

Symmetrically, the operation *last* : $\mathcal{A}^+ \to \mathcal{A}$ yields the last element of a non-empty stream:

$$\mathit{last}(X \triangleright x) \;=\; x$$

The operation *rest* : $\mathcal{A}^+ \to \mathcal{A}^\star$ applied to a non-empty stream yields the stream without its first element:

$$\mathit{rest}(x \triangleleft X) \;=\; X$$

The operation *lead* : $\mathcal{A}^+ \to \mathcal{A}^\star$ applied to a non-empty stream yields the stream without its last element:

$$\mathit{lead}(X \triangleright x) \;=\; X \hspace{4cm} \Box$$

As with the prefix relation, the basic operations on streams are extended point-wisely to tuples of arguments. The extension to infinite streams will be discussed in connection with continuity, cf. Subsection 2.3.2.

2.3 Stream Processing Functions

The history of data passing a communication channel between components and, possibly, their environment is mathematically captured by the notion of a stream. Thus, a deterministic component which continuously processes data from its input ports and emits data at its output ports is considered as a function mapping input histories to output histories.

Definition 2.13 (function on streams)
A *function on streams* maps a tuple of input streams to a tuple of output streams:

$$f : \mathcal{A}_1^\infty \times \ldots \times \mathcal{A}_m^\infty \to \mathcal{B}_1^\infty \times \ldots \times \mathcal{B}_n^\infty$$

The input types $(\mathcal{A}_1, \ldots, \mathcal{A}_m)$ $(m \geq 0)$ and the output types $(\mathcal{B}_1, \ldots, \mathcal{B}_n)$ $(n \geq 0)$ determine the syntactic *interface* of the component, cf. Figure 2.1. The interface is divided into an *input interface* $(\mathcal{A}_1, \ldots, \mathcal{A}_m)$ and an *output interface* $(\mathcal{B}_1, \ldots, \mathcal{B}_n)$. □

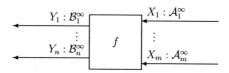

Figure 2.1: Component modelled by a function f with m input and n output streams

A function on streams describes the *input / output behaviour*, for short *behaviour*, of a component.

As every multi-valued function, a function on streams with n results can be split into n single-valued functions each providing exactly one output stream.

The prefix order on streams is transferred to functions $f, g : \mathcal{A}_1^\infty \times \ldots \times \mathcal{A}_m^\infty \to \mathcal{B}_1^\infty \times \ldots \times \mathcal{B}_n^\infty$ on streams by setting

$$f \sqsubseteq g \iff \forall (X_1, \ldots, X_m) \in \mathcal{A}_1^\infty \times \ldots \times \mathcal{A}_m^\infty : \tag{2.1}$$
$$f(X_1, \ldots, X_m) \sqsubseteq g(X_1, \ldots, X_m).$$

2.3.1 Monotonicity

The history-based description of components needs to respect causality, and thus requires order-preserving functions.

Definition 2.14 (causality)
A function $f : \mathcal{A}_1^\infty \times \ldots \times \mathcal{A}_m^\infty \to \mathcal{B}_1^\infty \times \ldots \times \mathcal{B}_n^\infty$ on streams respects *causality* if it is monotonic with respect to the prefix order:

$$f(X_1, \ldots, X_m) \sqsubseteq f(X_1 \& Y_1, \ldots, X_m \& Y_m)$$

for all $X_i, Y_i \in \mathcal{A}_i$ $(1 \leq i \leq m)$. □

The monotonicity requirement stems from the idea that more information on the input leads to an extension of the output, or in other words: interactive components cannot change previous output.

In order to make sure that specifications indeed respect causality, the monotonicity must be proved for each specification. In the following, we show that if the specification of a function on streams shows a particular syntactic pattern, its monotonicity can be guaranteed.

A criterion for monotonicity

We investigate functions on streams which are specified by *terminating* equations yielding empty streams, and by *recursive* equations operating on a prefix of input streams.

We consider a function $f : \mathcal{A}_1^\star \times \ldots \times \mathcal{A}_m^\star \to \mathcal{B}_1^\star \times \ldots \times \mathcal{B}_n^\star$ on finite streams which is defined by simple-structured terminating equations $((T_1, \ldots, T_m) \in \mathcal{T})$

$$f(T_1, \ldots, T_m) = \underbrace{(\langle \rangle, \ldots, \langle \rangle)}_{n-\text{times}} \tag{2.2}$$

such that the non-empty set $\mathcal{T} \subseteq \mathcal{A}_1^\star \times \ldots \times \mathcal{A}_m^\star$ of input stream tuples that are specified through these terminating equations is prefix closed. If $\mathcal{T} = \mathcal{A}_1^\star \times \ldots \times \mathcal{A}_m^\star$, then the function f is only specified by terminating equations like (2.2) and is therefore the monotonic function always yielding the tuple of empty streams.

All the other input stream tuples can be decomposed into a prefix which lies in the set of minimal elements $\mathcal{M}$ of $\mathcal{A}_1^\star \times \ldots \times \mathcal{A}_m^\star \setminus \mathcal{T}$ and an arbitrary rest. For all these other input stream tuples, we require that f is specified uniquely and completely by recursive equations with the pattern

$$f(M_1 \& X_1, \ldots, M_m \& X_m) = \tag{2.3}$$
$$g(M_1, \ldots, M_m) \& f(h(M_1, \ldots, M_m) \& (X_1, \ldots, X_m))$$

such that $(M_1, \ldots, M_m) \in \mathcal{M}$ and for each input stream tuple exactly one equation is applicable. The function $g : \mathcal{M} \to \mathcal{B}_1^\star \times \ldots \times \mathcal{B}_n^\star$ determines a segment of the output depending on a prefix of the input streams, and the *reduction function* $h : \mathcal{M} \to \mathcal{A}_1^\star \times \ldots \times \mathcal{A}_m^\star$ reduces the input streams.

We require that the recursion terminates for all input stream tuples. That means that the *termination function* $\tau : \mathcal{A}_1^\star \times \ldots \times \mathcal{A}_m^\star \to \mathcal{T}$ defined by

$$(T_1, \ldots, T_m) \in \mathcal{T} \implies \tau(T_1, \ldots, T_m) = (T_1, \ldots, T_m) \tag{2.4}$$
$$(M_1, \ldots, M_m) \in \mathcal{M} \implies \tau(M_1 \& X_1, \ldots, M_m \& X_m) = \tag{2.5}$$
$$\tau(h(M_1, \ldots, M_m) \& (X_1, \ldots, X_m))$$

is terminating: $\forall(X_1, \ldots, X_m) \in \mathcal{A}_1^\star \times \ldots \times \mathcal{A}_m^\star \, \exists p \in \mathbb{N} : \tau^p(X_1, \ldots, X_m) \in \mathcal{T}$. The existence of the termination function implies that $\mathcal{T} \neq \emptyset$. The termination function τ induces a termination order on the input streams.

Under these assumptions, the stream processing function f validates a decomposition property ensuring monotonicity. In the following theorem capital letters denote stream tuples.

Theorem 2.15
Let $f : \mathcal{A}_1^\star \times \ldots \times \mathcal{A}_m^\star \to \mathcal{B}_1^\star \times \ldots \times \mathcal{B}_n^\star$ be a stream processing function and $\mathcal{T} \subseteq \mathcal{A}_1^\star \times \ldots \times \mathcal{A}_m^\star$ be a non-empty prefix closed subset of the input streams. Let $\mathcal{M}$ denote the set of minimal elements of $\mathcal{A}_1^\star \times \ldots \times \mathcal{A}_m^\star \setminus \mathcal{T}$ and

$$g : \mathcal{M} \to \mathcal{B}_1^\star \times \ldots \times \mathcal{B}_n^\star$$
$$h : \mathcal{M} \to \mathcal{A}_1^\star \times \ldots \times \mathcal{A}_m^\star$$

be functions on this set. Let f be specified by equations

$$f(T) \;=\; \underbrace{(\langle\rangle, \ldots, \langle\rangle)}_{n-\text{times}}$$
$$f(M \& X) \;=\; g(M) \,\&\, f(h(M) \& X)$$

with $T \in \mathcal{T}$, $M \in \mathcal{M}$, such that for each input stream exactly one equation is applicable.
If the function $\tau : \mathcal{A}_1^\star \times \ldots \times \mathcal{A}_m^\star \to \mathcal{T}$ defined by

$$\tau(T) \;=\; T$$
$$\tau(M \& X) \;=\; \tau(h(M) \& X)$$

is terminating, then f validates the *decomposition property*

$$f(X \& Y) \;=\; f(X) \,\&\, f(\tau(X) \& Y).$$

Thus the function f is monotonic. □

The proof proceeds by induction on the termination order:

Proof: IB: $X = T \in \mathcal{T}$:
$$\begin{aligned} & f(T \& Y) \\ = \; & \underbrace{(\langle\rangle, \ldots, \langle\rangle)}_{n-\text{times}} \,\&\, f(\tau(T) \& Y) \\ = \; & f(T) \,\&\, f(\tau(T) \& Y) \end{aligned}$$

IS: $X \notin \mathcal{T}$, that is $X = M\&Z$ for an $M \in \mathcal{M}$, and the induction hypothesis holds for $h(M)\&Z$:

$$
\begin{aligned}
& f(M\&Z\&Y) \\
= {}& g(M) \,\&\, f(h(M)\&Z\&Y) \\
\overset{IH}{=} {}& g(M) \,\&\, f(h(M)\&Z) \,\&\, f(\tau(h(M)\&Z)\&Y) \\
= {}& f(M\&Z) \,\&\, f(\tau(h(M)\&Z)\&Y) \\
= {}& f(M\&Z) \,\&\, f(\tau(M\&Z)\&Y) \hspace{3cm} \square
\end{aligned}
$$

This syntactic criterion for monotonicity is sufficient, however not necessary. The following example demonstrates an application of the criterion.

Example 2.16 (monotonicity of a shift register)
A shift register is a component with one input and one output channel of the same type, cf. Figure 2.2.

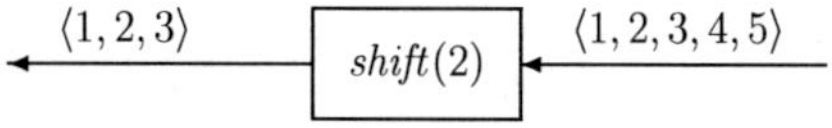

$$\langle 1, 2, 3 \rangle \qquad shift(2) \qquad \langle 1, 2, 3, 4, 5 \rangle$$

Figure 2.2: Shift register with size 2

The shift register $shift : \mathbb{P} \to (\mathcal{A}^\star \to \mathcal{A}^\star)$, where $\mathbb{P} = \mathbb{N} \setminus \{0\}$ denotes the set of positive natural numbers, is parameterized with its positive size. We suppose that initially the shift register is empty. As long as the length of the input stream does not exceed the size of the shift register, no output will appear. Otherwise, at least the first input element is shifted out of the shift register:

$$|X| \leq n \implies shift(n)(X) = \langle \rangle \tag{2.6}$$
$$|x \triangleleft X| > n \implies shift(n)(x \triangleleft X) = x \triangleleft shift(n)(X) \tag{2.7}$$

For each $n \in \mathbb{P}$, the set $\mathcal{T}_n = \mathcal{A}^{\leq n}$ of input streams leading to a direct termination is prefix closed. The set of minimal elements of $\mathcal{A}^\star \setminus \mathcal{T}_n$ is $\mathcal{M}_n = \mathcal{A}^{n+1}$. We rewrite the second equation (2.7) so that it meets the pattern of the recursive Equation (2.3):

$$shift(n)(\langle x_1, x_2, \ldots, x_{n+1} \rangle \& X) = x_1 \triangleleft shift(n)(\langle x_2, \ldots, x_{n+1} \rangle \& X) \tag{2.8}$$

The corresponding reduction function $h_n : \mathcal{A}^{n+1} \to \mathcal{A}^\star$ can now be abstracted from Equation (2.8):

$$h_n(M) = rest(M) \tag{2.9}$$

Since the reduction function h_n deletes the first element, the termination function $\tau_n : \mathcal{A}^* \to \mathcal{A}^{\leq n}$ yields the last n elements of the input stream as far as they exist:

$$\tau_n(X) \;=\; \begin{cases} X & \text{if } |X| \leq n \\ \tau_n(\mathit{rest}(X)) & \text{otherwise} \end{cases} \qquad (2.10)$$

By Theorem 2.15, $\mathit{shift}(n)$ is monotonic and validates the decomposition property

$$\mathit{shift}(n)(X \& Y) \;=\; \mathit{shift}(n)(X) \& \mathit{shift}(n)(\tau_n(X) \& Y). \qquad (2.11)$$

$\square$

2.3.2 Continuity

Interactive components continually process input. Since we are going to approximate the output for an infinite input stream via the outputs of its finite prefixes, we require stream processing functions to be continuous.

Definition 2.17 (stream processing function)
A monotonic function $f : \mathcal{A}_1^\infty \times \ldots \times \mathcal{A}_m^\infty \to \mathcal{B}_1^\infty \times \ldots \times \mathcal{B}_n^\infty$ on streams is called a *stream processing function* if it is continuous:

$$f(\bigsqcup D) \;=\; \bigsqcup f(D)$$

for all directed sets $D \subseteq \mathcal{A}_1^\infty \times \ldots \times \mathcal{A}_m^\infty$ where $\bigsqcup$ in each case denotes the least upper bound with respect to the order on the corresponding stream domains. $\square$

Analogous to predicate transformers [Dij75, Dij76], stream processing functions are also called *stream transformers*, because they transform input streams to output streams.

In the following we illustrate how monotonic functions on finite streams can be extended to continuous functions on finite and infinite streams. For reasons of clarity we denote the cpo of streams over $\mathcal{B}$ by $Idl(\mathcal{B}^*)$ ordered by subset inclusion $\subseteq$ instead of the usual shorthand notation $\mathcal{B}^\infty$, and concentrate on functions with a single input and output stream. According to Proposition 2.6, every monotonic function $f : \mathcal{A}^* \to Idl(\mathcal{B}^*)$ on finite streams can naturally be extended to a unique continuous function $\widehat{f} : Idl(\mathcal{A}^*) \to Idl(\mathcal{B}^*)$ on finite and infinite streams by setting

$$\widehat{f}(I) = \bigcup_{X \in I} f(X) \qquad (2.12)$$

for $I \in Idl(\mathcal{A}^\star)$, where $f(X) \in Idl(\mathcal{B}^\star)$ is an ideal representing a stream and the set union $\bigcup$ denotes the least upper bound with respect to subset inclusion.

The following example illustrates how the unique continuous extension is obtained from a specification on finite streams.

Example 2.18 (duplicate)
The stream processing function $dupl : \mathbb{N}^\star \to Idl(\mathbb{N}^\star)$ duplicates every element of a finite input stream:

$$dupl(\langle\rangle) \;=\; \langle\rangle \tag{2.13}$$
$$dupl(x \triangleleft X) \;=\; x \triangleleft x \triangleleft dupl(X) \tag{2.14}$$

In the ideal presentation we get for example for the input streams $\langle\rangle$, $\langle 1 \rangle$, and $\langle 1, 2 \rangle$:

$$
\begin{aligned}
dupl(\langle\rangle) &= \{\langle\rangle\} \\
dupl(\langle 1 \rangle) &= \{\langle\rangle, \langle 1 \rangle, \langle 1, 1 \rangle\} \\
dupl(\langle 1, 2 \rangle) &= \{\langle\rangle, \langle 1 \rangle, \langle 1, 1 \rangle, \langle 1, 1, 2 \rangle, \langle 1, 1, 2, 2 \rangle\}
\end{aligned}
$$

The unique continuous extension $\widehat{dupl} : Idl(\mathbb{N}^\star) \to Idl(\mathbb{N}^\star)$ for an ideal $I \in Idl(\mathbb{N}^\star)$ is

$$\widehat{dupl}(I) \;=\; \bigcup_{X \in I} dupl(X). \tag{2.15}$$

For example, for the input stream $\langle 1, 2 \rangle$, we get

$$
\begin{aligned}
\widehat{dupl}(\{\langle\rangle, \langle 1 \rangle, \langle 1, 2 \rangle\}) &= \{\langle\rangle\} \\
&\cup \{\langle\rangle, \langle 1 \rangle, \langle 1, 1 \rangle\} \\
&\cup \{\langle\rangle, \langle 1 \rangle, \langle 1, 1 \rangle, \langle 1, 1, 2 \rangle, \langle 1, 1, 2, 2 \rangle\}
\end{aligned}
$$

and for the infinite input stream $\langle 1, 2, 3, \ldots \rangle$ we get

$$
\begin{aligned}
\widehat{dupl}(\{\langle\rangle, \langle 1 \rangle, \langle 1, 2 \rangle, \langle 1, 2, 3 \rangle, \ldots\}) & \\
= \{\langle\rangle\} & \\
\cup \{\langle\rangle, \langle 1 \rangle, \langle 1, 1 \rangle\} & \\
\cup \{\langle\rangle, \langle 1 \rangle, \langle 1, 1 \rangle, \langle 1, 1, 2 \rangle, \langle 1, 1, 2, 2 \rangle\} & \\
\cup \{\langle\rangle, \langle 1 \rangle, \langle 1, 1 \rangle, \langle 1, 1, 2 \rangle, \langle 1, 1, 2, 2 \rangle, \langle 1, 1, 2, 2, 3 \rangle, \langle 1, 1, 2, 2, 3, 3 \rangle\} & \\
\cup \ldots & \\
= \{\langle\rangle, \langle 1 \rangle, \langle 1, 1 \rangle, \langle 1, 1, 2 \rangle, \langle 1, 1, 2, 2 \rangle, \langle 1, 1, 2, 2, 3 \rangle, \langle 1, 1, 2, 2, 3, 3 \rangle, \ldots\}. \quad \square &
\end{aligned}
$$

The unique continuous extension can often be obtained in a more convenient way. If a stream processing function $f : \mathcal{A}^\star \to \mathcal{B}^\star$ yields only finite output streams for finite input streams, then the range $\mathcal{B}^\star$ manages without ideal completion. The output ideal for an input ideal $I \in Idl(\mathcal{A}^\star)$ is the downward closure ($\downarrow$) of the output streams for all the input streams in the ideal I:

$$\widehat{f}(I) \;\; = \;\; \downarrow \bigcup_{X \in I} \{f(X)\} \tag{2.16}$$

If even the image of the continuous extension $\widehat{f}$ would contain only finite ideals, that means $\widehat{f}(I) = \downarrow\{Y\}$ is the principal ideal of a finite stream $Y \in \mathcal{B}^\star$, then the unique continuous extension $\widehat{f} : \mathcal{A}^\infty \to \mathcal{B}^\star$ can be simplified to

$$\widehat{f}(I) \;\; = \;\; Y \,. \tag{2.17}$$

The above considerations generalize to stream processing functions with more than one input channel and more than one output channel.

On the other hand, since the set of finite and infinite streams is a consistently complete algebraic cpo, the set of stream processing functions with the same interface forms a consistently complete algebraic cpo, and every continuous function on streams is the unique continuous extension of its restriction to finite streams. Therefore, a stream processing function is in general specified only on its finite input streams, and the behaviour on infinite input streams is inferred from the behaviour on finite streams.

With the above technique, some of the *basic operations* on streams can be extended to infinite streams. Concatenation is monotonic in its second argument, though not in its first argument. Hence, the concatenation is extended to infinite streams in the second argument and prefixing is also extended to infinite streams in its stream argument. Usually, concatenation is extended to infinite streams in the first argument by setting for $X \in \mathcal{A}^\omega$, $Y \in \mathcal{A}^\infty$:

$$X \& Y \;\; = \;\; X \tag{2.18}$$

The operations *rest* and *lead* are monotonic on non-empty streams and are therefore extended to infinite streams. *lead* is the identity on infinite streams $X \in \mathcal{A}^\omega$:

$$rest(x \lhd X) \;\; = \;\; X \tag{2.19}$$

$$lead(X) \;\; = \;\; X \tag{2.20}$$

The operation *first* from non-empty input streams into a set ordered by equality can also be extended to infinite streams: $(X \in \mathcal{A}^\omega)$

$$first(x \lhd X) \;\; = \;\; x \tag{2.21}$$

Safety and liveness properties

System specifications are often separated into safety aspects and liveness aspects [AS85, Kin94]. Safety properties are predicates which can be violated by finite streams [BS01b]. In order to express liveness properties such as fairness [Fra86], we need predicates on finite and infinite streams, because the violation of a liveness property can only be observed for infinite input streams. Möller [Möl98] investigates safety and liveness properties for behaviours which are considered as sets of streams from the algebraic point of view. The characterization and the methodological aspects of safety and liveness are much-discussed, see for example [Gum93] and the discussion [DW90, AAA+91, DW91]. In this thesis we are not going to deal with safety and liveness any further.

2.3.3 Selected Stream Processing Functions

Strict stream processing functions model non-spontaneous components which do not emit output before receiving input on at least one of the input channels.

Definition 2.19 (strict function, reactive part)
A stream processing function $f : \mathcal{A}_1^\infty \times \ldots \times \mathcal{A}_m^\infty \to \mathcal{B}_1^\infty \times \ldots \times \mathcal{B}_n^\infty$ is called *strict* iff it preserves the bottom elements:

$$f(\langle\rangle, \ldots, \langle\rangle) \;=\; (\langle\rangle, \ldots, \langle\rangle)$$

For a stream processing function $f : \mathcal{A}_1^\infty \times \ldots \times \mathcal{A}_m^\infty \to \mathcal{B}_1^\infty \times \ldots \times \mathcal{B}_n^\infty$, the function $react_f : \mathcal{A}_1^\infty \times \ldots \times \mathcal{A}_m^\infty \to \mathcal{B}_1^\infty \times \ldots \times \mathcal{B}_n^\infty$, defined by

$$f(X) \;=\; f(\langle\rangle, \ldots, \langle\rangle) \,\&\, react_f(X) \,,$$

constitutes the *reactive part* of f, provided $f(\langle\rangle, \ldots, \langle\rangle) \in \mathcal{B}_1^\star \times \ldots \times \mathcal{B}_n^\star$. □

The reactive part of a stream processing function describes the output of a component which is emitted only in reaction to input data while dropping the spontaneous output. The reactive part of a stream processing function is always a strict function.

In pulse-controlled systems such as hardware, the components synchronously repeatedly consume the first element on each input channel and emit an element on each output channel. IO-synchronous systems are characterized by a relationship between the length of input streams and of the corresponding output streams.

Definition 2.20 (io-synchronous, offset, instantaneous)
A component $f : \mathcal{A}_1^\infty \times \ldots \times \mathcal{A}_m^\infty \to \mathcal{B}_1^\infty \times \ldots \times \mathcal{B}_n^\infty$ is called *io-synchronous*, if it validates

$$react_f(X_1, \ldots, X_m) \in \mathcal{B}_1^p \times \ldots \times \mathcal{B}_n^p$$

for all finite input streams $X_1, \ldots, X_m$ and $p = \min\{|X_1|, \ldots, |X_m|\}$.
Let $(Y_1, \ldots, Y_n) = f(\langle\rangle, \ldots, \langle\rangle)$. Then $d_i = |Y_i|$ is called the *offset* of the ith output channel $(i = 1, \ldots, n)$.
If $d_i = 0$ for all output channels $1 \leq i \leq n$, then an io-synchronous component is called *instantaneous*.   □

Synchronous concurrent algorithms [PTH98] describe io-synchronous components.

A crucial kind of stream processing functions describe the behaviour of *routing components*. Simple basic routing components are for example components without input channels, called *sources*, and components without output channels, called sinks, *identities*, and *copy* components.

A basic routing component that is worth being specified is a cross component. Cross components are an important element for composing systems out of components, because they help to overcome the inflexibility of the mathematical view of interfaces being tuples of streams.

Example 2.21 (cross component)
A cross component $\mathsf{X}_n(\sigma) : \mathcal{A}_1^\star \times \ldots \times \mathcal{A}_n^\star \to \mathcal{A}_{\sigma^{-1}(1)}^\infty \times \ldots \times \mathcal{A}_{\sigma^{-1}(n)}^\infty$ rearranges its n input streams according to a permutation function σ of $\{1, \ldots, n\}$:

$$\mathsf{X}_n(\sigma)(X_1, \ldots, X_n) = (X_{\sigma^{-1}(1)}, \ldots, X_{\sigma^{-1}(n)}) \qquad (2.22)$$

For $n = 2$ and $\tau(1) = 2, \tau(2) = 1$, we obtain $\mathsf{X} = \mathsf{X}_2(\tau)$ crossing two streams.
                                                                □

Routing components play a significant role in architecture refinement, cf. Chapter 11.1. Cross components are also relevant for a particular application of interface refinement, cf. Chapter 10.

2.4   History Abstractions

While stream processing functions summarize the behaviour of a component by mapping input streams to output streams, a finer view reveals the causal relationship between single elements in the input stream and segments of the output stream depending on the corresponding prehistories. History abstractions identify input histories each with the same effect on future output for any extension of the input history. History abstractions will be the key for state refinements, cf. Theorem 4.9.

In this section, we restrict ourselves to stream processing functions with a single finite input stream producing a tuple of finite output streams.

First, we isolate the effect of an input element on the output stream after processing a prehistory, cf. Figure 2.3.

Definition 2.22 (output extension)
The *output extension* $\varepsilon_f : \mathcal{A}^* \times \mathcal{A} \to \mathcal{B}_1^* \times \ldots \times \mathcal{B}_n^*$ of a stream transformer $f : \mathcal{A}^* \to \mathcal{B}_1^* \times \ldots \times \mathcal{B}_n^*$ is defined by

$$f(X \triangleright x) \;\; = \;\; f(X) \,\&\, \varepsilon_f(X,x) \,. \qquad \qquad \square$$

We may omit the index f if the stream transformer is determined by the context.

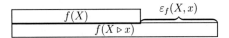

Figure 2.3: Extension of the output history

The output extension is in fact a skolem function of the equation

$$\forall X \in \mathcal{A}^* \, \forall x \in \mathcal{A} \, \exists R \in \mathcal{B}_1^* \times \ldots \times \mathcal{B}_n^* : \quad f(X \triangleright x) = f(X) \,\&\, R \quad (2.23)$$

guaranteeing the monotonicity of a stream transformer $f : \mathcal{A}^* \to \mathcal{B}_1^* \times \ldots \times \mathcal{B}_n^*$, which is equivalent to the equation given in Definition 2.14. The output extension completely determines the behaviour of a stream processing function apart from its result for empty input.

Proposition 2.23
Let $f, g : \mathcal{A}^* \to \mathcal{B}_1^* \times \ldots \times \mathcal{B}_n^*$ be stream processing functions with the same interface. Then the output extensions of f and g agree iff their reactive parts agree:

$$\varepsilon_f = \varepsilon_g \quad \Longleftrightarrow \quad react_f = react_g \qquad \qquad \square$$

Proof: We derive a direct specification of $react_f$:

$$f(\langle\rangle) \,\&\, react_f(\langle\rangle)$$
$$= \; f(\langle\rangle)$$
$$= \; f(\langle\rangle) \,\&\, (\langle\rangle, \ldots, \langle\rangle)$$

$$f(\langle\rangle) \,\&\, react_f(X \triangleright x)$$
$$= \; f(X \triangleright x)$$
$$= \; f(X) \,\&\, \varepsilon_f(X, x)$$
$$= \; f(\langle\rangle) \,\&\, react_f(X) \,\&\, \varepsilon_f(X, x)$$

Consequently, $react_f$ is strict, and ε_f is the output extension of $react_f$:

$$react_f(\langle\rangle) \;=\; (\langle\rangle, \ldots, \langle\rangle)$$
$$react_f(X \triangleright x) \;=\; react_f(X) \,\&\, \varepsilon_f(X, x)$$

Analogously, we get the following direct specification of $react_g$:

$$react_g(\langle\rangle) \;=\; (\langle\rangle, \ldots, \langle\rangle)$$
$$react_g(X \triangleright x) \;=\; react_g(X) \,\&\, \varepsilon_g(X, x)$$

The direct specifications immediately prove the implication.

They also prove the other direction. Assume $react_f = react_g$:

$$react_f(X) \,\&\, \varepsilon_f(X, x)$$
$$= \; react_f(X \triangleright x)$$
$$= \; react_g(X \triangleright x)$$
$$= \; react_g(X) \,\&\, \varepsilon_g(X, x)$$
$$= \; react_f(X) \,\&\, \varepsilon_g(X, x) \qquad\qquad\qquad \Box$$

The following two definitions characterize properties of stream functions which identify certain subsets of input streams. Output compatible functions may identify input histories if they have the same effect on the next output.

Definition 2.24 (output compatible)

A function $\beta : \mathcal{A}^\star \to \mathcal{Q}$ is called *output compatible* with respect to an output extension $\varepsilon : \mathcal{A}^\star \times \mathcal{A} \to \mathcal{B}_1^\star \times \ldots \times \mathcal{B}_n^\star$, if it identifies only histories with the same effect on ε:

$$\beta(X) = \beta(Y) \;\implies\; \varepsilon(X, x) = \varepsilon(Y, x) \qquad\qquad \Box$$

Transition closed functions may identify input histories only if their prolongations are also identified.

Definition 2.25 (transition closed)
A function $\beta : \mathcal{A}^\star \to \mathcal{Q}$ is called *transition closed*, if it identifies only histories whose extensions are not distinguished:

$$\beta(X) = \beta(Y) \quad \Longrightarrow \quad \beta(X \triangleright x) = \beta(Y \triangleright x) \qquad \qquad \square$$

A transition closed function indeed identifies all the prolongations of identified streams:

$$\beta(X) = \beta(Y) \quad \Longrightarrow \quad \beta(X \& Z) = \beta(Y \& Z) \qquad (2.24)$$

The proof proceeds by induction on the prolongating stream Z.

Transition closed functions will be used in order to map input histories to states, cf. Section 4.4, and thus they identify the input histories leading to the same state. Since the functions validating the property "transition closed" play an important role for state refinement, they are given a proper name.

Definition 2.26 (history abstraction)
Any transition closed function $\alpha : \mathcal{A}^\star \to \mathcal{Q}$ on streams is called a *history abstraction*. A history abstraction $\alpha : \mathcal{A}^\star \to \mathcal{Q}$ is called *history abstraction for a stream processing function* $f : \mathcal{A}^\star \to \mathcal{B}_1^\star \times \ldots \times \mathcal{B}_n^\star$ if it is output compatible with respect to the output extension $\varepsilon_f : \mathcal{A}^\star \times \mathcal{A} \to \mathcal{B}_1^\star \times \ldots \times \mathcal{B}_n^\star$ of f. $\qquad \square$

Definition 2.26 separates the requirements for a history abstraction into two conditions: the property "transition closed" is independent of a particular stream processing function, whereas "output compatible" refers to a particular stream processing function.

Stream processing functions which agree on their reactive part share the same history abstractions.

Example 2.27 (last(n))
The function $last(n)$ yields the final segment of the last n elements of the input as far as they exist. The specification of $last : \mathbb{N} \to (\mathcal{A}^\star \to \mathcal{A}^\star)$ proceeds by structural induction on the input stream and on the number of elements to be extracted:

$$last(n)(\langle\rangle) \;=\; \langle\rangle \qquad (2.25)$$
$$last(0)(X) \;=\; \langle\rangle \qquad (2.26)$$
$$last(n+1)(X \triangleright x) \;=\; last(n)(X) \triangleright x \qquad (2.27)$$

For every $n \in \mathbb{N}$, the function $last(n) : \mathcal{A}^\star \to \mathcal{A}^{\leq n}$ is transition closed:

$$last(n)(X) = last(n)(Y) \quad \Longrightarrow \quad last(n)(X \triangleright x) = last(n)(Y \triangleright x) \quad (2.28)$$

The proof proceeds by induction on the input stream X or Y and on n.
Consequently, for every $n \in \mathbb{N}$, $last(n)$ is a history abstraction.   □

Further common history abstractions are, for example, the constant function always giving the same result independent of the history, filter functions, the length function, $take(n)$ functions yielding the first n elements of a history as far as they exist, set and multiset abstractions or reductions of the history. Some of these history abstractions together with the sets of functions with the respective history abstraction are investigated in Chapter 5.

2.5 Composition of Stream Processing Functions

Composite networks are built from communicating components. The behaviour of the composite system can be inferred from the behaviour of the components. For composing stream processing functions we define composition operators for sequential and parallel composition and feedback.

2.5.1 Sequential Composition

A component whose output ports are connected to all the input ports of another component is sequentially composed with the other component. The behaviour of the composite system is obtained by function composition of the stream processing functions specifying the behaviour of the two components.

Definition 2.28 (sequential composition)
The *sequential composition* of a component $f : \mathcal{A}_1^\infty \times \ldots \times \mathcal{A}_m^\infty \to \mathcal{B}_1^\infty \times \ldots \times \mathcal{B}_n^\infty$ and a component $g : \mathcal{B}_1^\infty \times \ldots \times \mathcal{B}_n^\infty \to \mathcal{C}_1^\infty \times \ldots \times \mathcal{C}_p^\infty$ with a compatible interface is denoted $f \mathbin{;} g : \mathcal{A}_1^\infty \times \ldots \times \mathcal{A}_m^\infty \to \mathcal{C}_1^\infty \times \ldots \times \mathcal{C}_p^\infty$ with

$$f \mathbin{;} g \;=\; g \circ f$$

where the operator $\circ$ denotes function composition: $(g \circ f)(X_1, \ldots, X_m) = g(f(X_1, \ldots, X_m))$.   □

The composite system $f \mathbin{;} g$ can thus be considered as a new component, cf. Figure 2.4. Chapter 10 proposes techniques how to adapt interfaces so that components can be sequentially composed.

The sequential composition is associative. The identity function of the appropriate type is its neutral element. The sequential composition of two

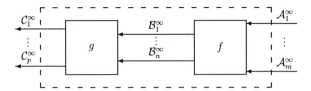

Figure 2.4: Sequential composition of f and g

strict, monotonic or continuous functions results in a strict, monotonic or continuous function, respectively.

If f and g are io-synchronous, then the composition $f;g$ is also io-synchronous. The offset of an output channel of f ; g is the offset of the respective output channel of g increased by the minimal offset of the output channels of f. In particular, the sequential composition of instantaneous components yields an instantaneous component again.

2.5.2 Parallel Composition

Components that work independently of each other are composed by parallel composition. The behaviour of the composite system is obtained by juxtaposing the input channels and the output channels of both components, cf. Figure 2.5.

Definition 2.29 (parallel composition)
The *parallel composition* of a component $f : \mathcal{A}_1^\infty \times \ldots \times \mathcal{A}_m^\infty \to \mathcal{B}_1^\infty \times \ldots \times \mathcal{B}_n^\infty$ and a component $g : \mathcal{C}_1^\infty \times \ldots \times \mathcal{C}_p^\infty \to \mathcal{D}_1^\infty \times \ldots \times \mathcal{D}_q^\infty$ is denoted $f \parallel g :$ $\mathcal{A}_1^\infty \times \ldots \times \mathcal{A}_m^\infty \times \mathcal{C}_1^\infty \times \ldots \times \mathcal{C}_p^\infty \to \mathcal{B}_1^\infty \times \ldots \times \mathcal{B}_n^\infty \times \mathcal{D}_1^\infty \times \ldots \times \mathcal{D}_q^\infty$ with

$$(f \parallel g)(X_1, \ldots, X_{m+p}) = f(X_1, \ldots, X_m) \,\hat{}\, g(X_{m+1}, \ldots X_{m+p})$$

where the operator $\hat{}$ denotes tuple concatenation:

$$(R_1, \ldots, R_n) \,\hat{}\, (S_1, \ldots, S_q) = (R_1, \ldots, R_n, S_1, \ldots, S_q) \qquad \square$$

The parallel composition of strict, monotonic or continuous functions yields a strict, monotonic or continuous function, respectively.

The parallel composition of io-synchronous components yields an io-synchronous component. Parallel composition preserves the offsets. In particular, the parallel composition of instantaneous components yields an instantaneous component again.

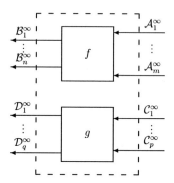

Figure 2.5: Parallel composition of f and g

The parallel composition is associative. The neutral element of the parallel composition is the *null component* with neither input nor output channels.

Since the parallel composition is a juxtaposition in space, the parallel composition is not commutative. In connection with channel crossing we have

$$f \parallel g = \mathsf{X}_{m+p}(\sigma) \,; (g \parallel f) \,; \mathsf{X}_{n+q}(\tau) \tag{2.29}$$

with the input permutation function

$$\sigma(i) = \begin{cases} i + p & \text{if } 1 \leq i \leq m \\ i - m & \text{if } m < i \leq m + p \end{cases}$$

and the output permutation function

$$\tau(i) = \begin{cases} i + n & \text{if } 1 \leq i \leq q \\ i - q & \text{if } q < i \leq q + n. \end{cases}$$

The tuple-based notation requires channel crossing because it is bound up with an arrangement of the input and output channels. If we considered named channels (cf. Subsection 2.5.5), the parallel composition would be commutative.

2.5.3   Feedback

In order to specify cyclic networks we need feedback. The feedback operation, cf. Figure 2.6, is defined with the least fixpoint operator.

Definition 2.30 (feedback)

A *k-feedback* connects the rear $k \geq 1$ output channels of a component $f :$
$\mathcal{A}_1^\infty \times \ldots \times \mathcal{A}_m^\infty \times \mathcal{B}_1^\infty \times \ldots \times \mathcal{B}_k^\infty \to \mathcal{C}_1^\infty \times \ldots \times \mathcal{C}_n^\infty \times \mathcal{B}_1^\infty \times \ldots \times \mathcal{B}_k^\infty$ to its rear
input channels. The behaviour of this system is specified by the feedback
operator $\circlearrowleft_k f : \mathcal{A}_1^\infty \times \ldots \times \mathcal{A}_m^\infty \to \mathcal{C}_1^\infty \times \ldots \times \mathcal{C}_n^\infty$ defined by

$$(\circlearrowleft_k f)(X_1, \ldots, X_m) = \Pi_{1,\ldots,n} f(X_1, \ldots, X_m, Z_1, \ldots, Z_k)$$

where $\Pi_{i,\ldots,j}$ denotes the projection on the components i through j of a tuple,
and where $(Z_1, \ldots, Z_k)$ is the least fixpoint of the equation

$$(Z_1, \ldots, Z_k) = \Pi_{n+1,\ldots,n+k} f(X_1, \ldots, X_m, Z_1, \ldots, Z_k). \qquad \square$$

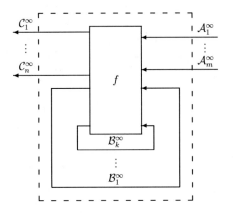

Figure 2.6: Feedback of k channels

Since a stream processing function is a continuous function on a complete
partial order, the least fixpoint exists and can be iterated from the least element of the underlying complete partial order, the k-tuple of empty streams
(due to the fixpoint theorem on complete partial orders [Kle52]):

$$(\circlearrowleft_k f)(X_1, \ldots, X_m) = \bigsqcup_{i>0} (Y_1^i, \ldots, Y_n^i) \qquad (2.30)$$

where

$$(Z_1^0, \ldots, Z_k^0) = (\langle\rangle, \ldots, \langle\rangle) \qquad (2.31)$$
$$(Y_1^{i+1}, \ldots, Y_n^{i+1}, Z_1^{i+1}, \ldots, Z_k^{i+1}) = f(X_1, \ldots, X_m, Z_1^i, \ldots, Z_k^i). \qquad (2.32)$$

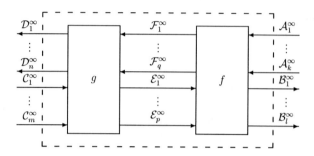

Figure 2.7: Universal composition of two components

k-feedback applied to an io-synchronous component f yields the constant function $(\circlearrowleft_k f)(X_1, \ldots, X_m) = \Pi_{1,\ldots,n} f(\langle\rangle, \ldots, \langle\rangle)$ if the offset of at least one of the k channels fed back is 0, because the least fixpoint contains an empty stream. In particular, feedback applied to an instantaneous component yields no output. If the offset of all the channels fed back exceeds 0, then the feedback preserves the offsets of the respective output channels.

The feedback operator connects the rear output channels of a component to the rear input channels, cf. Figure 2.6. This commitment does not restrict generality because we can rearrange the input and output channels of a component by inserting a cross component before and after the component before applying the feedback operator. In this way any output channel can be connected to any input channel.

For further *algebraic laws* concerning the composition operators and basic routing components refer to [DDM86], the book [Şte00] on network algebra, and Chapter 11.1 on architecture refinement.

2.5.4   Universal Composition

The representation of the connections of a network of distributed components by sequential and parallel composition and feedback is not unique, even not for two components. Components in a cyclic network can, for example, be considered as a sequential composition with feedback where each of the components could be the first component in the sequence. Therefore, we provide a more general composition operator which abstracts from the misleading notions "parallel" and "sequential" and indeed reflects that the components operate concurrently. The universal composition, cf. Figure 2.7, abstracts

from the layout of systems and concentrates on the connections between the
ports of components.

A universal composition of two components f and g which are each connected
to the environment with k and m input channels and l and n output channels
is a bidirectional connection with as much channels as needed. Each bidirectional channel can then be split into two unidirectional channels in opposite
directions, cf. Figure 2.7.

Broy [Bro98a] introduces a similar general composition of two components
with mutual feedback, cf. Figure 2.8. His definition of the composition is
based on sets of input and output channel names. We explain the universal composition in terms of the composition operations defined so far. The
universal composition of two components can be interpreted as a parallel
composition with feedback.

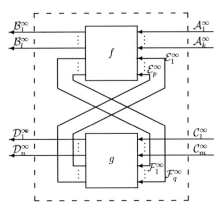

Figure 2.8: Universal composition as mutual feedback

Definition 2.31 (universal composition)

The universal composition $f^p \oplus^q g : \mathcal{A}_1^\infty \times \ldots \times \mathcal{A}_k^\infty \times \mathcal{C}_1^\infty \times \ldots \times \mathcal{C}_m^\infty \rightarrow$
$\mathcal{B}_1^\infty \times \ldots \times \mathcal{B}_l^\infty \times \mathcal{D}_1^\infty \times \ldots \times \mathcal{D}_n^\infty$ of a component

$$f : \mathcal{A}_1^\infty \times \ldots \times \mathcal{A}_k^\infty \times \mathcal{E}_1^\infty \times \ldots \times \mathcal{E}_p^\infty \rightarrow \mathcal{B}_1^\infty \times \ldots \times \mathcal{B}_l^\infty \times \mathcal{F}_1^\infty \times \ldots \times \mathcal{F}_q^\infty$$

and a component

$$g : \mathcal{C}_1^\infty \times \ldots \times \mathcal{C}_m^\infty \times \mathcal{F}_1^\infty \times \ldots \times \mathcal{F}_q^\infty \rightarrow \mathcal{D}_1^\infty \times \ldots \times \mathcal{D}_n^\infty \times \mathcal{E}_1^\infty \times \ldots \times \mathcal{E}_p^\infty$$

is defined by a parallel composition with feedback in connection with cross
components

$$f^p \oplus^q g \;=\; \circlearrowleft_{p+q} (\mathsf{X}_{k+m+q+p}(\sigma)\,;\,(f \parallel g)\,;\,\mathsf{X}_{l+q+n+p}(\tau))$$

with the input crossing

$$\sigma(i) \;=\; \begin{cases} i & \text{if } 1 \le i \le k \\ i+p & \text{if } k < i \le k+m \\ i+p & \text{if } k+m < i \le k+m+q \\ i-m-q & \text{if } k+m+q < i \le k+m+q+p \end{cases}$$

and the output crossing

$$\tau(i) \;=\; \begin{cases} i & \text{if } 1 \le i \le l \\ i+n & \text{if } l < i \le l+q \\ i-q & \text{if } l+q < i \le l+q+n \\ i & \text{if } l+q+n < i \le l+q+n+p \end{cases}$$

$\square$

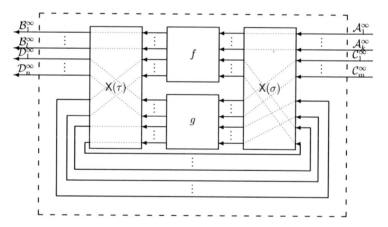

Figure 2.9: Universal composition as parallel composition with feedback and
cross components

The universal composition, cf. Figure 2.9, can also be defined by different
though equivalent equations involving the feedback operator, for example by

cross components realizing a different order on the feedback channels, or by sequential composition (in both directions) with identity components.

Sequential and parallel composition and feedback can be obtained as special cases of the general composition:

sequential composition $f \mathbin{;} g$ is obtained through the absence of feedback channels back from the second component g to the first component f and the absence of external output channels for f and external input channels for g: $p = l = m = 0$.

parallel composition $f \parallel g$ is characterized by the absence of the mutual feedback channels: $p = q = 0$.

feedback $\circlearrowright_q f$ is obtained by choosing the identity on the feedback channels for g, and thereby requiring that the types of the mutual feedback channels agree and that g neither has external input nor output channels: $g = id_q$, $p = q$, $m = n = 0$.

As with the parallel composition, the general composition is interchangeable only with channel crossing. The definition of the universal composition can be extended to an arbitrary number of components in a natural way.

2.5.5 Alternative Compositions

The connections of every finite network of components can always be expressed by sequential and parallel composition and feedback. However, the arrangement of the network components in space, which is based on tuples of streams, and the restriction to a basic set of three composition operators in general require routing components such as cross components, identity components, and copy components.

If we considered *named channels* [Kah74] instead of stream tuples, a stream processing function would map valuations to valuations. A *valuation* maps channel names to streams. A composite network is then described by a finite number of mutually recursive equations each with a correctly typed and dimensionated tuple of channel names (each and pairwise disjoint) on the left hand side and the application of a stream processing function provided with the corresponding number of channel names of suitable types as arguments on the right hand side.

Input channels do not occur on the left hand side of an equation. *Output channels* do not occur on the right hand side of an equation. The remaining channels are *internal channels*.

The disadvantage of named channels is that the composition of subsystems is based on channel names, and thus it requires channel renaming and a hiding concept for internal channels to avoid name conflicts.

The compositions through operators and through named channels are equally powerful. A network description with operators can be transformed into a description with channel names by marking each stream with a new name and adding an equation for each component of the network relating the tuple of output channel names with the application of a stream processing function to the tuple of input channel names. In the other direction, a description of a network with named channels can be transformed into a description with composition operators, for example, by enclosing the parallel composition of all components in cross components rearranging all streams such that the feedback operator connects output and input streams which belong to the same channel name. Channels which occur more than once on the right hand side of equations need a copy component in the description with unnamed channels.

Another idea for the composition of stream processing functions stems from synchronous concurrent algorithms (SCA) [MT88, PTH98]. The connections between the components are modelled by *port mappings* which map input ports to channels or sources.

Chapter 3

State Transition Machines with Input and Output

In the setting of stream processing functions, the behaviour of a component is specified by a stream processing function. The specification in general refers to the complete input and output streams and ignores the incremental construction of streams. We aim at transforming input / output specifications into specifications close to an implementation which access the input streams from the front element by element and which extend the output streams at the rear.

Usually, the implementation of the behaviour of a component requires a state, be it in the shape of attributes in the object oriented paradigm, of parameters in the applicative paradigm, or of local variables in the imperative paradigm. We employ an abstract machine model which makes use of an internal state. The abstract machine model gives us the freedom to postpone the decision about the programming language for the implementation of the component's behaviour.

A component continuously reads data from an input stream, and as a reaction it may produce output data and change its internal state. We define and analyse state transition machines with input and output which repeatedly perform these activities as long as input is provided at an input port.

Before analysing the relation between states of a state transition machine and investigating the connection between distinct state transition machines, we compare state transition machines with related approaches. We concentrate on state transition machines with one input channel and one output channel at first.

3.1   Basics

The behaviour of distributed systems is often formalized by a labelled state transition system specifying a transition relation between states associated with labels [WN95]. The transitions denote memory updates, inputs, outputs, or other actions. For the purposes of modelling communicating components, we associate a state transition with receiving an element on an input channel and sending data to an output channel.

Definition 3.1 (state transition machine with input and output)
A *state transition machine with input and output*, for short a state transition machine,

$$M \;=\; (\mathcal{Q}, \mathcal{A}, \mathcal{B}, next, out, q_0)$$

consists of

- a non-empty set $\mathcal{Q}$ of *states,*

- a non-empty set $\mathcal{A}$ of *input data,*

- a non-empty set $\mathcal{B}$ of *output data,*

- a (single-step) *state transition function* $next : \mathcal{Q} \times \mathcal{A} \to \mathcal{Q}$,

- a (single-step) *output function* $out : \mathcal{Q} \times \mathcal{A} \to \mathcal{B}^\star$, and

- an *initial state* $q_0 \in \mathcal{Q}$.

The types $\mathcal{A}$ and $\mathcal{B}$ determine the *interface* of the state transition machine.
□

In a given state, the current input datum completely determines the transition, since the transition functions are total and deterministic. The single-step output function yields a sequence of elements, not just a single element. The single-step functions can naturally be extended to finite input streams.

Definition 3.2 (multi-step state transition function)
The *multi-step state transition function* $next^\star : \mathcal{Q} \to (\mathcal{A}^\star \to \mathcal{Q})$ yields the state after processing a finite input stream:

$$
\begin{aligned}
next^\star(q)(\langle\rangle) &\;=\; q \\
next^\star(q)(x \lhd X) &\;=\; next^\star(next(q, x))(X)
\end{aligned}
$$
□

In each state $q \in \mathcal{Q}$, the multi-step state transition function cooperates with concatenation:

$$next^\star(q)(X \& Y) \;\; = \;\; next^\star(next^\star(q)(X))(Y) \tag{3.1}$$

Definition 3.3 (multi-step output function)
The *multi-step output function* $out^\star : \mathcal{Q} \rightarrow (\mathcal{A}^\star \rightarrow \mathcal{B}^\star)$ accumulates the output stream for a finite input stream:

$$out^\star(q)(\langle\rangle) \;\; = \;\; \langle\rangle$$
$$out^\star(q)(x \triangleleft X) \;\; = \;\; out(q, x) \,\&\, out^\star(next(q, x))(X)$$

The multi-step output function describes the *behaviour* of the state transition machine. □

In each state $q \in \mathcal{Q}$, the multi-step output function is monotonic:

$$out^\star(q)(X \& Y) \;\; = \;\; out^\star(q)(X) \,\&\, out^\star(next^\star(q)(X))(Y) \tag{3.2}$$

Hence, for each state the multi-step output function constitutes a stream processing function, which has a unique continuous extension to infinite input streams. It abstracts from the state transitions and offers a history-based view of a state transition machine. The proofs of Equations (3.1) and (3.2) proceed by induction on the initial part of the input stream.

In general, state transition machines may have unreachable states. For comparing state transition machines, we often reduce them to reachable states only.

Definition 3.4 (rooted state transition machine)
A state transition machine $M = (\mathcal{Q}, \mathcal{A}, \mathcal{B}, next, out, q_0)$ is called *rooted* if all its states are reachable from the initial state:

$$\mathcal{Q} \;\; = \;\; next^\star(q_0)(\mathcal{A}^\star)$$

The *reachable part* $reach(M)$ of a state transition machine $M = (\mathcal{Q}, \mathcal{A}, \mathcal{B}, next, out, q_0)$ is its restriction to the set of reachable states $\mathcal{Q}' = next^\star(q_0)(\mathcal{A}^\star)$:

$$reach(M) \;\; = \;\; (\mathcal{Q}', \mathcal{A}, \mathcal{B}, next|_{\mathcal{Q}' \times \mathcal{A}}, out|_{\mathcal{Q}' \times \mathcal{A}}, q_0) \qquad \square$$

The state transition machines introduced in this section model the input / output behaviour of components based on internal state transitions.

3.2   State Transition Graphs, Diagrams and Tables

State transition machines can be depicted as annotated directed graphs, transition tables or a combination thereof. For the intuitive representations of state transition machines, we adopt the concepts which are generally used for state-based descriptions.

A state transition machine $M = (\mathcal{Q}, \mathcal{A}, \mathcal{B}, next, out, q_0)$ can be taken as a directed, labelled graph, called *state transition graph*. The set $\mathcal{Q}$ of states corresponds to the nodes of the graph. An arc from a state q to the successor state $next(q, x)$ is labelled with the input / output pair $(x, out(q, x))$, cf. Figure 3.1.

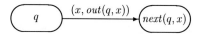

Figure 3.1: Arc of a state transition graph

The set of arcs of the state transition graph is

$$\left\{ q \xrightarrow{(x, out(q,x))} next(q, x) \mid q \in \mathcal{Q}, x \in \mathcal{A} \right\} . \tag{3.3}$$

The node representing the initial state is usually marked by an incoming arrow without source.

Large or even infinite state transition graphs can be described in a more compact form by parameterizing states and input data. The resulting *state transition diagram* offers a common representation of states showing uniform behaviour. An arc may, for example, be labelled by an expression for the new state depending on the previous state and the current input datum using primed notation for the new state. A condition for the current state and the current input can be annotated in square brackets, in the style of UML state diagrams.

That way, in the most compact form each state transition machine can be drawn with a single node, cf. Figure 3.2.

A *state transition table* consists of rows describing the state transitions. It contains columns for the current state, the current input datum, possibly a condition for the current state and the current input, the corresponding output, and the next state.

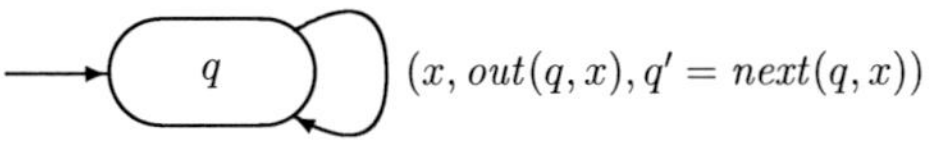
q
(x, out(q, x), q' = next(q, x))

Figure 3.2: Graphical representation with only one node

The following example exemplifies how to obtain a compact graphical representation for a state transition machine with an infinite number of states.

Example 3.5 (timer)
A timer emits a timeout after counting a number of unit signals. The timer is set by an input command $set(m)$ $(m > 0)$, and then lets the next m hiatons $\square$ pass until it emits the timeout signal denoted $!$. The timer can always be reset to a new number.

The timer is described by the state transition machine whose interface is determined by the set $\mathcal{A} = set(\mathbb{P}) \cup \{\square\}$ of input messages and the set $\mathcal{B} = \{\square, !\}$ of output messages. The state transition machine $M = (\mathbb{N}, \mathcal{A}, \mathcal{B}, next, out, 0)$ employs the state transition function

$$\begin{aligned} next(n, set(m)) &= m && (3.4)\\ next(0, \square) &= 0 && (3.5)\\ n > 0 \Longrightarrow next(n, \square) &= n - 1 && (3.6) \end{aligned}$$

and the output function

$$\begin{aligned} out(n, set(m)) &= \langle \square \rangle && (3.7)\\ out(0, \square) &= \langle\rangle && (3.8)\\ out(1, \square) &= \langle ! \rangle && (3.9)\\ n > 1 \Longrightarrow out(n, \square) &= \langle \square \rangle\,. && (3.10) \end{aligned}$$

The state transition graph of the timer has four types of arcs:

$$\begin{aligned} &\left\{ n \xrightarrow{(set(m), \langle \square \rangle)} m \mid n \in \mathbb{N}, m \in \mathbb{P} \right\} && (3.11)\\ \cup\ &\left\{ 0 \xrightarrow{(\square, \langle\rangle)} 0 \right\} && (3.12)\\ \cup\ &\left\{ 1 \xrightarrow{(\square, \langle ! \rangle)} 0 \right\} && (3.13)\\ \cup\ &\left\{ n \xrightarrow{(\square, \langle \square \rangle)} n - 1 \mid n > 1 \right\} && (3.14) \end{aligned}$$

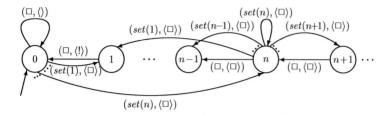

Figure 3.3: Part of the state transition graph for the timer $(n > 1)$

For reasons of clarity, the part of the state transition graph in Figure 3.3 contains only those arcs of type (3.11) which point from the node n to other nodes included in the presented part.

Figure 3.4 shows a condensed state transition diagram and Figure 3.5 the state transition table.

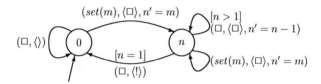

Figure 3.4: Condensed state transition diagram of the timer

q	x	where	$out(q, x)$	q'
n	$set(m)$		$\langle \Box \rangle$	m
0	$\Box$		$\langle \rangle$	0
1	$\Box$		$\langle ! \rangle$	0
n	$\Box$	$n > 1$	$\langle \Box \rangle$	$n - 1$

Figure 3.5: State transition table of the timer

The timer in [BS01b] differs from the version presented here in that it has a reset command and ignores set commands while counting.   □

3.3 Related Models

State transition machines with input and output are closely related to other state-based devices used to specify, verify, and analyse the behaviour of distributed systems.

3.3.1 Accepting Devices

Many of the related models have their origins in formal language theory and, hence, are accepting devices with a finite set of states. Accepting devices do not continuously produce output, but have an accepting condition instead, such as a set of accepting states.

Finite automata are not only applied to the analysis of regular languages. As accepting devices they also serve for the description of valid and invalid regular behaviour of processes. *ω-automata* [Tho90, Tho97], such as Büchi automata, Muller automata, or Rabin automata, are finite automata processing infinite streams which differ in their accepting conditions. Büchi automata, for example, accept an infinite word iff a final state occurs infinitely often in a run.

In contrast to state transition machines with input and output, all these accepting devices do not produce output, operate on a finite set of states, and are possibly restricted to a finite input alphabet.

3.3.2 Transition Systems

Transition systems are designed for modelling distributed systems by the set of state sequences the system may encounter during a run.

In particular, *finite transition systems* [Arn94] require a finite set of states and a finite set of transitions. One of the most common basic models describing the behaviour of processes are *labelled transition systems* [Kel76, Plo81, WN95] whose transitions carry actions. Labelled transition systems also serve as the basis for an operational semantics of formal process languages such as CSP [Hoa80] and CCS [Mil89].

In contrast to state transition machines, transition systems are not driven by input data.

3.3.3 State Machines with Input and Output

Most of the models for specifying and testing the behaviour of components with output originate in *finite state machines* [Nai97]. We distinguish between machines of Mealy type and machines of Moore type.

The widely used *Mealy machines* [HU79] produce exactly one output datum with each transition. Consequently, they can only describe the behaviour of io-synchronous components. Moreover, they operate on a finite set of states and have finite input and output alphabets. Mealy machines are a specialization of *generalized sequential machines* [Eil74], which show the closest relationship to state transition machines with input and output. As the only difference generalized sequential machines operate on finite sets.

Moore machines are dual to Mealy machines: the states of a Moore machine correspond to the outputs of a Mealy machine, and the outputs of the Moore machine correspond to states of the Mealy machine. Moore machines can describe the same systems as Mealy machines. If we described the behaviour of a component with a Moore machine derivative, the components would have to emit exactly one output element before input is processed. Moore machines are used for modelling systems which continually provide a datum at the output port which may only be replaced as a reaction to a new input datum. Since we do not want to observe single output elements in a transition, but sequences of output elements, Moore machine like models are not suited for our purposes.

A transition of a *port input/output automaton* [LS89, LT89] is labelled with either an input, or an output or an internal action. Transitions may depend on a condition. However, in each state each input action is enabled. Consequently, there is no direct connection between an input and the corresponding output. The input stream is not processed step by step, and output can be arbitrarily delayed.

Input-output transition systems [Tre96b, Tre96a] applied in testing theory differ only marginally from input/output automata. Input-output transition systems have a weaker interpretation of the property "input enabled": they allow internal actions before the input action. The internal actions in input-output transition systems are indistinguishable. Furthermore, the set of states and the input and output sets in input-output transition systems must be countable.

Extended finite state machines [LY96], which are also used in the field of testing, are finite state machines with additional variables in the states and transitions with conditions depending on the additional information.

Stream X-machines [Bar98] are an extension of the basic X-machine model [Eil74]. Stream X-machines are automata with input and output which distinguish between states and memory values. A system of *communicating X-machines* [BWW96] is no more than an X-machine [BCG+99] if the content of the communication channels is coded in the memory of a single X-machine.

Harel's *statecharts* [Har87] are built upon Mealy machines. They allow a system to be hierarchically decomposed into state machines. Communication is conducted via a broadcast mechanism. Mini-statecharts [SNR96], later called μ-Charts [Sch98a, PS97, Sch98b], are a derivative of statecharts which employ multicast communication and avoid some problems with the semantics of statecharts.

UML state diagrams [RJB98] are based on statecharts. The inputs are events, and outputs are actions. State diagrams may have final states.

In *SDL* [EHS97] process instances communicate via input buffers. The reception of an input signal may cause a state transition of a process instance combined with output to the input buffer of another process instance.

State transition systems [BP00a, Bro00] originating in [Bro97b] are used for specifying the behaviour of components and, in particular, for the verification that components validate safety and liveness properties [BP00b, Bro01a]. In order to ease verification, state transition systems carry as much information as possible: states are labelled with the previous and the future content of the channels and additional attributes.

In summary, there exist many computational devices which are closely related to state transition machines with input and output, yet none of them is identical with the state transition machines presented here.

3.4   Output Equivalence

We aim at transforming a state transition machine into a more compact one with a reduced number of states without changing the behaviour. To this end, we are interested in states which result in equal behaviour when provided with the same further input. In some related fields, for example testing, researchers study "indistinguishable" states [LY96].

Definition 3.6 (output equivalence)
Two states $p, q \in \mathcal{Q}$ of a state transition machine $M = (\mathcal{Q}, \mathcal{A}, \mathcal{B}, next, out, q_0)$ are called *output equivalent*, denoted $p \approx q$, iff they generate the same output for all input streams:

$$out^{\star}(p) \;=\; out^{\star}(q) \qquad\qquad \Box$$

Output equivalent states are indistinguishable for an observer as they produce the same output stream for every input stream.

Proposition 3.7
Successor states of output equivalent states are also output equivalent:

$$p \approx q \quad \Longrightarrow \quad next^{\star}(p)(X) \approx next^{\star}(q)(X) \qquad \qquad \Box$$

Proof: Assume $p \approx q$.

$$
\begin{aligned}
& out^{\star}(p)(X) \,\&\, out^{\star}(next^{\star}(p)(X))(Y) \\
= {}& out^{\star}(p)(X\&Y) \\
= {}& out^{\star}(q)(X\&Y) \\
= {}& out^{\star}(q)(X) \,\&\, out^{\star}(next^{\star}(q)(X))(Y) \\
= {}& out^{\star}(p)(X) \,\&\, out^{\star}(next^{\star}(q)(X))(Y)
\end{aligned}
$$

From $out^{\star}(next^{\star}(p)(X)) = out^{\star}(next^{\star}(q)(X))$ we conclude $next^{\star}(p)(X) \approx next^{\star}(q)(X)$. $\qquad \Box$

[BN94] investigate special properties of Mealy machines which ease the recognition of output equivalent states in Mealy machines.

3.5   State Congruence

For reducing the number of states for a state transition machine, we consider congruences [DS01a] relating output equivalent states. State congruences range from the identity on states which is the finest state congruence to the output equivalence as the coarsest one.

Definition 3.8 (state congruence)
For a state transition machine $M = (\mathcal{Q}, \mathcal{A}, \mathcal{B}, next, out, q_0)$, an equivalence relation $\sim$ on $\mathcal{Q}$ is called a *state congruence* iff it is compatible with the transition functions:

$$p \sim q \quad \Longrightarrow \quad next(p, x) \sim next(q, x) \qquad (3.15)$$

$$p \sim q \quad \Longrightarrow \quad out(p, x) = out(q, x) \qquad (3.16)$$

$$\Box$$

From the point of view of universal algebra [MT92, Wec92], a state transition machine $M = (\mathcal{Q}, \mathcal{A}, \mathcal{B}, next, out, q_0)$ is a Σ-algebra with three sorts $\mathcal{Q}$, $\mathcal{A}$, and $\mathcal{B}^{\star}$, two functions *next* and *out*, and one constant q_0. A state congruence is a specialization of a Σ-congruence whose relations on the input set and on the output are the corresponding equalities. From the theory of universal algebra, we take over terms such as quotients and finer / coarser congruences. Moreover, we employ corresponding results, for example, that the set of congruences ordered by set inclusion forms a partial order whose least element is the equality.

Proposition 3.9

Successor states of congruent states are congruent as well:

$$p \sim q \quad \Longrightarrow \quad next^\star(p)(X) \sim next^\star(q)(X)$$

Congruent states generate the same output:

$$p \sim q \quad \Longrightarrow \quad out^\star(p) = out^\star(q)$$

Hence, they are output equivalent.   □

The proofs proceed by induction on the input stream.

The other way round, the output equivalence relation forms a state congruence.

Proposition 3.10

The set of state congruences of a state transition machine ordered by set inclusion forms a *complete lattice*. The *least state congruence* is the equality, and the *greatest state congruence* is the output equivalence. The *meet operation* is the intersection of state congruences, and the *join operation* is the transitive closure of the union of state congruences.   □

In Section 4.3, this proposition will provide the foundation for comparing state refinements.

Definition 3.11 (quotient state transition machine)

Let $\sim$ be a state congruence on the state transition machine $M = (\mathcal{Q}, \mathcal{A}, \mathcal{B},$ $next, out, q_0)$. Then the state transition machine $M/_\sim = ([\mathcal{Q}]_\sim, \mathcal{A}, \mathcal{B}, next_\sim,$ $out_\sim, [q_0]_\sim)$ with

$$
\begin{aligned}
next_\sim([q]_\sim, x) &= [next(q, x)]_\sim \\
out_\sim([q]_\sim, x) &= out(q, x)
\end{aligned}
$$

is called the *quotient state transition machine* of M with respect to $\sim$.   □

The properties of state congruences guarantee that the transition functions of the quotient state transition machine are well-defined. The quotient state transition machine shows the same behaviour as the original state transition machine (cf. Equation (3.22)), but it manages with fewer states.

The problem of finding a state congruence corresponds to the problem of finding a (bi-)simulation relation for labelled transition systems or sequential machines [Gor80].

3.6   State Homomorphism

A quotient state transition machine for a state congruence which is not the
equality indeed reduces the number of states in a state transition machine.
Operating with congruence classes requires the choice of suitable representatives and prevents the addition of further states for a uniform treatment,
though.

For identifying output equivalent states, we now consider homomorphisms.
While a state congruence relates states in the same state transition machine,
a state homomorphism links the states of one state transition machine to
states in another state transition machine with the same interface and the
same input / output behaviour when started in compatible initial states.

Definition 3.12 (state homomorphism)
A *state homomorphism* $hom : \mathcal{Q} \to \mathcal{Q}'$ from a state transition machine $M =$
$(\mathcal{Q}, \mathcal{A}, \mathcal{B}, next, out, q_0)$ to a state transition machine $M' = (\mathcal{Q}', \mathcal{A}, \mathcal{B}, next',$
$out', q_0')$ with the same interface is compatible with the operations and con-
stants of the machines:

$$
\begin{aligned}
hom(next(q, x)) &= next'(hom(q), x) \\
out(q, x) &= out'(hom(q), x) \\
hom(q_0) &= q_0'
\end{aligned}
$$

A state homomorphism hom from the state transition machine M to the
state transition machine M' is denoted by $hom : M \to M'$.   □

A state homomorphism is compatible with the multi-step state transition
function

$$ hom(next^\star(q)(X)) = (next')^\star(hom(q))(X) \qquad (3.17) $$

and with the multi-step output function:

$$ out^\star(q) = (out')^\star(hom(q)) \qquad (3.18) $$

The proofs of Equations (3.17) and (3.18) proceed by induction on the input
stream. [Gor80] obtained the second result (3.18) for sequential machines
which produce exactly one output datum with each transition.

Consequently, states identified by a state homomorphism are output equivalent:

$$ hom(p) = hom(q) \implies p \approx q \qquad (3.19) $$

From the point of view of universal algebra, state homomorphisms are indeed a specialization of Σ-homomorphisms on state transition machines as three-sorted algebras. Thus, we obtain the well-known definitions and results from universal algebra [MT92, Wec92] about Σ-homomorphisms for state homomorphisms. For example, a bijective state homomorphism is a *state isomorphism*, the composition of state homomorphisms yields a state homomorphism, and the kernel of a state homomorphism is a state congruence.

Vice versa, if $\sim$ is a state congruence on a state transition machine $M = (\mathcal{Q}, \mathcal{A}, \mathcal{B}, next, out, q_0)$, then the quotient map $\phi_\sim : \mathcal{Q} \to [\mathcal{Q}]_\sim$ associating with each state its congruence class

$$\phi_\sim(q) \;=\; [q]_\sim \tag{3.20}$$

is a state homomorphism from M to the quotient state transition machine $M/_\sim = ([\mathcal{Q}]_\sim, \mathcal{A}, \mathcal{B}, next_\sim, out_\sim, [q_0]_\sim)$. With Equation (3.17), we get the multi-step state transition function

$$next_\sim^\star([q]_\sim)(X) \;=\; [next^\star(q)(X)]_\sim \tag{3.21}$$

and by Equation (3.18) the multi-step output function:

$$out_\sim^\star([q]_\sim) \;=\; out^\star(q) \tag{3.22}$$

The following proposition relates the existence of a state homomorphism from a rooted state transition machine to uniqueness.

Proposition 3.13
Let $M = (\mathcal{Q}, \mathcal{A}, \mathcal{B}, next, out, q_0)$ be a rooted state transition machine. A state homomorphism $hom : \mathcal{Q} \to \mathcal{Q}'$ from M to a state transition machine $M' = (\mathcal{Q}', \mathcal{A}, \mathcal{B}, next', out', q_0')$ is uniquely determined by

$$hom(next^\star(q_0)(X)) = (next')^\star(q_0')(X) \,. \qquad \qquad \square$$

The proof proceeds by induction on the input stream.

Consequently, there is at most one state homomorphism between two rooted state transition machines. In particular, rooted state transition machines related by state homomorphisms are isomorphic.

State homomorphisms have a close connection to state congruences and quotient state transition machines. They relate states of state transition machines with the same input / output behaviour. A state homomorphism on reachable states is determined by the the multi-step state transition function.

Concluding remarks

In this chapter, we gained an understanding of state transition machines, output equivalent states, and state congruences. We related state transition machines with the same behaviour through state homomorphisms.

The behaviour of a state transition machine given by the multi-step output function constitutes the step from a state-based view to a history-based view [Bro00]. In the next chapter, we address the opposite direction: we want to find concepts for a systematic introduction of states for a history-based description. State homomorphisms are a means for comparing different state-based views of the same input / output behaviour.

Chapter 4

State Refinement

The specification of a component's behaviour by a stream processing function supports a black box view mapping complete input histories to output histories. A state refinement offers a finer view of a component since it reveals the internal state transitions performed while processing an input stream element by element.

We give a definition for state refinement guaranteeing the existence of a naïve state refinement for every stream transformer. We analyse the set of all state refinements of a stream transformer and provide a constructive method for obtaining state refinements for stream processing functions carefully distinguishing between design decisions and derivations.

4.1   Introduction of State Refinement

A state refinement discloses the states of a component. Since the multistep output function of a state transition machine is a stream transformer which abstracts from the internal state transitions, we can introduce states by refining a stream transformer into a state transition machine.

A state refinement is a state transition machine with the same input / output behaviour as a given stream processing function.

Definition 4.1 (state refinement)
A state transition machine $M = (\mathcal{Q}, \mathcal{A}, \mathcal{B}, next, out, q_0)$ is called a *state refinement* for a stream transformer $f : \mathcal{A}^\star \to \mathcal{B}^\star$ iff the multi-step output function in the initial state agrees with the reactive part of the stream transformer f:

$$react_f \;=\; out^\star(q_0) \tag{4.1}$$

49

We say that M is a *refining state transition machine* for f and notate
$f \leadsto_{state} M$.   □

Since state transition machines produce output only in reaction to input,
they cannot deliver output if they do not receive input. Non-strict stream
transformers, however, yield output even if they are not (yet) provided with
input. For strict stream transformers, Equation (4.1) specializes to

$$f \;=\; out^{\star}(q_0)\,. \tag{4.2}$$

If the state transition machine $M = (\mathcal{Q}, \mathcal{A}, \mathcal{B}, next, out, q_0)$ is a state refinement of a stream transformer $f : \mathcal{A}^{\star} \to \mathcal{B}^{\star}$ and the state transition machine
M' is a state refinement of the multi-step output function $out^{\star}(q_0)$ of M,
then M' is also a state refinement of f:

$$f \leadsto_{state} M \wedge out^{\star}(q_0) \leadsto_{state} M' \;\;\Longrightarrow\;\; f \leadsto_{state} M' \tag{4.3}$$

After presenting a definition for state refinement, we validate the definition in
the following sections. We show that there is at least a naïve state refinement
for every stream transformer, and we compare state refinements before we
discuss the methodology for constructing state refinements.

4.2   Canonical State Refinement

The definition of a state refinement of a stream transformer guarantees that
there exists a state refinement for every stream transformer. Every stream
transformer has a state refinement whose set of states corresponds to the set
of input streams. In this section, we investigate the relationship of this naïve
state refinement to other state refinements of the same stream transformer.

For every stream transformer, there is a canonical state transition machine
recording the complete previous input history in its states.

Definition 4.2 (canonical state transition machine)
For a stream transformer $f : \mathcal{A}^{\star} \to \mathcal{B}^{\star}$, the *canonical state transition machine*, for short canonical state refinement, $M[f] = (\mathcal{A}^{\star}, \mathcal{A}, \mathcal{B}, next, out, \langle\rangle)$
is given with

$$\begin{aligned}
next(X, x) &= X \triangleright x \\
f(X) \,\&\, out(X, x) &= f(X \triangleright x)\,.
\end{aligned}$$ □

The state transition function appends the current input datum to the state. The output function is well-defined, because the stream transformer is monotonic. The output extension, cf. Definition 2.22, of a stream transformer coincides with the single-step output function of its canonical state transition machine.

In [Den96] the same basic idea is employed for a specification scheme for agents by so-called strategies. There, states which agree with previous inputs are called implicit states. With the same principle, [Rum96] presents the construction of a total "spelling" automaton for a stream processing function. The multi-step state transition function accumulates the input stream:

$$next^\star(X)(Y) \;=\; X\&Y \tag{4.4}$$

The multi-step output function extends the output history:

$$f(X) \,\&\, out^\star(X)(Y) \;=\; f(X\&Y) \tag{4.5}$$

The proofs of Equations (4.4) and (4.5) proceed by induction on the input stream Y.

Equation (4.5) guarantees that a stream transformer is refined by its canonical state transition machine.

Proposition 4.3
The canonical state transition machine $M[f] = (\mathcal{A}^\star, \mathcal{A}, \mathcal{B}, next, out, \langle\rangle)$ of a stream transformer $f : \mathcal{A}^\star \to \mathcal{B}^\star$ is a state refinement of f:

$$f \;\leadsto_{state}\; M[f] \qquad\qquad \Box$$

Knowing that input streams are the states of the canonical state transition machine, we transfer the terms output equivalence and state congruence to input streams of a stream transformer by considering the input streams to be the states of the canonical state transition machine.

By construction, a history abstraction, cf. Definition 2.26, induces a state congruence on the canonical state transition machine.

Proposition 4.4
Given a history abstraction $\alpha : \mathcal{A}^\star \to \mathcal{Q}$ for a stream transformer $f : \mathcal{A}^\star \to \mathcal{B}^\star$, the relation $\sim$ on $\mathcal{A}^\star$ defined by

$$X \sim Y \quad\Longleftrightarrow\quad \alpha(X) = \alpha(Y)$$

is a state congruence on the canonical state transition machine $M[f]$.

Vice versa, a state congruence $\sim$ on the canonical state transition machine $M[f] = (\mathcal{A}^\star, \mathcal{A}, \mathcal{B}, next, out, \langle\rangle)$ of a stream transformer $f : \mathcal{A}^\star \to \mathcal{B}^\star$ induces a history abstraction $\alpha : \mathcal{A}^\star \to [\mathcal{A}^\star]_\sim$ for f with $\alpha(X) = [X]_\sim$. $\qquad \Box$

The proof relates the output property (3.16) of a state congruence to output compatibility, cf. Definition 2.24, and the next state property of a state congruence (3.15) to the property "transition closed", cf. Definition 2.25.

The following proposition names the unique state homomorphism from a canonical state transition machine to another state refinement of the same stream transformer.

Proposition 4.5
For every state refinement $M = (\mathcal{Q}, \mathcal{A}, \mathcal{B}, next', out', q_0')$ of a stream transformer $f : \mathcal{A}^\star \to \mathcal{B}^\star$, the multi-step state transition function $(next')^\star(q_0') :$ $\mathcal{A}^\star \to \mathcal{Q}$ is the unique state homomorphism from the canonical state transition machine $M[f] = (\mathcal{A}^\star, \mathcal{A}, \mathcal{B}, next, out, q_0)$ to M. $\square$

Proof: We show directly that $(next')^\star(q_0')$ is a state homomorphism, cf. Definition 3.12:

$$\begin{aligned}
& (next')^\star(q_0')(q_0) \\
= {} & (next')^\star(q_0')(\langle\rangle) \\
= {} & q_0'
\end{aligned}$$

$$\begin{aligned}
& (next')^\star(q_0')(next(X, x)) \\
= {} & (next')^\star(q_0')(X \rhd x) \\
= {} & next'((next')^\star(q_0')(X), x)
\end{aligned}$$

$$\begin{aligned}
& f(X) \,\&\, out(X, x) \\
= {} & f(X \rhd x) \\
= {} & f(\langle\rangle) \,\&\, (out')^\star(q_0')(X \rhd x) \\
= {} & f(\langle\rangle) \,\&\, (out')^\star(q_0')(X) \,\&\, (out')((next')^\star(q_0')(X), x) \\
= {} & f(X) \,\&\, out'((next')^\star(q_0')(X), x)
\end{aligned}$$

The uniqueness of the state homomorphism follows from Proposition 3.13. $\square$

The canonical state transition machine of a stream transformer serves as a starting point for obtaining other state refinements, because state homomorphisms relate the canonical state refinement to all the other state refinements of the stream transformer.

4.3   Comparing State Refinements

A stream transformer has a variety of state refinements related by state homomorphisms. In this section we provide a criterion for comparing state refinements and analyse the space of possible state refinements.

We compare state refinements of the same stream transformer by falling back on the order of the state congruences which generate the quotient state transition machines of the canonical state refinement.

Proposition 4.6
The reachable parts of the state transition machines refining the same stream transformer ordered by state homomorphisms form a complete lattice up to isomorphism. □

Proof: The quotient state transition machines of the canonical state transition machine $M[f]$ ordered with the relation $\leq$ defined by

$$M[f]/_{\sim_1} \leq M[f]/_{\sim_2} \quad \Longleftrightarrow \quad \sim_1 \subseteq \sim_2$$

form a complete lattice, because each quotient state transition machine is uniquely determined by a state congruence.

Furthermore, for every rooted state transition machine $M = (Q, \mathcal{A}, \mathcal{B}, next, out, q_0)$ refining a stream transformer f, there is a unique quotient state transition machine $M[f]/_{\sim}$ isomorphic to M. The congruence $\sim$ relates input streams that take the state transition machine into the same state:

$$X \sim Y \quad \Longleftrightarrow \quad next^\star(q_0)(X) = next^\star(q_0)(Y)$$

According to Proposition 3.13, the unique isomorphism $iso : Q \rightarrow [\mathcal{A}^\star]_\sim$ is defined by $iso(next^\star(q_0)(X)) = [X]_\sim$. □

State transition machines ordered by state homomorphisms only form a preorder because isomorphic state transition machines are not identified. Arbitrary state refinements of a stream transformer do not form a complete lattice up to isomorphism because unreachable states violate the existence of the least element.

The canonical state transition machine, which is the least state refinement among the refining rooted state transition machines up to isomorphism, is also called the *finest state refinement*. A state transition machine whose states correspond to the output equivalence classes, which is the greatest state refinement up to isomorphism, is also called the *coarsest state refinement*.

4.4 Construction of a State Refinement

The theory of state transition machines elaborated so far suggests a four step procedure for finding a state refinement of a stream transformer.

In the first step, the *canonical state transition machine* is constructed. This step follows a scheme whereas the following two steps require a design decision.

In the second step, we select a *state congruence* on the set of input histories. In general, the output function of the canonical state transition machine suggests a state congruence.

In the third step, we choose a *representation* for the congruence classes.

In the forth step, the components of the *refining state transition machine* are derived.

In this section, we fuse steps two and three using history abstractions, cf. Definition 2.26. We also combine the derivation of the canonical state transition machine and of the refining state transition machine. The chosen history abstraction is the state homomorphism from the canonical state transition machine to the refining state transition machine.

Definition 4.7 (state refinement through a history abstraction)
Let $\alpha : \mathcal{A}^\star \to \mathcal{Q}$ be a history abstraction for a stream transformer $f : \mathcal{A}^\star \to \mathcal{B}^\star$. Then a state transition machine $M[f, \alpha] = (\mathcal{Q}, \mathcal{A}, \mathcal{B}, next, out, \alpha(\langle\rangle))$ with

$$next(\alpha(X), x) = \alpha(X \triangleright x)$$
$$out(\alpha(X), x) = \varepsilon_f(X, x)$$

is called a *state refinement for f through the history abstraction α*.   □

The properties "transition closed", cf. Definition 2.25, and "output compatible", cf. Definition 2.24, guarantee that the transition functions are well-defined. The output function can alternatively be defined implicitly without the output extension:

$$f(X) \,\&\, out(\alpha(X), x) = f(X \triangleright x) \tag{4.6}$$

By construction, a history abstraction is the state homomorphism from the canonical state transition machine to the state transition machine constructed in Definition 4.7.

Proposition 4.8
A history abstraction $\alpha : \mathcal{A}^\star \to \mathcal{Q}$ for a stream transformer $f : \mathcal{A}^\star \to \mathcal{B}^\star$ is the unique state homomorphism from the canonical state transition machine $M[f]$ to a state refinement $M[f, \alpha]$ of f through α.   □

Vice versa, the unique state homomorphism from a canonical state transition machine to any state refinement is a history abstraction, cf. Proposition 4.5. The following theorem justifies the terminology "state refinement through a history abstraction" from Definition 4.7.

Theorem 4.9

If $\alpha : \mathcal{A}^\star \to \mathcal{Q}$ is a history abstraction for a stream transformer $f : \mathcal{A}^\star \to \mathcal{B}^\star$, then a state transition machine $M[f, \alpha]$ forms a state refinement of the stream transformer f. □

Definition 4.7 specifies the state transition function and the output function only on the subset of reachable states. Their definition on unreachable states does not affect the behaviour of the state transition machine started in the initial state.

The history abstraction generates the set of reachable states:

$$\alpha = next^\star(q_0) \tag{4.7}$$

Consequently, we have

$$f(X) \,\&\, out^\star(\alpha(X))(Y) = f(X \& Y) \,. \tag{4.8}$$

If the history abstraction is the identity function on the input streams, we retrieve the canonical state transition machine:

$$M[f] = M[f, id_{\mathcal{A}^\star}] \tag{4.9}$$

If a surjective history abstraction identifies all input streams of each class of output equivalent input streams, then we get a refining state transition machine with the minimal number of states.

The history abstraction uniquely determines the reachable part of a state refinement. Consequently, the choice of the history abstraction also affects the size of the state space and the cost of the state transition and of the output function.

A history abstraction can be combined with a state homomorphism to obtain a coarser history abstraction: The function composition $hom \circ \alpha$ of a history abstraction $\alpha : \mathcal{A}^\star \to \mathcal{Q}$ for a stream transformer $f : \mathcal{A}^\star \to \mathcal{B}^\star$ and a state homomorphism $hom : \mathcal{Q} \to \mathcal{Q}'$ from the state refinement $M[f, \alpha]$ to $M' = (\mathcal{Q}', \mathcal{A}, \mathcal{B}, next', out', q_0')$ is again a history abstraction. The reachable parts of the state transition machine M' and the state refinement $M[f, hom \circ \alpha]$ agree, cf. Figure 4.1.

The procedure for constructing a state refinement for a stream transformer now consists of three steps.

In the first step, the *output extension* of the stream transformer is determined.

In the second step, a *history abstraction* is chosen, and the initial state and
the state transition function are derived.

In the third step, the *output function* of the state refinement is derived.

The first and the third step are mechanical whereas the second step requires
the design decision. In general, the output extension suggests a history abstraction.

Concluding Remarks

Figure 4.1 sketches different ways how to obtain state refinements for a stream
transformer.

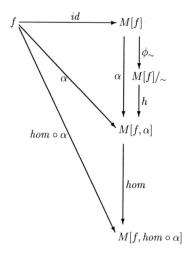

Figure 4.1: State refinements with state homomorphisms and history abstractions

Vertical arrows, annotated with state homomorphisms, denote transformations of a state refinement into a coarser state refinement. A quotient state

transition machine $M[f]/_\sim$, obtained with the quotient map $\phi_\sim$, can be refined with a state homomorphism h with $h([X]_\sim) = \alpha(X)$, choosing representatives for the congruence classes and, possibly, completing the set of states with unreachable states. In Figure 4.1 however, we assume that the state homomorphisms α, *hom*, and h are surjective so that all the state transition machines are rooted.

The other arrows denote state introductions for a stream transformer with history abstractions. A history abstraction constitutes the design decision which completely determines a state refinement on reachable states. The history abstraction yielding the canonical state refinement is the identity. A history abstraction can be combined with a state homomorphism to a history abstraction leading to a coarser state refinement.

Chapter 5

Applications of State Refinement

The previous chapter showed that history abstractions play a key role for a systematic state refinement. In this chapter we analyse the influence of particular history abstractions on state refinements. Thereby we start with a history abstraction and determine the associated state refinement as far as possible. This leads to a characterization of the refined stream transformers.

A history abstraction determines a state refinement apart from the output function, since the initial state and the state transition function are both independent of the refined stream transformer.

Therefore we investigate sets of stream transformers with the same history abstraction. In the following sections, we derive the initial state and the state transition function for various significant history abstractions using Theorem 4.9. We illustrate some representative stream transformers sharing the same state transition function, but differing in their output function. Furthermore, we evaluate and compare the applicability of the selected history abstractions.

5.1 History Independent Components

The simplest history abstraction is a constant function. We provide a state refinement for all the components with this history abstraction. Then we also characterize the set of stream processing function which can be implemented with this most simple state transition machine.

A constant function $const : \mathcal{A}^\star \to \{q_0\}$ on streams defined by

$$const(X) = q_0 \tag{5.1}$$

forms a history abstraction.

Definition 5.1 (history independent components)
The stream processing functions for which a constant function is a history abstraction describe *history independent* components.   □

The set of states of a state refinement for a history independent component can be a singleton set.

Proposition 5.2
For every history independent stream transformer $f : \mathcal{A}^* \to \mathcal{B}^*$, the state transition machine $M[f, const] = (\{q_0\}, \mathcal{A}, \mathcal{B}, next, out, q_0)$ with the trivial state transition function $next(q_0, x) = q_0$ and the output function $out(q_0, x) = \varepsilon_f(X, x)$ is the derived state refinement through the history abstraction *const*.
                                                                              □

In the following we first investigate a parameterized history independent component and, with that, characterize the set of history independent components.

Characterization of history independent components

Components which construct their output stream by applying a *basic function* to the single elements of the input stream are uniformly described by the functional $map' : (\mathcal{A} \to \mathcal{B}^*) \to (\mathcal{A}^* \to \mathcal{B}^*)$ with

$$map'(g)(\langle\rangle) \;=\; \langle\rangle \tag{5.2}$$
$$map'(g)(x \triangleleft X) \;=\; g(x) \,\&\, map'(g)(X)\,. \tag{5.3}$$

The function concatenates the substreams generated by the single input elements to form the output stream.

By Theorem 2.15, the function $map'(g)$ distributes over concatenation for every basic function g:

$$map'(g)(X \& Y) \;=\; map'(g)(X) \,\&\, map'(g)(Y) \tag{5.4}$$

Hence it is monotonic.

In the field of parallel programming on finite lists, a function $map'(g)$ on finite lists is a list homomorphism [DW98]. This means that $map'(g)$ applied to a finite list can be computed from the results of $map'(g)$ on segments of the input only, which can themselves be computed in parallel.

The output extension $\varepsilon_{map'(g)}(X, x) = g(x)$ only depends on the current input. Since it is independent of the previous input history, the history abstraction need not preserve any information of the previous input. Thus any transition closed function on $\mathcal{A}^\star$, in particular any constant function, is a history abstraction for $map'(g)$.

The refining state transition machine $M[map'(g), const] = (\{q_0\}, \mathcal{A}, \mathcal{B}, next, out, q_0)$ of a component $map'(g) : \mathcal{A}^\star \to \mathcal{B}^\star$ employs the output function $out(q_0, x) = g(x)$.

So every component whose behaviour can be described by the functional map' can be implemented by a state transition machine with a singleton state or without a state, respectively.

Vice versa, the behaviour of every strict component which can be implemented with a state transition machine $M = (\{q_0\}, \mathcal{A}, \mathcal{B}, next, out, q_0)$ with only a singleton state can be described as a function $map'(g)$ where the basic function $g : \mathcal{A} \to \mathcal{B}^\star$ is

$$g(x) = out(q_0, x). \tag{5.5}$$

In a word, the history independent components are exactly the functions map'.

Proposition 5.3
The stream transformer $f : \mathcal{A}^\star \to \mathcal{B}^\star$ is history independent iff there exists a basic function $g : \mathcal{A} \to \mathcal{B}^\star$ such that

$$react_f \;=\; map'(g) \qquad\qquad \square$$

We now present some history independent components, their notation in terms of map', and their state refinement. As the first example we revisit the duplicating component from Example 2.18.

Example 5.4 (duplicate — revisited)
The component $dupl : \mathcal{A}^\star \to \mathcal{A}^\star$ duplicating every element in the input stream is specified by $dupl = map'(g)$ employing the basic function $g : \mathcal{A} \to \mathcal{A}^\star$ with

$$g(x) \;=\; \langle x, x \rangle. \tag{5.6}$$

This history independent component has the refining state transition machine $M[dupl, const] = (\{q_0\}, \mathcal{A}, \mathcal{A}, next, out, q_0)$ with the output function $out(q_0, x) = \langle x, x \rangle$. $\qquad\qquad \square$

While the duplicating component outputs exactly two elements for each element in the input stream, a filter component outputs at most one element.

Example 5.5 (filter)

Filter components let elements from an input stream pass only if they validate a predicate. Filters $\textit{filter} : (\mathcal{A} \to \mathbb{B}) \to (\mathcal{A}^\star \to \mathcal{A}^\star)$ are defined by

$$\textit{filter}(P)(\langle\rangle) = \langle\rangle \tag{5.7}$$

$$\textit{filter}(P)(x \triangleleft X) = \begin{cases} x \triangleleft \textit{filter}(P)(X) & \text{if } P(x) \\ \textit{filter}(P)(X) & \text{if not } P(x). \end{cases} \tag{5.8}$$

The set $\mathbb{B}$ denotes the set of Boolean values. Filters are history independent components through $\textit{filter}(P) = \textit{map}'(\textit{validates}(P))$ where the basic function $\textit{validates} : (\mathcal{A} \to \mathbb{B}) \to (\mathcal{A} \to \mathcal{A}^\star)$ is defined by

$$\textit{validates}(P)(x) = \begin{cases} \langle x \rangle & \text{if } P(x) \\ \langle\rangle & \text{if not } P(x). \end{cases} \tag{5.9}$$

The state refinement $M[\textit{filter}(P), \textit{const}] = (\{q_0\}, \mathcal{A}, \mathcal{A}, \textit{next}, \textit{out}, q_0)$ employs the output function $\textit{out}(q_0, x) = \textit{validates}(P)(x)$. □

Instances of the filter function are at times relevant for the specification of other functions. Therefore we introduce some notation.

Definition 5.6 (notation for filters)

If the predicate P tests for the containment of an element in a set $\mathcal{M}$, we use the shorthand notation $\textit{filter}(\mathcal{M})$ for $\textit{filter}(\in \mathcal{M})$. If $\mathcal{M} = \{m\}$ is a singleton set, we notate $\textit{filter}(m)$ instead of $\textit{filter}(\{m\})$. For the length of a filtered stream $|\textit{filter}(\mathcal{M})(X)|$, we notate $\|X\|_{\mathcal{M}}$. □

Intuitive representatives of the class of history independent stream transformers are iterators.

Example 5.7 (iterator)

An iterator component $\textit{map} : (\mathcal{A} \to \mathcal{B}) \to (\mathcal{A}^\star \to \mathcal{B}^\star)$ applies a basic function to the single elements of its input stream:

$$\textit{map}(g)(\langle\rangle) = \langle\rangle \tag{5.10}$$

$$\textit{map}(g)(x \triangleleft X) = g(x) \triangleleft \textit{map}(g)(X) \tag{5.11}$$

The iterator is a history independent component through $\textit{map}(g) = \textit{map}'(\langle\cdot\rangle \circ g)$ where the operator $\langle\cdot\rangle$ wraps an element into a singleton stream.

The refining state transition machine $M[\textit{map}(g), \textit{const}] = (\{q_0\}, \mathcal{A}, \mathcal{B}, \textit{next}, \textit{out}, q_0)$ employs the output function $\textit{out}(q_0, x) = (\langle\cdot\rangle \circ g)(x) = \langle g(x)\rangle$. □

We now have an understanding of the components whose future behaviour does not depend on previous input. Their state refinement employs a singleton state only. Their output function depends only on the current input datum and is independent of the state.

5.2 Stationing Components

Input streams may cause various kinds of breaks in the behaviour of components. A break may, for example, arise from an unexpected datum or an end-of-transmission message indicating that no proper input can eventually be received on that channel. After processing a prehistory causing a break, a component often shows a uniform behaviour depending only on the current input. Thus a broken component behaves history insensitively.

If a component breaks on an input stream, it remains broken on all the prolongations of this input stream. We investigate history abstractions which identify such streams.

Definition 5.8 (history abstraction with stationing input)
Let the set

$$\mathcal{A}^{\star} = \mathcal{R} \,\dot\cup\, \bigcup_{i \in I} \mathcal{S}_i$$

of input streams be partitioned into non-empty, mutually disjoint, upward closed sets $\mathcal{S}_i$ ($i \in I$ for an index set I) of *stationing* input streams, and the non-empty set $\mathcal{R}$ of *regular* input streams which is then prefix closed.
The history abstraction $break : \mathcal{A}^{\star} \to \mathcal{R} \,\dot\cup\, \{s_i \mid i \in I\}$ with $s_i \neq s_j$ for $i \neq j$ identifies the stationing streams leading to the same break:

$$break(X) = \left\{ \begin{array}{ll} s_i & \text{if } X \in \mathcal{S}_i \\ X & \text{if } X \in \mathcal{R} \end{array} \right.$$

$\square$

$break$ is indeed transition closed, because $break(X) = break(Y)$ implies $X = Y$ or $X, Y \in \mathcal{S}_i$ for an $i \in I$. In both cases $break(X \rhd x) = break(Y \rhd x)$.

Definition 5.9 (stationary components)
The stream processing functions for which $break$ is a history abstraction describe *stationary* components. $\square$

The state refinement for a stationary component consequently operates on the set $\mathcal{Q} = \mathcal{R} \,\dot\cup\, \{s_i \mid i \in I\}$ of states. As the empty input stream is regular, the initial state of the derived state refinement is the empty stream.

Proposition 5.10
For stationary stream transformers $f : \mathcal{A}^{\star} \to \mathcal{B}^{\star}$, the state transition machine $M[f, break] = (\mathcal{R} \,\dot\cup\, \{s_i \mid i \in I\}, \mathcal{A}, \mathcal{B}, next, out, \langle\rangle)$ with the state transition

function

$$next(s_i, x) = s_i$$
$$next(X, x) = \left\{ \begin{array}{ll} s_i & \text{if } X \rhd x \in \mathcal{S}_i \\ X \rhd x & \text{if } X \rhd x \in \mathcal{R} \end{array} \right.$$

is a state refinement of f through the history abstraction *break*. The output function is

$$out(s_i, x) = \varepsilon_f(S_i, x) \quad \text{for an arbitrary } S_i \in \mathcal{S}_i$$
$$out(X, x) = \varepsilon_f(X, x). \qquad\qquad \square$$

After processing a stationing input stream the state transition machine always stays in the same absorbing state.

In general, this history abstraction does not yield the best reduction, because the regular input streams are not properly abstracted. However, it lays the basis for further reduction steps.

An intuitive example for stationary components are components which do not emit output any more if a stationing input stream has been processed. In that case the state refinement need not distinguish different stationary states.

Example 5.11 (breakdown)
Components are in general not designed to operate in an arbitrary environment, instead they put requirements on the input streams. Input streams which do not validate these requirements are called *erroneous*. One of the characteristic features of erroneous input streams is that they cannot be corrected by further input, which means that the set $\mathcal{E} \subseteq \mathcal{A}^\star$ of erroneous input streams is upward closed. *Fault sensitive components* $f : \mathcal{A}^\star \to \mathcal{B}^\star$ break down on erroneous input $E \in \mathcal{E}$:

$$f(E\&X) = f(E) \qquad\qquad (5.12)$$

For $E \in \mathcal{E}$ the output extension ε_f is

$$\varepsilon_f(E\&X, x) = \langle\rangle. \qquad\qquad (5.13)$$

Hence, *break* is indeed a history abstraction for fault sensitive components.

The set $\mathcal{Q} = (\mathcal{A}^\star \backslash \mathcal{E}) \cup \{\textit{fail}\}$ of states of the derived state transition machine has an absorbing control state *fail*. The output function of the derived state refinement is $(Q \neq \textit{fail})$

$$out(\textit{fail}, x) = \langle\rangle \qquad\qquad (5.14)$$
$$out(Q, x) = \varepsilon_f(Q, x). \qquad\qquad (5.15)$$

In summary, the multi-step output function $out^* : \mathcal{Q} \to (\mathcal{A}^* \to \mathcal{B}^*)$ of a fault sensitive component is an instantiation of $(q \in \mathcal{Q}, Q \neq \mathit{fail})$

$$out^*(q)(\langle\rangle) = \langle\rangle \tag{5.16}$$

$$out^*(\mathit{fail})(x \triangleleft X) = out^*(\mathit{fail})(X) \tag{5.17}$$

$$out^*(Q)(x \triangleleft X) = \begin{cases} \varepsilon_f(Q, x) \,\&\, out^*(\mathit{fail})(X) & \text{if } Q \triangleright x \in \mathcal{E} \\ \varepsilon_f(Q, x) \,\&\, out^*(Q \triangleright x)(X) & \text{if } Q \triangleright x \notin \mathcal{E} \,. \end{cases} \tag{5.18}$$

□

Instantiations are fault sensitive memory components, such as a bounded buffer, an interactive stack, a priority queue [Dos03b], or a double-ended queue [Dos03a], which break down when a datum is requested which has not been stored.

Not only components which break down on erroneous input streams can be implemented with a history abstraction *break*, but also history insensitive components with an initialization phase.

Example 5.12 (self-initializing filter)
A self-initializing filter component $\mathit{filterinit} : \mathcal{A}^* \to \mathcal{A}^*$ filters the remainder of its input stream for its first element provided it exists:

$$\mathit{filterinit}(\langle\rangle) = \langle\rangle \tag{5.19}$$

$$\mathit{filterinit}(\langle x \rangle) = \langle\rangle \tag{5.20}$$

$$\mathit{filterinit}(x \triangleleft y \triangleleft X) = \begin{cases} y \triangleleft \mathit{filterinit}(x \triangleleft X) & \text{if } x = y \\ \mathit{filterinit}(x \triangleleft X) & \text{if } x \neq y \end{cases} \tag{5.21}$$

We partition the set of input streams into stationing inputs $\mathcal{S}_i = \{i \triangleleft X \mid X \in \mathcal{A}^*\}$ $(i \in \mathcal{A})$ and the set $\mathcal{R} = \{\langle\rangle\}$ of regular input streams. The history abstraction $\mathit{break} : \mathcal{A}^* \to (\{\langle\rangle\} \cup \mathcal{A})$ whose absorbing states $\mathcal{A}$ are determined by the first element of stationing streams is indeed output compatible with respect to the output extension

$$\varepsilon(\langle\rangle, x) = \langle\rangle \tag{5.22}$$

$$\varepsilon(i \triangleleft X, x) = \begin{cases} \langle x \rangle & \text{if } x = i \\ \langle\rangle & \text{if } x \neq i \,. \end{cases} \tag{5.23}$$

Hence, $\mathit{filterinit}$ is a stationary component.
The output function of the refining state refinement specializes to $(i \in \mathcal{A})$

$$out(\langle\rangle, x) = \langle\rangle \tag{5.24}$$

$$out(i, x) = \begin{cases} \langle x \rangle & \text{if } x = i \\ \langle\rangle & \text{if } x \neq i \,. \end{cases} \tag{5.25}$$

In summary, the multi-step output function $out^\star : (\{\langle\rangle\} \cup \mathcal{A}) \to (\mathcal{A}^\star \to \mathcal{A}^\star)$ of the self-initializing filter is: $(Q \in \{\langle\rangle\} \cup \mathcal{A},\ i \in \mathcal{A})$

$$out^\star(Q)(\langle\rangle) = \langle\rangle \tag{5.26}$$

$$out^\star(\langle\rangle)(x \triangleleft X) = out^\star(x)(X) \tag{5.27}$$

$$out^\star(i)(x \triangleleft X) = \left\{ \begin{array}{ll} x \triangleleft out^\star(i)(X) & \text{if } x = i \\ out^\star(i)(X) & \text{if } x \neq i \end{array} \right. \tag{5.28}$$

For a non-empty input stream, the self-initializing filter can be obtained from an ordinary filter as follows:

$$filterinit(x \triangleleft X) = filter(x)(X) \tag{5.29}$$

$\square$

Although any component which behaves history insensitively after processing a breaking prehistory is a stationary component, the main field of application of the history abstraction *break* lies in the introduction of failure states.

5.3   Components with a Bounded Short-Term Memory

The states of a component are sometimes substreams of the history. Their length may be bounded, and they can be either scattered or contiguous. The history abstractions yielding a contiguous substream – except for a suffix of the history – with a constant length of a sufficiently long input history lead to state refinements whose filled states are absorbing. Hence, in this section we derive a state refinement for components whose reaction to further input only depends on the suffix of its input history with a fixed length as far as it exists.

The function $last(n)$, cf. Example 2.27, yielding the last n elements of an input stream as far as they exist, is a history abstraction.

Definition 5.13 (components with a bounded short-term memory)
The stream processing functions for which $last(n)$ is a history abstraction $(n > 0)$ describe *components with a bounded short-term memory* with capacity n. $\square$

The state refinement of components with short-term memory capacity n employs the set $\mathcal{Q} = \mathcal{A}^{\leq n}$ of states. The derived initial state of a state refinement of stream transformers with a bounded short-term memory is $q_0 = last(n)(\langle\rangle) = \langle\rangle$.

The derivation of the state transition function $next : \mathcal{A}^{\leq n} \times \mathcal{A} \to \mathcal{A}^{\leq n}$, and also of the output function, aims at eliminating occurrences of the input history and replacing them with occurrences of the abstraction of the input history. The properties of the abstraction function guarantee that the elimination of occurrences of the input history is always possible:

$$
\begin{aligned}
next(last(n)(X), x) &= last(n)(X \rhd x) \\
&= \begin{cases} X \rhd x & \text{if } |X \rhd x| \leq n \\ last(n-1)(X) \rhd x & \text{if } |X \rhd x| > n \end{cases} \\
&= \begin{cases} last(n)(X) \rhd x & \text{if } |X| < n \\ rest(last(n)(X)) \rhd x & \text{if } |X| \geq n \end{cases} \\
&= \begin{cases} last(n)(X) \rhd x & \text{if } |last(n)(X)| < n \\ rest(last(n)(X)) \rhd x & \text{if } |last(n)(X)| = n \end{cases}
\end{aligned}
$$

We do not consider stream transformers with the short-term memory capacity $n = 0$ because they coincide with the history independent components.

The following proposition summarizes the state refinement.

Proposition 5.14
For stream transformers $f : \mathcal{A}^\star \to \mathcal{B}^\star$ with short-term memory capacity $n > 0$, the state transition machine $M[f, last(n)] = (\mathcal{A}^{\leq n}, \mathcal{A}, \mathcal{B}, next, \varepsilon_f|_{\mathcal{A}^{\leq n} \times \mathcal{A}}, \langle\rangle)$ with the state transition function

$$
next(Q, x) = \begin{cases} Q \rhd x & \text{if } |Q| < n \\ rest(Q) \rhd x & \text{if } |Q| = n \end{cases}
$$

is a state refinement of f through the history abstraction $last(n)$. □

The state transitions of components with a bounded short-term memory are independent of the particular values which constitute the state. Once the state is filled it remains filled.

The standard component with a bounded short-term memory is a shift register because for each input datum, the shift register outputs the element which is removed from the state, if at all.

Example 5.15 (shift register — revisited)
The shift register $shift(n)$ $(n > 0)$ specified in Example 2.16 validates

$$
shift(n)(X \& Y) = shift(n)(X) \& shift(n)(last(n)(X) \& Y). \tag{5.30}
$$

Since its output extension

$$\varepsilon(X, x) \;=\; shift(n)(last(n)(X) \rhd x) \tag{5.31}$$

$$=\; \begin{cases} \langle\rangle & \text{if } |last(n)(X)| < n \\ \langle first(last(n)(X)) \rangle & \text{if } |last(n)(X)| = n \end{cases} \tag{5.32}$$

only depends on the $last(n)$ abstraction of an input history, $last(n)$ is a history abstraction for $shift(n)$. The output function of the state refinement is the output extension restricted to $\mathcal{A}^{\leq n} \times \mathcal{A}$. In summary, the multi-step output function $out^{\star} : \mathcal{A}^{\leq n} \rightarrow (\mathcal{A}^{\star} \rightarrow \mathcal{A}^{\star})$ describes a state-based implementation of the n-place shift register:

$$out^{\star}(Q)(\langle\rangle) \;=\; \langle\rangle \tag{5.33}$$

$$out^{\star}(Q)(x \lhd X) \;=\; \begin{cases} out^{\star}(Q \rhd x)(X) & \text{if } |Q| < n \\ first(Q) \lhd out^{\star}(rest(Q) \rhd x)(X) & \text{if } |Q| = n \end{cases} \tag{5.34}$$

$\square$

The following example gives a state refinement for a component whose future behaviour depends only on the previous input datum provided it exists.

Example 5.16 (stuttering removal)
Sometimes elements may be duplicated during a transmission through stuttering. The stream transformer $unstutter : \mathcal{A}^{\star} \rightarrow \mathcal{A}^{\star}$ eliminates all consecutive duplicates of elements in its input stream:

$$unstutter(\langle\rangle) \;=\; \langle\rangle \tag{5.35}$$

$$unstutter(\langle x \rangle) \;=\; \langle x \rangle \tag{5.36}$$

$$unstutter(x \lhd x \lhd X) \;=\; unstutter(x \lhd X) \tag{5.37}$$

$$x \neq y \implies unstutter(x \lhd y \lhd X) \;=\; x \lhd unstutter(y \lhd X) \tag{5.38}$$

The function $unstutter$ is monotonic:

$$unstutter(X \rhd x) \;=\; \begin{cases} unstutter(X) & \text{if } last(1)(X) = \langle x \rangle \\ unstutter(X) \rhd x & \text{if } last(1)(X) \neq \langle x \rangle \end{cases} \tag{5.39}$$

Its output extension

$$\varepsilon(X, x) \;=\; \begin{cases} \langle\rangle & \text{if } last(1)(X) = \langle x \rangle \\ \langle x \rangle & \text{if } last(1)(X) \neq \langle x \rangle \end{cases} \tag{5.40}$$

shows that $last(1)$ is a history abstraction for $unstutter$.

We obtain the output function $out : \mathcal{A}^{\leq 1} \times \mathcal{A} \to \mathcal{A}^{\star}$ with

$$out(\langle x \rangle, x) = \langle \rangle \qquad (5.41)$$
$$Q \neq \langle x \rangle \implies out(Q, x) = \langle x \rangle . \qquad (5.42)$$

In summary, the multi-step output function $out^{\star} : \mathcal{A}^{\leq 1} \to (\mathcal{A}^{\star} \to \mathcal{A}^{\star})$ with

$$out^{\star}(Q)(\langle \rangle) = \langle \rangle \qquad (5.43)$$
$$out^{\star}(\langle \rangle)(x \lhd X) = x \lhd out^{\star}(\langle x \rangle)(X) \qquad (5.44)$$
$$out^{\star}(\langle q \rangle)(x \lhd X) = \left\{ \begin{array}{ll} out^{\star}(\langle x \rangle)(X) & \text{if } q = x \\ x \lhd out^{\star}(\langle x \rangle)(X) & \text{if } q \neq x \end{array} \right. \qquad (5.45)$$

stores in its state the datum which has last been emitted. □

Further representatives of components with a bounded short-term memory are, for example, a single pulser, cf. Example 7.4, simple delaying components, smoothing components emitting the average value of the last inputs, or analysers recording particular pairs, triples etc. in the input stream.

5.4 Components with Requests

The input data of interactive components can often be split into a subset of data which may have an effect on further output and a subset of data without any effect on the future output of the component. The data of the first type are called *updates* and the ones of the latter type *requests*. In this section we give a state refinement for components whose set of input data contains requests.

Such requests can be filtered away with the history abstraction *filter*, cf. Example 5.5. *filter*($\mathcal{U}$) is transition closed for every set $\mathcal{U}$ and is therefore a history abstraction.

Definition 5.17 (components with requests)
The stream processing functions for which *filter*($\mathcal{U}$) is a history abstraction describe *components with requests*. The elements in the set $\mathcal{U}$ are called *updates*, the others are called *requests*. □

The input streams without requests constitute the set of states for a state refinement of such components. The following proposition provides a state refinement for components with requests apart from the output function.

Proposition 5.18

For stream transformers with requests $f : \mathcal{A}^\star \to \mathcal{B}^\star$ with the history abstraction $filter(\mathcal{U})$ ($\mathcal{U} \subseteq \mathcal{A}$), the state transition machine $M[f, filter(\mathcal{U})] = (\mathcal{U}^\star, \mathcal{A}, \mathcal{B}, next, \varepsilon_f|_{\mathcal{U}^\star \times \mathcal{A}}, \langle\rangle)$ with the state transition function

$$next(X, x) = \begin{cases} X & \text{if } x \notin \mathcal{U} \\ X \triangleright x & \text{if } x \in \mathcal{U} \end{cases}$$

appending the current input datum to the state if it is an update, is a state refinement of f through the history abstraction $filter(\mathcal{U})$. $\square$

Typical examples in the set of components with requests are stream processing functions whose set of input data is split in write commands and read commands. The following example presents the introduction of a state refinement for a component with requests by an addressable memory component.

Example 5.19 (memory component with acknowledgements)

An addressable memory receives write commands combined with an address and the datum to be written, and read commands combined with an address. Let $\mathcal{A} \neq \emptyset$ denote the set of addresses and $\mathcal{D} \neq \emptyset$ denote the set of data. Then $\mathcal{I} = \mathsf{w}(\mathcal{A}, \mathcal{D}) \cup \mathsf{r}(\mathcal{A})$ denotes the set of input messages. The memory sends an acknowledgement @ on each (successful) write command. The set of output data is therefore $\mathcal{O} = \mathcal{D} \cup \{@\}$. Illegal read commands are ignored. In the following specifications, let $W, W_1, W_2 \in \mathsf{w}(\mathcal{A}, \mathcal{D})^\star$ and $V_a \in \mathsf{w}(\mathcal{A} \setminus \{a\}, \mathcal{D})^\star$.

The behaviour $memloc : \mathcal{I}^\star \to \mathcal{O}^\star$ of the memory component

$$memloc(W) = @^{|W|} \tag{5.46}$$
$$memloc(W \& \langle \mathsf{r}(a) \rangle \& X) = @^{|W|} \& memloc_{@'ed}(W \& \langle \mathsf{r}(a) \rangle \& X) \tag{5.47}$$

is defined via an auxiliary function $memloc_{@'ed} : (\mathsf{w}(\mathcal{A}, \mathcal{D}))^\star \& \langle \mathsf{r}(\mathcal{A}) \rangle \& \mathcal{I}^\star \to \mathcal{O}^\star$ which yields the output of the above memory assuming that the longest prefix containing only write commands has already been acknowledged:

$$memloc_{@'ed}(V_a \& \langle \mathsf{r}(a) \rangle \& W) = @^{|W|} \tag{5.48}$$
$$memloc_{@'ed}(V_a \& \langle \mathsf{r}(a) \rangle \& W \& \langle \mathsf{r}(b) \rangle \& X) =$$
$$@^{|W|} \& memloc_{@'ed}(V_a \& W \& \langle \mathsf{r}(b) \rangle \& X) \tag{5.49}$$
$$memloc_{@'ed}(W_1 \& \langle \mathsf{w}(a, d) \rangle \& V_a \& \langle \mathsf{r}(a) \rangle \& W_2) = d \triangleleft @^{|W_2|} \tag{5.50}$$
$$memloc_{@'ed}(W_1 \& \langle \mathsf{w}(a, d) \rangle \& V_a \& \langle \mathsf{r}(a) \rangle \& W_2 \& \langle \mathsf{r}(b) \rangle \& X) =$$
$$d \triangleleft @^{|W_2|} \& memloc_{@'ed}(W_1 \& \langle \mathsf{w}(a, d) \rangle \& V_a \& W_2 \& \langle \mathsf{r}(b) \rangle \& X) \tag{5.51}$$

memloc is monotonic:

$$memloc(X \& W) \quad = \quad memloc(X) \& @^{|W|} \tag{5.52}$$

$$memloc(X \& W \& \langle r(a)\rangle \& Y) \quad = \quad memloc(X) \& @^{|W|}$$
$$\& \, memloc_{@'ed}(filter(\mathsf{w}(\mathcal{A},\mathcal{D}))(X)\& W \& \langle r(a)\rangle \& Y) \tag{5.53}$$

Thus the output extension of *memloc* is $(Y \in (\mathsf{w}(\mathcal{A} \setminus \{a\}, \mathcal{D}) \cup \mathsf{r}(\mathcal{A}))^\star)$

$$\varepsilon(Y, \mathsf{r}(a)) \quad = \quad \langle\rangle \tag{5.54}$$

$$\varepsilon(X \& \langle \mathsf{w}(a,d)\rangle \& Y, \mathsf{r}(a)) \quad = \quad \langle d \rangle \tag{5.55}$$

$$\varepsilon(X, \mathsf{w}(a,d)) \quad = \quad \langle @ \rangle \,. \tag{5.56}$$

Since the output extension is independent of read commands in the history, they are requests, write commands are updates, and $filter(\mathsf{w}(\mathcal{A},\mathcal{D}))$ is a history abstraction for *memloc*. The state transition function of the derived state transition machine $M[memloc, filter(\mathsf{w}(\mathcal{A},\mathcal{D}))] = (\mathsf{w}(\mathcal{A},\mathcal{D})^\star, \mathcal{I}, \mathcal{O}, next, out, \langle\rangle)$ specializes to

$$next(W, \mathsf{r}(a)) \quad = \quad W \tag{5.57}$$

$$next(W, \mathsf{w}(a,d)) \quad = \quad W \rhd \mathsf{w}(a,d) \tag{5.58}$$

and the output function is

$$out(V_a, \mathsf{r}(a)) \quad = \quad \langle\rangle \tag{5.59}$$

$$out(W \& \langle \mathsf{w}(a,d)\rangle \& V_a, \mathsf{r}(a)) \quad = \quad \langle d \rangle \tag{5.60}$$

$$out(W, \mathsf{w}(a,d)) \quad = \quad \langle @ \rangle \,. \tag{5.61}$$

Coarser state refinements exist, because only the last write command to an address has an effect on the future output. The coarsest history abstraction filters the write commands, drops all but the last write command to each address and abstracts from the order of these last write commands.   □

Further examples for components with requests are fault tolerant memory components without acknowledgements or database components processing updates and queries. Fault sensitive memory components, which break on an illegal request command, are not components with requests as defined in this section because illegal request commands have an effect on the future behaviour of the component.

5.5   Scan Components

Many network components such as counters accumulate their input with an operation. The history abstraction for such components reduces the input stream with this operation. We present the state refinement for components with such a history abstraction, and we evaluate the significance of this history abstraction for the introduction of a state refinement for arbitrary stream transformers.

Quite a powerful history abstraction is a reduce functional $red : (\mathcal{C} \times \mathcal{A} \to \mathcal{C}) \to (\mathcal{C} \to (\mathcal{A}^\star \to \mathcal{C}))$ for an operation and an initial value:

$$red(\oplus)(e)(\langle\rangle) \;=\; e \tag{5.62}$$
$$red(\oplus)(e)(x \triangleleft X) \;=\; red(\oplus)(e \oplus x)(X) \tag{5.63}$$

For every state transition machine, the multi-step state transition function is an instance of the reduce function $next^\star = red(next)$.

For every $\oplus$ and e, the function $red(\oplus)(e)$ is transition closed, because it validates

$$red(\oplus)(e)(X \triangleright x) \;=\; red(\oplus)(e)(X) \oplus x\,. \tag{5.64}$$

Definition 5.20 (scan components)
The stream processing functions for which $red(\oplus)(e)$ is a history abstraction describe *scan components*.   □

The refining state transition machine employs the set $\mathcal{C}$ as its set of states. We derive the initial state

$$q_0 \;=\; red(\oplus)(e)(\langle\rangle) = e \tag{5.65}$$

and the state transition function for states that are reductions of an input history with the initial element e:

$$next(red(\oplus)(e)(X), x) \;=\; red(\oplus)(e)(X \triangleright x) = red(\oplus)(e)(X) \oplus x \tag{5.66}$$

The results of the state transition function on the other values in $\mathcal{C}$ can be chosen arbitrarily, for example as $next(q, x) = q \oplus x$ so that the state transition function is uniformly described.

Also for the output function, the result for those states that are not reductions of input histories with the initial state e can be chosen arbitrarily.

Proposition 5.21
For scan components $f : \mathcal{A}^\star \to \mathcal{B}^\star$ with the history abstraction $red(\oplus)(e)$, the state transition machine $M[f, red(\oplus)(e)] = (\mathcal{C}, \mathcal{A}, \mathcal{B}, next, out, e)$ with the state transition

$$next(q, x) = q \oplus x$$

and the output function validating

$$out(red(\oplus)(e)(X), x) = \varepsilon_f(X, x)$$

is a state refinement of f through the history abstraction $red(\oplus)(e)$. □

In the following, we demonstrate the state refinement of a scan component with an example which helps characterizing scan components.

Characterization of scan components

We now investigate a particular scan component and present a state refinement. This particular scan component also provides a characterization of the set of scan components.

A component $scan' : ((\mathcal{C} \times \mathcal{A} \to \mathcal{B}^\star) \times (\mathcal{C} \times \mathcal{A} \to \mathcal{C})) \to (\mathcal{C} \to (\mathcal{A}^\star \to \mathcal{B}^\star))$ constructs its output stream by applying the first dyadic operation to the proper prefixes of its input stream reduced under the second dyadic operation and the subsequent datum:

$$scan'(\otimes, \oplus)(e)(\langle\rangle) = \langle\rangle \tag{5.67}$$
$$scan'(\otimes, \oplus)(e)(x \triangleleft X) = (e \otimes x) \,\&\, scan'(\otimes, \oplus)(e \oplus x)(X) \tag{5.68}$$

The function $scan'(\otimes, \oplus)(e)$ validates the decomposition property

$$scan'(\otimes, \oplus)(e)(X \& Y) = \tag{5.69}$$
$$scan'(\otimes, \oplus)(e)(X) \,\&\, scan'(\otimes, \oplus)(red(\oplus)(e)(X))(Y) \,.$$

Hence, it is monotonic.

Since its output extension

$$\varepsilon(X, x) = red(\oplus)(e)(X) \otimes x \tag{5.70}$$

depends only on the reduced value of the input history, $red(\oplus)(e)$ is a history abstraction for $scan'(\otimes, \oplus)(e)$, and hence $scan'(\otimes, \oplus)(e)$ is a scan component.

For states q which are not reductions of an input stream we choose $out(q, x) = q \otimes x$. Together with the derived part of the output function we get for all states $q \in \mathcal{C}$:

$$out(q, x) \quad = \quad q \otimes x \tag{5.71}$$

Then the derived state transition machine is $M[scan'(\otimes, \oplus)(e), red(\oplus)(e)] = (\mathcal{C}, \mathcal{A}, \mathcal{B}, \oplus, \otimes, e)$. Since the operation $\oplus$ is the state transition function of the derived state transition machine, the multi-step state transition function $\oplus^* = red(\oplus)$ agrees with the reduce function.

As the specification pattern for $scan'$ in Equations (5.67) and (5.68) coincides with the specification pattern of the multi-step output function of any state transition machine in Definition 3.3 by matching the operation $\otimes$ with the output function and $\oplus$ with the state transition function, the multi-step output function of a state transition machine is a scan component. As every stream transformer possesses a state refinement, every stream transformer is a scan component.

Proposition 5.22
Every stream transformer $f : \mathcal{A}^* \rightarrow \mathcal{B}^*$, which has a state refinement $M = (\mathcal{Q}, \mathcal{A}, \mathcal{B}, next, out, q_0)$, is a scan component through $react_f = scan'(out, next)(q_0)$.

Vice versa, every strict component f with the history abstraction $red(\oplus)(e)$ can be specified as $f = scan'(\otimes, \oplus)(e)$ where $\otimes$ is defined by $red(\oplus)(e)(X) \otimes x = \varepsilon_f(X, x)$. □

Consequently, the scan components constitute the most general class of stream transformers with the same history abstraction, because it is the set of all stream transformers.

Although every stream processing function is a scan component, we present an intuitive example which is a specialization of the general scan.

Example 5.23 (ordinary scan)
We now specialize the above function $scan'(\otimes, \oplus)(e)$ concerning two aspects. First we assume that the contribution to the output and the next state are computed by the same operation $\oplus$. The second aspect is already known from the specialization of map' to map: the operation $\oplus$ now computes only single elements of the output stream. The specialization

$$scan(\oplus)(e) \quad = \quad scan'(\langle \cdot \rangle \circ \oplus)(\oplus)(e) \tag{5.72}$$

leads to

$$scan(\oplus)(e)(\langle \rangle) \quad = \quad \langle \rangle \tag{5.73}$$
$$scan(\oplus)(e)(x \triangleleft X) \quad = \quad (e \oplus x) \triangleleft scan(\oplus)(e \oplus x)(X) \,. \tag{5.74}$$

The output function the state refinement for *scan'* specializes to:

$$out(red(\oplus)(e)(X), x) \;=\; \langle red(\oplus)(e)(X) \oplus x \rangle \qquad (5.75)$$

For those states which are not reductions of input histories with the initial state e we choose for example $out(q, x) = \langle q \oplus x \rangle$. The resulting output function is

$$out(q, x) = \langle q \oplus x \rangle. \qquad (5.76)$$

Instantiations of the ordinary scan component are for example counters, modulo-counters, and counters with reset. [Dos02] investigates further examples and analyses (de-)composition properties of ordinary scan components.
□

In summary, the investigation showed that scan components are the most general class because every stream transformer can be considered to be a scan component. If a stream transformer is specified as a general scan function, the machine functions of the state refinement can directly be taken from the specification.

5.6 History Requiring Components

So far in this chapter we investigated history abstractions leading, in general, to coarser state refinements than the canonical state transition machine. In this section, we study the respective identity on the input streams, which is a history abstraction for every stream processing function, leading to the canonical state refinement. So in contrast to the previous sections we now do not investigate the class of components with the same history abstraction. Instead we find out whether for some components the identity is the coarsest surjective history abstraction.

Definition 5.24 (history requiring component)
A component is called *history requiring* if none of its input histories are output equivalent.
□

We now show that history requiring components indeed exist by giving an example for a history requiring component.

Example 5.25 (positions)
The stream transformer *positions* : $\mathbb{N}^\star \to \mathbb{N}^\star$ receives an input stream containing position numbers. For each position in its input stream it outputs

the value on this position in the input stream provided it has already been
processed:

$$positions(X) \;=\; history(\langle\rangle)(X) \tag{5.77}$$

positions is specified through an auxiliary function *history* : $\mathbb{N}^\star \to (\mathbb{N}^\star \to \mathbb{N}^\star)$:

$$history(X)(\langle\rangle) \;=\; \langle\rangle \tag{5.78}$$
$$history(X)(x \triangleleft Y) \;=\; lookup(X, x) \,\&\, history(X \triangleright x)(Y) \tag{5.79}$$

history is again specified with an auxiliary function *lookup* : $\mathbb{N}^\star \times \mathbb{N} \to \mathbb{N}^\star$
determining the value at a given position in a prehistory:

$$lookup(\langle\rangle, n) \;=\; \langle\rangle \tag{5.80}$$
$$lookup(x \triangleleft X, n) \;=\; \begin{cases} \langle x\rangle & \text{if } n = 0 \\ lookup(X, n-1) & \text{if } n > 0 \end{cases} \tag{5.81}$$

Obviously, *positions* is defined as its canonical state transition machine:
history is the multi-step output function, the (single-step) output function
is *lookup*, and the state transition function appends the current input datum
to the state.

The output equivalence classes of *positions* each contain only a single input
history:

$$X_1 \approx X_2 \quad\Longleftrightarrow\quad X_1 = X_2 \tag{5.82}$$

Proof: Outline for $\Longrightarrow$: Let $X_1 \neq X_2$, and let $k \geq 0$ be the length of
the maximal common prefix of X_1 and X_2, that means either one
of the streams is shorter than the other and its length is k, or X_1
and X_2 differ at position k. Since *lookup* is the output function of
positions, we have

$$positions(X_1 \triangleright k) \;=\; positions(X_1) \,\&\, lookup(X_1, k)$$
$$positions(X_2 \triangleright k) \;=\; positions(X_2) \,\&\, lookup(X_2, k)$$

X_1 and X_2 consequently cannot be output equivalent, because
$lookup(X_1, k) \neq lookup(X_2, k)$.   □

Consequently, a history abstraction cannot identify any input streams.   □

In summary, although the canonical state refinement is the finest rooted state
refinement, it is sometimes also the coarsest state refinement.

Concluding remarks

This chapter highlighted the significance of history abstractions for state refinement. The history abstractions of the same stream transformer lead to state refinements with a different degree of granularity. We investigated some important history abstractions independent of a stream transformer and determined the corresponding state refinement as far as possible with the construction scheme given in the previous chapter.

We characterized the components which can be refined by the simplest state refinement: a trivial state transition machine with a singleton state. We also encountered a history abstraction which is powerful enough to determine any state refinement for any arbitrary stream transformer, which need not be the canonical state transition machine, which is the finest state refinement. We also showed that there exist components whose coarsest state refinement coincides with the finest (rooted) state refinement.

Besides the classes we investigated in this chapter, there are many more interesting classes determined by history abstractions, for example by set or multiset abstraction or the length function or combinations of these history abstractions.

Chapter 6

State Refinements with History Condensing Functions

A history abstraction for a stream transformer determines a state refinement. Therefore, the choice of a history abstraction is a decisive step for the systematic introduction of states. The developer has to get an idea for a history abstraction based on the output extension of the stream transformer.

In this chapter, we show that if the stream transformer validates a decomposition property involving a function called history condensing function, then the history condensing function provides a history abstraction, with which we get a state refinement.

The history condensing function reduces an input stream to a stream containing the relevant information while the stream transformer does not deliver output when provided with the reduced input stream.

6.1 History Condensing Functions

In this section, we introduce a property which is validated by many stream transformers. The characterizing equation employs an auxiliary function from which a history abstraction can be obtained.

The behaviour of a stream transformer for composed input can often be inferred from the behaviour for an initial part of the input and the behaviour for the rear part preceded by some stream extracting the essential information from the initial part of the input.

Definition 6.1 (history condensing function)
A stream transformer $f : \mathcal{A}^\star \to \mathcal{B}^\star$ is said to validate the *decomposition*

property with a *history condensing function* $h : \mathcal{A}^* \rightarrow \mathcal{A}^*$, if

$$f(X \& Y) \;\; = \;\; f(X) \& f(h(X) \& Y)$$

holds. In this case, h is called *a history condensing function for the stream transformer* f.   □

This decomposition applies, for example, to functions validating the criterion for monotonicity, cf. Theorem 2.15. A corresponding decomposition of functions on finite lists leads to list homomorphisms with accumulation and indexing [DW00].

The history condensing function yields an input stream which does not evoke output and which nevertheless keeps the relevant information from the initial part determining the behaviour on further input.

For the rest of the chapter, we assume that the stream transformer $f : \mathcal{A}^* \rightarrow \mathcal{B}^*$ validates the decomposition property with a history condensing function $h : \mathcal{A}^* \rightarrow \mathcal{A}^*$.

Now we investigate basic properties of history condensing functions. First we specialize the decomposition such that the rear stream and the initial stream respectively are empty.

Lemma 6.2
The result of the history condensing function evokes no output:

$$f(h(X)) \;\; = \;\; \langle\rangle$$

The monotonicity of f requires that f is strict.

The result of the history condensing function h applied to the empty stream at the beginning of an input stream of f has no effect on the output:

$$f(Y) \;\; = \;\; f(h(\langle\rangle) \& Y)$$ □

The following lemma is necessary in order to show that the history condensing function h is output compatible.

Lemma 6.3
Multiple applications of h to initial parts of the input do not affect further output:

$$f(h(h(X) \& Y) \& Z) \;\; = \;\; f(h(X \& Y) \& Z)$$ □

Proof:

$$
\begin{aligned}
&\quad\; f(X\&Y) \,\&\, f(h(X\&Y)\&Z) \\
&= f(X\&Y\&Z) \\
&= f(X) \,\&\, f(h(X)\&Y\&Z) \\
&= f(X) \,\&\, f(h(X)\&Y) \,\&\, f(h(h(X)\&Y)\&Z) \\
&= f(X\&Y) \,\&\, f(h(h(X)\&Y)\&Z) \qquad\qquad\qquad\qquad \square
\end{aligned}
$$

Since the output extension $\varepsilon_f(X, x) = f(h(X) \triangleright x)$ of f is also invariant concerning multiple applications of h

$$
\varepsilon_f(X, x) = \varepsilon_f(h(X), x), \tag{6.1}
$$

the history condensing function h is output compatible with respect to the output extension of f.

Despite of all the useful properties a history condensing function validates, it does not generally form a history abstraction, because it may not be transition closed. Consequently, we pursue another way to derive a state refinement employing the history condensing function.

6.2 Construction of a State Refinement

For constructing a state refinement whose states are particular input streams, we transform the specification into a syntactic pattern meeting the definition of the multi-step output function of a state transition machine.

In order to find a state refinement, we try to directly derive a function $g : \mathcal{Q} \to (\mathcal{A}^\star \to \mathcal{B}^\star)$ whose equations follow the recursion structure of the multi-step output function of a state transition machine from the specification

$$
g(Q)(X) = f(Q\&X). \tag{6.2}
$$

The state space is restricted to $\mathcal{Q} = f^{-1}(\langle\rangle) \subseteq \mathcal{A}^\star$ in order to enable a direct transformation of f. The set $\mathcal{Q}$ is not empty, because $f(h(X)) = \langle\rangle$ for all $X \in \mathcal{A}^\star$.

We retrieve $f(X) = g(Q_0)(X)$, if $Q_0 \in \mathcal{Q}_0$ has no effect on the output of f:

$$
\mathcal{Q}_0 = \{Q_0 \in \mathcal{A}^\star \mid f(Q_0\&X) = f(X) \text{ for all } X \in \mathcal{A}^\star\} \tag{6.3}
$$

Since the states $Q_0 \in \mathcal{Q}_0$ validate $f(Q_0) = \langle\rangle$, we have $\mathcal{Q}_0 \subseteq \mathcal{Q}$. $\mathcal{Q}_0$ is not empty, because $h(\langle\rangle) \in \mathcal{Q}_0$ and $\langle\rangle \in \mathcal{Q}_0$.

We now derive a direct recursive version of g:

$$
\begin{aligned}
g(Q)(\langle\rangle) &= f(Q \& \langle\rangle) \\
&= f(Q) \\
&\overset{(a)}{=} \langle\rangle \\
g(Q)(x \triangleleft X) &= f(Q \& x \triangleleft X) \\
&= f(Q \triangleright x) \& f(h(Q \triangleright x) \& X) \\
&= f(Q) \& \varepsilon_f(Q, x) \& f(h(Q \triangleright x) \& X) \\
&\overset{(b)}{=} \varepsilon_f(Q, x) \& f(h(Q \triangleright x) \& X) \\
&= \varepsilon_f(Q, x) \& g(h(Q \triangleright x))(X)
\end{aligned}
$$

For the derivation steps (a) and (b) we make use of the restriction that Q validates $f(Q) = \langle\rangle$.

In summary, the derivation yields:

$$
\begin{aligned}
g(Q)(\langle\rangle) &= \langle\rangle & (6.4) \\
g(Q)(x \triangleleft X) &= \varepsilon_f(Q, x) \& g(h(Q \triangleright x))(X) & (6.5)
\end{aligned}
$$

The function g now indeed has the structure of the multi-step output function $out^\star$ of a state refinement of f with an *initial state* $Q_0 \in \mathcal{Q}_0$.

The *state transition function*, which is abstracted from Equation (6.5), reads $next(Q, x) = h(Q \triangleright x)$. The function $\alpha = next^\star(Q_0)$ is the *history abstraction* for f leading to this state refinement:

$$
\begin{aligned}
\alpha(\langle\rangle) &= Q_0 & (6.6) \\
\alpha(X \triangleright x) &= h(\alpha(X) \triangleright x) & (6.7)
\end{aligned}
$$

The *output function* $out(Q, x) = f(Q \triangleright x)$ is abstracted from Equation (6.5) as follows:

$$
\begin{aligned}
out(Q, x) &= \varepsilon_f(Q, x) \\
&= f(Q) \& \varepsilon_f(Q, x) \\
&= f(Q \triangleright x)
\end{aligned}
$$

The following theorem summarizes the result.

Theorem 6.4

Let $h : \mathcal{A}^\star \to \mathcal{A}^\star$ be a history condensing function for the stream transformer $f : \mathcal{A}^\star \to \mathcal{B}^\star$. Then a refining state transition machine is $M = (next^\star(Q_0)(\mathcal{A}^\star), \mathcal{A}, \mathcal{B}, next, out, Q_0)$ with an initial state Q_0 validating

$$
f(Q_0 \& X) = f(X)
$$

and the transition functions

$$next(Q, x) = h(Q \triangleright x)$$
$$out(Q, x) = f(Q \triangleright x).$$

If the history condensing function h is invariant concerning multiple applications of itself to initial parts of its input

$$h(h(X)\&Y) = h(X\&Y),$$

then h is transition closed, and the multi-step state transition function is $next^*(h(X))(Y) = h(X\&Y)$. In particular, if the initial state is chosen as $Q_0 = h(\langle\rangle)$, then h is the history abstraction leading to this state refinement. □

The theorem directly yields a state refinement of a stream transformer validating a decomposition property which is often obtained as a by-product from the proof of the monotonicity. In particular, the stream transformers which validate the criterion for monotonicity, cf. Theorem 2.15, can be refined with this theorem.

Lemma 6.5
For stream transformers which validate the criterion for monotonicity from Theorem 2.15, the termination function τ is the history abstraction leading to the state refinement in Theorem 6.4 with initial state $Q_0 = \tau(\langle\rangle) = \langle\rangle$. □

This lemma follows from the property $\tau(\tau(X)\&Y) = \tau(X\&Y)$ which is proved by induction on the input stream analogous to the proof of Theorem 2.15.

However, the state refinement obtained with Theorem 6.4 need not be the coarsest state refinement.

To conclude, we summarize the relationship between state refinements obtained with history abstractions and those obtained with history condensing functions. Equations (6.6) and (6.7) determine the history abstraction leading to the state refinement which is obtained with a history condensing function. Theorem 6.4 characterizes the history condensing functions which are also history abstractions. In the other direction, a history abstraction $\alpha : \mathcal{A}^* \to \mathcal{A}^*$ for a stream transformer $f : \mathcal{A}^* \to \mathcal{B}^*$ is a history condensing function for f, if $f(\alpha(X)) = \langle\rangle$ holds for all $X \in \mathcal{A}^*$. In that case the state transition machine obtained with Theorem 6.4 agrees with the state transition machine $M[f, \alpha]$ if the initial state is chosen as $Q_0 = \alpha(\langle\rangle)$.

6.3   Applications

Memory components receive write commands which update the store, and read commands which do not change the store but request a datum from the store provided the requested datum is available. They differ in the types of their access operations, the storage strategy (FiFo, LiFo, priorities, addresses, etc), their capacity, and their reaction to illegal access.

Memory components often possess a history condensing function. For each input stream, the history condensing function yields an input stream that generates the same store without producing output. These state generating input streams usually contain update commands without legal requests and no outdated update commands. Possibly, the shortest input streams indicating illegal memory accesses also generate a state.

We illustrate state refinement with history condensing functions for two memory components, viz. a simple memory cell and an unbounded buffer.

Example 6.6 (memory cell ignoring illegal read commands)
A memory cell receives write commands with a datum to be stored and read commands requesting the datum written most recently into the memory cell. Let $\mathcal{D} \neq \emptyset$ denote the set of data and $\mathcal{C} = \{r\} \cup w(\mathcal{D})$ denote the set of input commands. The memory cell $mem : \mathcal{C}^\star \to \mathcal{D}^\star$ ignores illegal read commands:

$$mem(\langle\rangle) = \langle\rangle \tag{6.8}$$
$$mem(\langle w(d)\rangle) = \langle\rangle \tag{6.9}$$
$$mem(w(d) \lhd r \lhd X) = d \lhd mem(w(d) \lhd X) \tag{6.10}$$
$$mem(w(d) \lhd w(e) \lhd X) = mem(w(e) \lhd X) \tag{6.11}$$
$$mem(r \lhd X) = mem(X) \tag{6.12}$$

By Theorem 2.15, mem validates the decomposition property

$$mem(X \& Y) = mem(X) \& mem(write(X) \& Y) \tag{6.13}$$

where the auxiliary function $write : \mathcal{C}^\star \to (w(\mathcal{D}))^{\leq 1}$ resulting from the recursion structure of mem reduces an input history to the most recent write command if it exists:

$$write(\langle\rangle) = \langle\rangle \tag{6.14}$$
$$write(\langle w(d)\rangle) = \langle w(d)\rangle \tag{6.15}$$
$$write(w(d) \lhd r \lhd X) = write(w(d) \lhd X) \tag{6.16}$$
$$write(w(d) \lhd w(e) \lhd X) = write(w(e) \lhd X) \tag{6.17}$$
$$write(r \lhd X) = write(X) \tag{6.18}$$

By Lemma 6.5, the history condensing function *write* is a history abstraction.
Theorem 6.4 yields the refining state transition machine $M = ((\mathbf{w}(\mathcal{D}))^{\leq 1}, \mathcal{C},$
$\mathcal{D}, next, out, \langle \rangle)$ with the state transition function

$$
\begin{aligned}
next(Q, \mathsf{r}) &= write(Q \triangleright \mathsf{r}) \\
&= write(Q) \\
&= Q & (6.19) \\
next(\langle \rangle, \mathbf{w}(d)) &= write(\langle \mathbf{w}(d) \rangle) \\
&= \langle \mathbf{w}(d) \rangle \\
next(\langle \mathbf{w}(d) \rangle, \mathbf{w}(e)) &= write(\langle \mathbf{w}(d), \mathbf{w}(e) \rangle) \\
&= write(\langle \mathbf{w}(e) \rangle) \\
&= \langle \mathbf{w}(e) \rangle & (6.20)
\end{aligned}
$$

and the output function

$$
\begin{aligned}
out(Q, \mathbf{w}(d)) &= mem(Q \& \langle \mathbf{w}(d) \rangle) \\
&= \langle \rangle & (6.21) \\
out(\langle \rangle, \mathsf{r}) &= mem(\langle \mathsf{r} \rangle) \\
&= \langle \rangle & (6.22) \\
out(\langle \mathbf{w}(d) \rangle, \mathsf{r}) &= mem(\langle \mathbf{w}(d), \mathsf{r} \rangle) \\
&= d \triangleleft mem(\langle \mathbf{w}(d) \rangle) \\
&= \langle d \rangle & (6.23)
\end{aligned}
$$

With the state isomorphism dropping the constructor $\mathbf{w}$ in the state, we get
the state-based implementation $cell : \mathcal{D}^{\leq 1} \to (\mathcal{C}^{\star} \to \mathcal{D}^{\star})$ as the multi-step
output function:

$$
\begin{aligned}
cell(Q)(\langle \rangle) &= \langle \rangle & (6.24) \\
cell(\langle \rangle)(\mathbf{w}(d) \triangleleft X) &= cell(\langle d \rangle)(X) & (6.25) \\
cell(\langle \rangle)(\mathsf{r} \triangleleft X) &= cell(\langle \rangle)(X) & (6.26) \\
cell(\langle d \rangle)(\mathbf{w}(e) \triangleleft X) &= cell(\langle e \rangle)(X) & (6.27) \\
cell(\langle d \rangle)(\mathsf{r} \triangleleft X) &= d \triangleleft cell(\langle d \rangle)(X) & (6.28)
\end{aligned}
$$

The obtained state refinement is the coarsest state refinement. □

Theorem 6.4 cannot be applied to memory components which acknowledge
write commands, such as in Example 5.19, because in that case the state
generating input streams produce output.

While the request commands of the memory cell had no effect on the state,
in the next example write as well as request commands may change the state.

Example 6.7 (unbounded buffer)
An unbounded buffer [DS01b] receives input commands with a datum to be stored and request commands. When receiving a request command the component outputs the first datum which has been stored, but was not requested yet. A fault tolerant unbounded buffer $ubuf : (in(\mathcal{D}) \cup \{req\})^\star \to \mathcal{D}^\star$ ignores illegal request commands. We assume $d \in \mathcal{D} \neq \emptyset$ and $D \in in(\mathcal{D})^\star$:

$$ubuf(D) \;=\; \langle\rangle \tag{6.29}$$
$$ubuf(in(d) \vartriangleleft D \& \langle req \rangle \& X) \;=\; d \vartriangleleft ubuf(D\&X) \tag{6.30}$$
$$ubuf(req \vartriangleleft X) \;=\; ubuf(X) \tag{6.31}$$

$ubuf$ is monotonic, cf. Theorem 2.15:

$$ubuf(X\&Y) \;=\; ubuf(X) \,\&\, ubuf(queue(X)\&Y) \tag{6.32}$$

The auxiliary function $queue : (in(\mathcal{D}) \cup \{req\})^\star \to in(\mathcal{D})^\star$ resulting from the recursion structure of $ubuf$ deletes all request commands and retains the input commands as far as they have not been requested yet: $(D \in in(\mathcal{D})^\star)$

$$queue(D) \;=\; D \tag{6.33}$$
$$queue(in(d) \vartriangleleft D \& \langle req \rangle \& X) \;=\; queue(D\&X) \tag{6.34}$$
$$queue(req \vartriangleleft X) \;=\; queue(X) \tag{6.35}$$

According to Lemma 6.5, the history condensing function $queue$ is a history abstraction. By Theorem 6.4 the state transition function is obtained from the equation $next(queue(X), x) = queue(queue(X) \vartriangleright x)$. We drop the constructors in in the state, that means we represent each state $in^\star(D)$ by D:

$$next(Q, in(d)) \;=\; Q \vartriangleright d \tag{6.36}$$
$$next(q \vartriangleleft Q, req) \;=\; Q \tag{6.37}$$
$$next(\langle\rangle, req) \;=\; \langle\rangle \tag{6.38}$$

The equation $out(queue(X), x) = ubuf(queue(X) \vartriangleright x)$ yields the output function:

$$out(Q, in(d)) \;=\; \langle\rangle \tag{6.39}$$
$$out(q \vartriangleleft Q, req) \;=\; \langle q \rangle \tag{6.40}$$
$$out(\langle\rangle, req) \;=\; \langle\rangle \tag{6.41}$$

The obtained state transition machine with the initial state $\langle\rangle$ is the coarsest state refinement.   □

Also many of the examples presented in the previous chapter can be refined with the technique presented in this chapter.

Concluding remarks

In this chapter, we derived a theorem which provides a state refinement for stream transformers based on a history condensing function. The refinement applies to stream transformers whose output can be composed of the behaviour for an initial part of the input and the behaviour for the rest of the input stream if a history condensing function codes the essential information of the initial part of the input into an input stream which causes no output.

The states of the refining state transition machine are input streams which cause no output. The state transition function applies the history condensing function, and the output function applies the refined stream transformer to the current state extended by the current input. The history condensing function represents information which may be relevant for the future behaviour without producing any output. Thus it may code more information in a state than is actually necessary. Then the obtained state transition machine can be further improved with state homomorphisms.

Chapter 7

Control and Data States

Many state-based development methodologies employ the notions of control and data states. In general, we find combinations thereof in the form of a finite set of (control) states each with a set of variables for example in statecharts, UML state diagrams, extended finite state machines, SDL, or in X-machines [BWW96, Bar98, BCG$^+$99]. From the theoretical point of view, there is no obvious formal difference between data and control states. Control states can always be considered to be data states, just as control flow can be reduced to data flow [BJP91].

A specification employs in general only a small or at least a finite number of control states. Control systems, for example, have a reasonably small number of states. From the conceptual point of view, we expect the data part of a state to concentrate on input data aspects and the control part to concentrate on aspects which are independent of the particular set of input data. Since control aspects often stick out from a specification, they give rise to particular concepts for the introduction of control states.

We present a general method how to transform a specification of a component with mutually recursive functions into a state-based version where the function names correspond to control states. We illustrate the method with several examples, and suggest a strategy how to try transforming a specification into the required structure.

7.1 Lifting Function Names to Control States

We aim at a formal method how to introduce control states. If a stream processing function is specified by a system of mutually recursive functions with a uniform recursion structure, then, lifting the function names to states, each of the mutually recursive functions corresponds to a control state.

If the mutually recursive functions show a particular uniform recursion pattern in their stream argument then the result is indeed a state transition machine.

Definition 7.1 (recursion scheme for control states)
Let $\mathcal{F} \subseteq \{f : \mathcal{Q}_f \to (\mathcal{A}^\star \to \mathcal{B}^\star)\}$ be a non-empty set of state-based stream processing functions with the same domain $\mathcal{A}^\star$ and range $\mathcal{B}^\star$, and possibly different state spaces $\mathcal{Q}_f$. The functions in $\mathcal{F}$ follow a *recursion scheme for control states* if they are mutually recursive and are described according to the following structure ($f \in \mathcal{F}$):

$$
\begin{aligned}
f(q)(\langle\rangle) &= \langle\rangle \\
f(q)(x \triangleleft X) &= out_f(q, x) \,\&\, (funct_f(q, x))(next_f(q, x))(X)
\end{aligned}
$$

$out_f : \mathcal{Q}_f \times \mathcal{A} \to \mathcal{B}^\star$ determines the output of the stream processing function f produced by the current input in the current state.
$funct_f : \mathcal{Q}_f \times \mathcal{A} \to \mathcal{F}$ determines the next function to be called depending on the current state and on the current input.
$next_f : \mathcal{Q}_f \times \mathcal{A} \to \cup_{g \in \mathcal{F}} \mathcal{Q}_g$ determines the state in which the next function is to be called depending on the current state and on the current input. We assume that the next state lies in the state space of the function called next: $next_f(q, x) \in \mathcal{Q}_{funct_f(q,x)}$.
The tuple $(\mathcal{F}, out_\mathcal{F}, funct_\mathcal{F}, next_\mathcal{F})$ characterizes the recursion scheme.   □

Such a system of functions indeed specifies a stream processing function.

Proposition 7.2
Let a recursion scheme for control states be described by $(\mathcal{F}, out_\mathcal{F}, funct_\mathcal{F}, next_\mathcal{F})$ as in Definition 7.1. Each function $f \in \mathcal{F}$ defines a monotonic stream transformer with state:

$$
f(q)(X \& Y) = f(q)(X) \,\&\, (funct_f^\star(q)(X))(next_f^\star(q)(X))(Y)   \qquad □
$$

The term $funct_f^\star(q)(X)$ determines the function which is applied when the input stream X has been processed by the start function f in the start state q. The function $funct_f^\star : \mathcal{Q}_f \to (\mathcal{A}^\star \to \mathcal{F})$ is defined by:

$$
\begin{aligned}
funct_f^\star(q)(\langle\rangle) &= f &\qquad (7.1) \\
funct_f^\star(q)(x \triangleleft X) &= funct_{funct_f(q,x)}^\star(next_f(q,x))(X) &\qquad (7.2)
\end{aligned}
$$

The function $next_f^\star : \mathcal{Q}_f \to (\mathcal{A}^\star \to \cup_{g \in \mathcal{F}} \mathcal{Q}_g)$ determines the state in which the above function $funct_f^\star(q)(X)$ will be called:

$$next_f^\star(q)(\langle\rangle) \;=\; q \tag{7.3}$$

$$next_f^\star(q)(x \triangleleft X) \;=\; next_{funct_f(q,x)}^\star(next_f(q,x))(X) \tag{7.4}$$

Each function in $\mathcal{F}$ can be transformed into a state refinement by lifting the function names to states:

$$\mathcal{Q} \;=\; \{(f,q) \mid f \in \mathcal{F}, q \in \mathcal{Q}_f\} \tag{7.5}$$

$$next((f,q),x) \;=\; (funct_f(q,x), next_f(q,x)) \tag{7.6}$$

$$out((f,q),x) \;=\; out_f(q,x) \tag{7.7}$$

New names for the states may be set through a bijection $name : \mathcal{F} \to \mathcal{C}$. If $\mathcal{F}$ is finite, that is $|\mathcal{F}| = n \in \mathbb{N}$, then we choose, for example, $\mathcal{C} = \{1, \ldots, n\}$. The following theorem summarizes the results.

Theorem 7.3
Let a recursion scheme for control states be described by $(\mathcal{F}, out_{\mathcal{F}}, funct_{\mathcal{F}}, next_{\mathcal{F}})$ as in Definition 7.1 with a designated initial function $f_0 \in \mathcal{F}$ and an initial state $q_0 \in \mathcal{Q}_{f_0}$. Let $name : \mathcal{F} \to \mathcal{C}$ be a bijection into a set $\mathcal{C}$ of names for states. Then the state transition machine $M = (\{(name(f),q) \mid f \in \mathcal{F}, q \in \mathcal{Q}_f\}, \mathcal{A}, \mathcal{B}, next, out, (name(f_0), q_0))$ is a state refinement for $f_0(q_0)$ with the state transition and output functions

$$next((name(f),q),x) \;=\; (name(funct_f(q,x)), next_f(q,x))$$
$$out((name(f),q),x) \;=\; out_f(q,x).$$

The multi-step output function is:

$$out^\star(name(f),q)(\langle\rangle) \;=\; \langle\rangle$$
$$out^\star(name(f),q)(x \triangleleft X) \;=\;$$
$$out((name(f),q),x) \,\&\, out^\star(next((name(f),q),x))(X) \qquad \Box$$

A function in the set of defining stream processing functions which does not really operate on states is assumed to have the trivial state space with only a single state. The multi-step output function is directly obtained by pairing the state with the function name.

The names of the mutually recursive functions with states generate the control states. The states combine control and data aspects in the form of a tuple with a control flag and the corresponding data. The uniform recursion structure which removes the first element from its non-empty input stream ensures that the input stream is processed element by element so that lifting the function names to states indeed leads to a state transition machine.

We now demonstrate the application of Theorem 7.3 with an example.

Example 7.4 (single pulser)
A single pulser [Dos00a] is a clocked digital component which records a unit pulse (i.e. 1, representing high current, preceded by 0, representing low current) with 1 in its output stream. Otherwise it emits 0. A single pulser can be specified by two mutually recursive functions $low, high : \{0, 1\}^\star \to \{0, 1\}^\star$. The function low describes the behaviour after processing 0:

$$low(\langle\rangle) \;=\; \langle\rangle \tag{7.8}$$
$$low(0 \triangleleft X) \;=\; 0 \triangleleft low(X) \tag{7.9}$$
$$low(1 \triangleleft X) \;=\; 1 \triangleleft high(X) \tag{7.10}$$

The function $high$ describes the behaviour after processing 1:

$$high(\langle\rangle) \;=\; \langle\rangle \tag{7.11}$$
$$high(0 \triangleleft X) \;=\; 0 \triangleleft low(X) \tag{7.12}$$
$$high(1 \triangleleft X) \;=\; 0 \triangleleft high(X) \tag{7.13}$$

The two mutually recursive functions match the recursion scheme required for the application of Theorem 7.3. A state refinement $pulse : \{0, 1\} \to (\{0, 1\}^\star \to \{0, 1\}^\star)$ of the single pulser can, for example, code the function low by 0 and the function $high$ by 1:

$$low \;\mapsto\; 0 \tag{7.14}$$
$$high \;\mapsto\; 1 \tag{7.15}$$

Then the following equations describe the multi-step output function of the single pulser:

$$pulse(q)(\langle\rangle) \;=\; \langle\rangle \tag{7.16}$$
$$pulse(0)(0 \triangleleft X) \;=\; 0 \triangleleft pulse(0)(X) \tag{7.17}$$
$$pulse(0)(1 \triangleleft X) \;=\; 1 \triangleleft pulse(1)(X) \tag{7.18}$$
$$pulse(1)(0 \triangleleft X) \;=\; 0 \triangleleft pulse(0)(X) \tag{7.19}$$
$$pulse(1)(1 \triangleleft X) \;=\; 0 \triangleleft pulse(1)(X) \tag{7.20}$$

Both states of the single pulser are pure control states without data aspects.
□

The single pulser employs two control states without data aspects whereas the states of a differentiator, cf. Subsection 10.2.3, – of which the single pulser is an instantiation – are pure data states retaining the last datum of the prehistory. The single pulser emphasizes that a component in general employs only a finite number of control states, whereas the size of a set of data states is insignificant.

This section demonstrated that a specification of a stream processing function with mutually recursive functions following the required recursion scheme can straightforwardly be transformed into a state refinement by lifting function names to control states. The recursion scheme determines the size of the states and the costs of the machine functions.

7.2 Transfer of the Approach

The introduction of control states in the previous section was based on the idea of lifting function names of a specification with mutually recursive functions to states. We now investigate whether this idea can be applied to specifications with mutually recursive functions which do not follow the required recursion scheme because they have more than one input port. We cannot expect the resulting specifications to be state transition machines. However, we arrive at specifications which may help to find history abstractions for the introduction of a state refinement for components with more than one input stream, cf. Section 8.4.

With two examples we demonstrate how the introduction of control states through lifting function names to states transforms a specification with two mutually recursive functions or with a non-uniform recursion pattern concerning the streams in its argument into a recursive function with a uniform recursion pattern. Both examples deal with components with more than one input channel. In the first example, control states are combined with data aspects.

Example 7.5 (sender and receiver synchronized)
A synchronized sender waits for the expected Boolean acknowledgement before sending the next datum with the new expected acknowledgement (similar to the Alternating Bit Protocol [BS01b]). If a wrong acknowledgement arrives, it resends the previous datum together with the expected acknowledgement. The synchronized sender is specified by two mutually recursive

functions:

$$send : \mathbb{B} \to ((\mathcal{D}^{\star} \times \mathbb{B}^{\star}) \to (\mathcal{D} \times \mathbb{B})^{\star})$$
$$wait : (\mathbb{B} \times \mathcal{D}) \to ((\mathcal{D}^{\star} \times \mathbb{B}^{\star}) \to (\mathcal{D} \times \mathbb{B})^{\star})$$

The function $send$ specifies the behaviour of the sender when it is ready to send the next datum:

$$send(b)(\langle\rangle, A) \;=\; \langle\rangle \tag{7.21}$$
$$send(b)(x \lhd X, A) \;=\; (x, b) \lhd wait(b, x)(X, A) \tag{7.22}$$

When the sender receives a datum, it sends the datum together with the expected acknowledgement. Afterwards, when it waits for the expected acknowledgement, its behaviour follows the specification of the function $wait$:

$$wait(b, x)(X, \langle\rangle) \;=\; \langle\rangle \tag{7.23}$$
$$wait(b, x)(X, b \lhd A) \;=\; send(not(b))(X, A) \tag{7.24}$$
$$wait(b, x)(X, not(b) \lhd A) \;=\; (x, b) \lhd wait(b, x)(X, A) \tag{7.25}$$

When the expected acknowledgement arrives, the component is ready to send the next datum and expects the alternated acknowledgement. If a wrong acknowledgement arrives, it resends the previous datum together with the expected acknowledgement and continues waiting for the correct acknowledgement.

We code $send$ by 0 and $wait$ by 1 and thus define

$$sender : (((\{0\} \times \mathbb{B}) \cup (\{1\} \times (\mathbb{B} \times \mathcal{D}))) \to ((\mathcal{D}^{\star} \times \mathbb{B}^{\star}) \to (\mathcal{D} \times \mathbb{B})^{\star})$$

by replacing

$$send(b) \;\mapsto\; sender(0, b) \tag{7.26}$$
$$wait(b, x) \;\mapsto\; sender(1, (b, x)) \,. \tag{7.27}$$

The obtained result is:

$$sender(0, b)(\langle\rangle, A) \;=\; \langle\rangle \tag{7.28}$$
$$sender(1, q)(X, \langle\rangle) \;=\; \langle\rangle \tag{7.29}$$
$$sender(0, b)(x \lhd X, A) \;=\; (x, b) \lhd sender(1, (b, x))(X, A) \tag{7.30}$$
$$sender(1, (b, x))(X, b \lhd A) \;=\; sender(0, not(b))(X, A) \tag{7.31}$$
$$sender(1, (b, x))(X, not(b) \lhd A) \;=\; (x, b) \lhd sender(1, (b, x))(X, A) \tag{7.32}$$

The obtained equations process the input streams respecting the construction principle apart from Equations (7.28) and (7.29). Based on these two equations, a history abstraction for components with more than one input stream, cf. Section 8.4, only needs to introduce buffers for the consumption of data or acknowledgements, respectively, in case there are no messages on the other input stream. □

In the next example the introduction of control states transforms a specification permuting the tuple of input streams in each recursive call into a specification maintaining the order of the input streams.

Example 7.6 (demultiplexer)
A demultiplexer is a merge component which cyclically passes the data from its input channels to its output channel according to the round robin strategy.

For the specification of a demultiplexer, we need a particular cross operation $left_n : (\mathcal{A}^\star)^n \to (\mathcal{A}^\star)^n$ ($n > 0$) realizing a left shift of the tuple of input streams:

$$left_n(X_1, X_2, \ldots, X_n) = (X_2, \ldots, X_n, X_1) \qquad (7.33)$$

The recursive call in the specification of the merge function $demux_n : (\mathcal{A}^\star)^n \to \mathcal{A}^\star$ changes the order of the input streams in the tuple with the left shift:

$$demux_n(\langle\rangle, X_2, \ldots, X_n) = \langle\rangle \qquad (7.34)$$
$$demux_n(x_1 \lhd X_1, X_2, \ldots, X_n) = x_1 \lhd demux_n(left_n(X_1, \ldots, X_n)) \qquad (7.35)$$

Making use of the summary description of the left shift ($1 < i \leq n$)

$$(X_1, \ldots, X_n) = left_n^{i-1}(X_{n-i+2} \ldots, X_n, X_1, \ldots, X_{n-i+1}) \qquad (7.36)$$

we rewrite the specification of $demux_n$ such that the arrangement of the streams in the argument is maintained in the recursive calls ($1 < i \leq n$):

$$demux_n(left_n^{i-1}(X_{n-i+2} \ldots, X_n, \langle\rangle, X_2, \ldots, X_{n-i+1})) = \langle\rangle \qquad (7.37)$$
$$demux_n(left_n^0(\langle\rangle, X_2, \ldots, X_n)) = \langle\rangle \qquad (7.38)$$
$$demux_n(left_n^{i-1}(X_{n-i+2} \ldots, X_n, x_1 \lhd X_1, X_2, \ldots, X_{n-i+1})) =$$
$$x_1 \lhd demux_n(left_n^i(X_{n-i+2} \ldots, X_n, X_1, \ldots, X_{n-i+1})) \qquad (7.39)$$
$$demux_n(left_n^0(x_1 \lhd X_1, X_2, \ldots, X_n)) =$$
$$x_1 \lhd demux_n(left_n^1(X_1, \ldots, X_n)) \qquad (7.40)$$

$demux_n$ is now specified by n mutually recursive functions $demux_n \circ left_n^{i-1}$ for $1 \leq i \leq n$. We specify the state-based round robin merge component $rrmerge_n : \{1, \ldots, n\} \to (\mathcal{A}^\star)^n \to \mathcal{A}^\star$ with the replacement

$$demux_n \circ left_n^{i-1} \mapsto rrmerge_n(i) . \qquad (7.41)$$

The parameter of the function *merge* indicates the next element which is to be emitted to the output. With this replacement and a renaming of the input streams, we immediately get a direct specification of merge:

$$rrmerge_n(i)(Y_1, \ldots, Y_{i-1}, \langle\rangle, Y_{i+1}, \ldots, Y_n) \;\; = \;\; \langle\rangle \qquad (7.42)$$

$$rrmerge_n(i)(Y_1, \ldots, Y_{i-1}, y_i \lhd Y_i, Y_{i+1}, \ldots, Y_n) \;\; =$$
$$y_i \lhd rrmerge_n(i \bmod n + 1)(Y_1, \ldots, Y_n) \quad (7.43)$$

Thus we obtained a definition of merge which does not change the arrangement of the input streams in the tuple, but the index instead. □

These examples show that a specification by mutually recursive functions implicitly carries control aspects, and they exemplify the systematic extraction of control states.

7.3　Transformation into Mutually Recursive Functions

In the previous example the specification of the demultiplexer originally did not employ mutually recursive functions. Only after a short transformation, we obtained a specification with mutually recursive functions. In this section, we demonstrate a method how a stream processing function may be transformed into the recursion scheme required for the introduction of control states with help of an example.

The transformation principle we present is applicable to stream processing functions which are specified by terminating and recursive equations inspecting a prefix of the input stream each. The transformation assumes that there exists an equivalent specification which shows the required syntactic pattern of mutually recursive functions which process the input stream element by element, and which employ a state which carries information from the input history. We do not know in advance how many mutually recursive functions are necessary and how the output function, the next-function function and the next-state function look like.

We start deriving these mutually recursive functions $f_1, f_2, \ldots$ by assuming that a given function f is specified by the function f_1 with the required pattern. If, during the derivation, we cannot employ functions which already arose during the derivation, we introduce a new function.

We demonstrate the principle by an example.

Example 7.7 (door access system)

A door access system allows the users to open the door if they have got the right key. The door can be closed with any key. Moreover, a new key can be set by first providing the old key and then providing the new key.

The set $\mathcal{I}$ of input commands of the door access controller with a set $\mathcal{K} \neq \emptyset$ of keys consists of commands $door(\mathcal{K})$ for opening and closing the door with a key, and the commands $key(\mathcal{K})$ for providing keys for a reset. The output $\mathcal{O} = \{open, close\}$ records opening and closing of the door.

The door access controller is defined by equations inspecting the input stream in different depths. For this example, we assume $k, l, m \in \mathcal{K}$, $m \neq k$ and $y \in \mathcal{I} \setminus \{key(k), door(k)\}$.

$$f(\langle\rangle) = \langle\rangle \tag{7.44}$$

$$f(door(k) \triangleleft X) = f(X) \tag{7.45}$$

$$f(\langle key(k)\rangle) = \langle\rangle \tag{7.46}$$

$$f(\langle key(k), door(k)\rangle) = \langle open\rangle \tag{7.47}$$

$$f(key(k) \triangleleft door(k) \triangleleft door(l) \triangleleft X) = open \triangleleft close \triangleleft f(key(k) \triangleleft X) \tag{7.48}$$

$$f(key(k) \triangleleft door(k) \triangleleft key(m) \triangleleft X) = open \triangleleft close \triangleleft f(key(k) \triangleleft X) \tag{7.49}$$

$$f(key(k) \triangleleft door(k) \triangleleft key(k) \triangleleft X) = open \triangleleft close \triangleleft f(X) \tag{7.50}$$

$$f(key(k) \triangleleft key(k) \triangleleft X) = f(X) \tag{7.51}$$

$$f(key(k) \triangleleft y \triangleleft X) = f(key(k) \triangleleft X) \tag{7.52}$$

An attempt to handle the door before a key is set has no effect (7.45). Handling the door with the previously provided key opens the door (7.47). If the door has been opened, then it can be closed with any key (7.48). Additionally, it closes automatically, if someone tries resetting the key (7.49), (7.50). Before a new key can be set, the previous key has to be provided to the access control system (7.51). Attempts to open the door with a wrong key or attempts to reset the key with the wrong key are ignored when the door is not open (7.52).

We try do derive a set of mutually recursive equations with the desired recursion structure and the start function $f_1 : \mathcal{I}^\star \to \mathcal{O}^\star$:

$$f_1 := f \tag{7.53}$$

The derivation strategy tries to reduce occurrences of the new functions to occurrences of the original function f. If no reduction is possible, then a new function is introduced which accumulates the previous input: $(z \in \mathcal{I} \setminus$

$\{key(k)\})$

$$
\begin{aligned}
f_1(\langle\rangle) &= f(\langle\rangle) = \langle\rangle && (7.54)\\
f_1(door(k) \vartriangleleft X) &= f(door(k) \vartriangleleft X) = f(X) = \langle\rangle \,\&\, f_1(X) && (7.55)\\
f_1(key(k) \vartriangleleft X) &=: f_1(\langle key(k)\rangle) \,\&\, f_2(k)(X)\\
&= f(\langle key(k)\rangle) \,\&\, f_2(k)(X)\\
&= \langle\rangle \,\&\, f_2(k)(X) && (7.56)\\
f_2(k)(\langle\rangle) &= f_1(key(k) \vartriangleleft \langle\rangle) = f(\langle key(k)\rangle) = \langle\rangle && (7.57)\\
f_2(k)(key(k) \vartriangleleft X) &= f_1(key(k) \vartriangleleft key(k) \vartriangleleft X)\\
&= f(key(k) \vartriangleleft key(k) \vartriangleleft X) = f(X)\\
&= \langle\rangle \,\&\, f_1(X) && (7.58)\\
f_2(k)(y \vartriangleleft X) &= f_1(key(k) \vartriangleleft y \vartriangleleft X) = f(key(k) \vartriangleleft y \vartriangleleft X)\\
&= f(key(k) \vartriangleleft X) = f_1(key(k) \vartriangleleft X)\\
&= \langle\rangle \,\&\, f_2(k)(X) && (7.59)\\
f_2(k)(door(k) \vartriangleleft X) &=: f_2(k)(\langle door(k)\rangle) \,\&\, f_3(k)(X)\\
&= f_1(\langle key(k), door(k)\rangle) \,\&\, f_3(k)(X)\\
&= f(\langle key(k), door(k)\rangle) \,\&\, f_3(k)(X)\\
&= \langle open\rangle \,\&\, f_3(k)(X) && (7.60)\\
open \vartriangleleft f_3(k)(\langle\rangle) &= f_2(door(k) \vartriangleleft \langle\rangle) = f_1(key(k) \vartriangleleft door(k) \vartriangleleft \langle\rangle)\\
&= f(key(k) \vartriangleleft door(k) \vartriangleleft \langle\rangle)\\
&= open \vartriangleleft \langle\rangle && (7.61)\\
open \vartriangleleft f_3(k)(key(k) \vartriangleleft X) &= f_2(k)(door(k) \vartriangleleft key(k) \vartriangleleft X)\\
&= f_1(key(k) \vartriangleleft door(k) \vartriangleleft key(k) \vartriangleleft X)\\
&= f(key(k) \vartriangleleft door(k) \vartriangleleft key(k) \vartriangleleft X)\\
&= open \vartriangleleft close \vartriangleleft f(X)\\
&= open \vartriangleleft close \vartriangleleft f_1(X) && (7.62)\\
open \vartriangleleft f_3(k)(z \vartriangleleft X) &= f_2(k)(door(k) \vartriangleleft z \vartriangleleft X)\\
&= f_1(key(k) \vartriangleleft door(k) \vartriangleleft z \vartriangleleft X)\\
&= f(key(k) \vartriangleleft door(k) \vartriangleleft z \vartriangleleft X)\\
&= open \vartriangleleft close \vartriangleleft f(key(k) \vartriangleleft X)\\
&= open \vartriangleleft close \vartriangleleft f_1(key(k) \vartriangleleft X)\\
&= open \vartriangleleft close \vartriangleleft f_2(k)(X) && (7.63)
\end{aligned}
$$

The new function $f_2 : \mathcal{K} \to (\mathcal{I}^\star \to \mathcal{O}^\star)$ is introduced when a key has been provided and the further input is unknown. The new function $f_3 : \mathcal{K} \to$

$(\mathcal{I}^\star \to \mathcal{O}^\star)$ is introduced for the case when the door has been opened with the correct key and the further input is unknown.

The following table summarizes the resulting mutually recursive equations with the functions f_1, f_2, and f_3.

i	$f_i(q)($	$x \triangleleft X)$	$=$	$out_{f_i}(q,x)$ &	$(funct_{f_i}(q,x))$	$(next_{f_i}(q,x))(X)$	
1	f_1 (	$\langle\rangle)$	$=$	$\langle\rangle$			
	f_1 (	$door(k) \triangleleft X)$	$=$		f_1		(X)
	f_1 (	$key(k) \triangleleft X)$	$=$		f_2	(k)	(X)
2	$f_2(k)($	$\langle\rangle)$	$=$	$\langle\rangle$			
	$f_2(k)($	$door(k) \triangleleft X)$	$=$	$open \triangleleft$	f_3	(k)	(X)
	$f_2(k)($	$door(m) \triangleleft X)$	$=$		f_2	(k)	(X)
	$f_2(k)($	$key(k) \triangleleft X)$	$=$		f_1		(X)
	$f_2(k)($	$key(m) \triangleleft X)$	$=$		f_2	(k)	(X)
3	$f_3(k)($	$\langle\rangle)$	$=$	$\langle\rangle$			
	$f_3(k)($	$door(l) \triangleleft X)$	$=$	$close \triangleleft$	f_2	(k)	(X)
	$f_3(k)($	$key(k) \triangleleft X)$	$=$	$close \triangleleft$	f_1		(X)
	$f_3(k)($	$key(m) \triangleleft X)$	$=$	$close \triangleleft$	f_2	(k)	(X)

We lift the function indices to states by setting

$$f_1 \mapsto 1 \tag{7.64}$$
$$f_2(k) \mapsto (2,k) \tag{7.65}$$
$$f_3(k) \mapsto (3,k). \tag{7.66}$$

Figure 7.1 shows the state transition diagram of the obtained state transition machine. □

The example exemplifies how it is sometimes possible to directly transform a specification into mutually recursive functions with the required pattern if the specification accesses prefixes of the respective input stream. However, there is no guarantee that this strategy is successful in a finite number of steps.

Concluding remarks

A state is in general a combination of information which depends on the particular set of input data and information which can be described independently of the set of input data. The latter information is called control aspect of a state.

A component specification by a system of mutually recursive functions implicitly carries control information. Lifting function names to parameters is

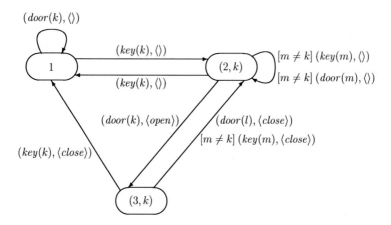

Figure 7.1: State transition diagram for the door access controller

universally applicable for obtaining a specification which is closer to a state-based specification. If the mutually recursive functions are specified with a uniform recursion pattern so that the input stream is processed element by element, then this transformation leads to a state transition machine. A direct transformation of an arbitrary specification into a specification with mutually recursive functions processing the input stream element by element is sometimes possible, however, it is not always feasible.

Chapter 8

Generalization to Arbitrary Stream Processing Functions

In the previous chapters, we discussed state refinement for components with exactly one input and one output channel processing finite input and generating finite output streams. In this chapter, we extend the approach to components processing and generating tuples of possibly infinite streams. The generalization to components with several output channels is straightforward, whereas the generalization to components with several input streams raises synchronization aspects. We discuss the extension of state refinement to infinite output streams prior to the extension to infinite input streams.

8.1 Extension to Infinite Output Streams

The first generalization of state refinement we discuss is the extension to infinite output streams for finite input streams. Thereby we make use of the fact that the behaviour of stream transformers after producing infinite output when consuming a finite input stream cannot be observed.

Formally, our methodology can be extended to stream transformers which produce infinite output for finite input, if we define the concatenation such that appending to an infinite stream $X \in \mathcal{B}^\omega$ leaves it unchanged, cf. Equation (2.18):

$$X \& Y = X \qquad (8.1)$$

In contrast to the concatenation to a finite stream, this extension to infinite streams is not left reducible.

With this agreement we generalize the definition of state transition machines to infinite output streams.

Definition 8.1 (state transition machine with infinite output streams)
$M = (Q, \mathcal{A}, \mathcal{B}, next, out, q_0)$ is a *state transition machine with finite and infinite output streams* if Q, $\mathcal{A}$, $\mathcal{B}$, $next$, and q_0 are as in Definition 3.1, and the output function $out : Q \times \mathcal{A} \to \mathcal{B}^\infty$ may yield infinite output streams. $\square$

The further output of the state transition machine after a transition with an infinite output stream remains invisible. If $out(q, x) \in \mathcal{B}^\omega$, we have

$$out^\star(q)(x \triangleleft X) \;=\; out(q, x). \tag{8.2}$$

This coincides with the behaviour of a stream transformer which has processed an input stream generating infinite output. If $f(X) \in \mathcal{B}^\omega$, we have

$$f(X) \;=\; f(X\&Y). \tag{8.3}$$

Consequently, as soon an an element in the input stream has caused an infinite output, the further behaviour of the multi-step output function as well as the extension of the output of a stream transformer becomes irrelevant and can be considered to be undetermined, cf. Section 9.3. We get a state refinement of a stream transformer with the methodology presented in the previous chapters without taking into account its behaviour for those input streams which are proper extensions of an input stream yielding an infinite output stream. In other words, we can assume an arbitrary extension of the output in this case.

The only concept which cannot directly be transferred to the extended approach is the output extension. The output extension $\varepsilon_f(X, x)$ for an input stream X such that $f(X) \in \mathcal{B}^\omega$ cannot be defined properly because its definition relies on the left reducibility of the concatenation. For a stream transformer $f : \mathcal{A}^\star \to \mathcal{B}^\infty$ the equation

$$f(X) \,\&\, \varepsilon_f(X, x) \;=\; f(X \triangleright x) \tag{8.4}$$

does not define the output extension for $X \in \mathcal{A}^\star$ with $f(X) \in \mathcal{B}^\omega$. However, this lack in the definition of the output extension coincides with the above result that the further output after an infinite output is invisible.

In summary, stream transformers which generate an infinite output stream for a finite input stream can be refined with the techniques in the previous chapters without taking the behaviour after the infinite output into account.

8.2   Extension to Infinite Input Streams

After investigating extensions of state refinement to infinite output streams, we discuss how state refinement can also be extended to stream processing functions with infinite input streams.

As every stream processing function $f : \mathcal{A}^\infty \to \mathcal{B}^\infty$ on finite and infinite streams is the unique continuous extension of its restriction $f|_{\mathcal{A}^\star}$ to finite streams, the methodology naturally extends to stream processing functions with finite and infinite input streams through the approximations on finite streams.

Proposition 8.2

Let $f|_{\mathcal{A}^\star}$ be the restriction of $f : \mathcal{A}^\infty \to \mathcal{B}^\infty$ to finite input streams. Then the output function $out^\infty : \mathcal{Q} \to (\mathcal{A}^\infty \to \mathcal{B}^\infty)$ for finite and infinite streams of a state refinement $M = (\mathcal{Q}, \mathcal{A}, \mathcal{B}, next, out, q_0)$ of $f|_{\mathcal{A}^\star}$, defined by

$$out^\infty(q)(X) \quad = \quad \bigsqcup_{Y \in \mathcal{A}^\star, Y \sqsubseteq X} out^\star(q)(Y)$$

coincides with f:

$$out^\infty(q_0) \quad = \quad react_f \qquad \qquad \square$$

Since the multi-step state transition function is not designed for interaction [Weg97, Weg98] and records only a snapshot of the internal state during a computation, an analogous extension of the multi-step state transition function to infinite input streams is not necessary and, consistently, in general not possible, because the range of the state transition function need not be a complete partial order. Also the concept of history abstraction need not explicitly be transferred to infinite input streams because considering infinite streams for the requirements "transition closed" and "output compatible" makes no sense.

Therefore, a state refinement of a stream transformer which is specified on finite and infinite streams is a state refinement of its restriction to finite input streams only. This state refinement on finite streams approximates the behaviour of the stream transformer on infinite streams.

8.3   Extension to Several Output Channels

So far, we only considered state transition machines with exactly one input channel and exactly one output channel. Hence, we only presented state refinements for stream transformers with a single input stream and a single output stream. In this section, we discuss two approaches to state refinements for components with more than one output channel. The first approach adapts the definition for state transition machines to several output streams. The other approach makes use of a product state transition machine.

In order to model stream processing functions $f : \mathcal{A}^\star \to \mathcal{B}_1^\star \times \ldots \times \mathcal{B}_n^\star$ with more than one output channel by a single state transition machine, we extend the definition of a state transition machine concerning the set of output data and the output function.

Definition 8.3 (state transition machine with several output channels)
$M = (\mathcal{Q}, \mathcal{A}, (\mathcal{B}_1, \ldots, \mathcal{B}_n), next, out, q_0)$ is a *state transition machine with n output channels* where $\mathcal{Q}$, $\mathcal{A}$, $next$, and q_0 are as in Definition 3.1 and the output function $out : \mathcal{Q} \times \mathcal{A} \to \mathcal{B}_1^\star \times \ldots \times \mathcal{B}_n^\star$ yields tuples of the corresponding stream types.   □

State transition machines were originally defined for a single output channel only for reasons of clarity of notation. All the definitions, constructions, and propositions in the previous chapters concerning state transition machines and state refinements carry over to stream processing functions with an arbitrary number of output streams.

A second approach for finding a state refinement for a stream processing function $f : \mathcal{A}^\star \to \mathcal{B}_1^\star \times \ldots \times \mathcal{B}_n^\star$ with several output streams is based on the decomposition of such a stream processing function into the sequential composition of a copy component and the parallel compositions of all the projections of the stream processing function onto its output streams:

$$ f \;=\; copy_n \,; (f_1 \parallel \ldots \parallel f_n) \qquad (8.5) $$

where $copy_n : \mathcal{A}^\star \to (\mathcal{A}^\star)^n$ defined by $copy_n(X) = (X, \ldots, X)$ copies the input stream n times, and $f_i : \mathcal{A}^\star \to \mathcal{B}_i^\star$ defined by $f_i = \Pi_i \circ f$ yields the projection onto the ith output stream of f. Each stream transformer f_i can then separately by refined into an ordinary state transition machine M_i.

Proposition 8.4
Let $f : \mathcal{A}^\star \to \mathcal{B}_1^\star \times \ldots \times \mathcal{B}_n^\star$ be a stream transformer with n output streams. If $M_i = (\mathcal{Q}_i, \mathcal{A}, \mathcal{B}_i, next_i, out_i, q_{0i})$ is a state refinement for $f_i = \Pi_i \circ f$ $(1 \leq i \leq n)$, then the *product state transition machine* $M = (\mathcal{Q}_1 \times \ldots \times \mathcal{Q}_n, \mathcal{A}, (\mathcal{B}_1, \ldots, \mathcal{B}_n), next, out, (q_{01}, \ldots, q_{0n}))$ where $next$ and out are applied to tuples

$$ next((q_1, \ldots, q_n), x) \;=\; (next_1(q_1, x), \ldots, next_n(q_n, x)) $$
$$ out((q_1, \ldots, q_n), x) \;=\; (out_1(q_1, x), \ldots, out_n(q_n, x)) $$

is a state refinement of f. □

The proof proceeds by induction on the input stream. In general, the construction of the product state transition machine introduces many unreachable states.

If $\alpha_i : \mathcal{A}^\star \to \mathcal{Q}_i$ ($1 \le i \le n$) are the history abstractions leading to the state refinements $M[f_i, \alpha_i]$ of f_i, then $\alpha : \mathcal{A}^\star \to \mathcal{Q}_1 \times \ldots \times \mathcal{Q}_n$ defined by $\alpha(X) = (\alpha_1(X), \ldots, \alpha_n(X))$ is a history abstraction for f, such that the reachable part $reach(M[f, \alpha])$ of the constructed state refinement agrees with the reachable part $reach(M)$ of the product state transition machine.

In summary, the concepts for state refinement generalize to components with several output channels and are compatible with the decomposition of a stream processing function into separate functions for each output stream.

8.4 Extension to Several Input Channels

The remaining extension of state refinement that is still to be presented is the generalization to components with more than one input stream. As with the extension of concepts for state refinement to several output channels, we first of all adapt the definition of state transition machines to machines with more than one input channel such that our methodology can be transferred to components with an arbitrary number of input streams.

An extension of the presented approach to state transition machines with more than one input channel needs to trigger a state transition by the consumption of a single datum at one of the input channels. We will explain later why it suffices to allow only for the consumption of single input data, and neglect the simultaneous consumption of input data from several channels at the moment. We extend the input set of state transition machines to tuples of channel numbers or names and data in the style of port input/output automata [LS89]. Furthermore we require that the multi-step state transition function and the multi-step output function are independent of the order of input data from different input channels.

Definition 8.5 (state transition machine with several input channels)
$M = (\mathcal{Q}, \mathcal{A}, \mathcal{B}, next, out, q_0)$ is a *state transition machine with input and output with n input channels* where $\mathcal{Q}$, $\mathcal{B}$, $next$, out, and q_0 are as in Definition 3.1 and the set of input data

$$\mathcal{A} = \bigcup_{i \in \{1, \ldots, n\}} \{i\} \times \mathcal{A}_i$$

contains tuples of a channel number and a datum from the respective channel. The machine functions of the extended state transition machine compensate the order of the consumption of data from two different input channels $i \neq j$:

$$next(next(q, (i, x)), (j, y)) \;=\; next(next(q, (j, y)), (i, x)) \quad (8.6)$$
$$out(q, (i, x)) \,\&\, out(next(q, (i, x)), (j, y)) \;=\;$$
$$out(q, (j, y)) \,\&\, out(next(q, (j, y)), (i, x)) \quad (8.7)$$

The multi-step state transition function reads

$$next^{\star}(q)(\langle\rangle, \ldots, \langle\rangle) \;=\; q$$
$$next^{\star}(q)(X_1, \ldots, X_{i-1}, x \triangleleft X_i, X_{i+1}, \ldots, X_n) \;=\;$$
$$next^{\star}(next(q, (i, x)))(X_1, \ldots, X_n)\,.$$

The multi-step output function reads

$$out^{\star}(q)(\langle\rangle, \ldots, \langle\rangle) \;=\; \langle\rangle$$
$$out^{\star}(q)(X_1, \ldots, X_{i-1}, x \triangleleft X_i, X_{i+1}, \ldots, X_n) \;=\;$$
$$out(q, (i, x)) \,\&\, out^{\star}(next(q, (i, x)))(X_1, \ldots, X_n)\,. \quad \square$$

The state transition machines for a single input stream are a specialization of these state transition machines with several input channels.

Equations (8.6) and (8.7) guarantee that the multi-step state transition function and the output function are well-defined. If there is input on more than one input channel, then the decision for the consumption of an element from a particular one of these input channels must not affect the future behaviour of an extended state transition machine refining a stream processing function with finite input streams. Disdained elements from another input channel can be consumed in later steps without changing the input / output behaviour, cf. Figure 8.1.

With the presented extensions, our methodology for state refinement can be transferred to stream processing functions with several input streams.

Proposition 8.6

If we transfer the definitions on which state refinement has been based (such as output extension, output compatible, transition closed, history abstraction, output equivalence, state congruence, state homomorphism, state refinement, canonical state transition machine) in the natural way (in the style of Definition 8.5), then the construction of a state refinement for a stream processing function from Theorem 4.9 also works for stream processing functions with several input streams. $\square$

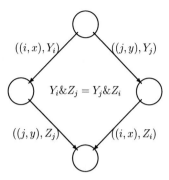

Figure 8.1: Input independence

The construction of the state transition machine with several input channels from a stream processing function automatically guarantees meeting the input independence conditions.

The extension of our approach to components with several input streams leads to the problem of interleaving versus true concurrency concerning the consumption of elements from different input channels. Therefore, our proposed solution falls back on respective solutions for labelled transition systems. *Transition systems with independence* [SNW93] extend ordinary transition systems with a relation on transitions identifying "independent" transitions. Independent transitions can occur *concurrently*, that is in any arbitrary order or even simultaneously without the future behaviour of the overall system being affected by their order, while the corresponding outputs are joined. The requirements for the independence relation (symmetry, irreflexivity, etc.) include the completeness of concurrency "diamonds", cf. Figure 8.1, where opposite transitions denote the same event and the other transitions are pairwise independent. In our framework, two transitions from the same state are considered to be independent iff different input channels are concerned.

Now we illustrate the extension of our approach to components with more than one input channel with examples. Some of the examples also illustrate the generalization to components with more than one output channel.

Example 8.7 (cross component — revisited)
We construct a state refinement for the cross component $X : \mathcal{A}_1^\star \times \mathcal{A}_2^\star \to \mathcal{A}_2^\star \times \mathcal{A}_1^\star$ from Example 2.21. The output extension is derived from the

equations

$$\mathsf{X}(X,Y) \,\&\, \varepsilon(X,Y)(1,x) \;=\; \mathsf{X}(X \triangleright x, Y) \tag{8.8}$$
$$\mathsf{X}(X,Y) \,\&\, \varepsilon(X,Y)(2,y) \;=\; \mathsf{X}(X, Y \triangleright y)\,. \tag{8.9}$$

The output extension

$$\varepsilon(X,Y)(1,x) \;=\; (\langle\rangle, \langle x\rangle) \tag{8.10}$$
$$\varepsilon(X,Y)(2,y) \;=\; (\langle y\rangle, \langle\rangle) \tag{8.11}$$

is independent of the previous input histories on each channel. The history abstraction

$$\alpha(X,Y) \;=\; q_0 \tag{8.12}$$

identifies all input histories. The refining state transition machine $M[\mathsf{X}, \alpha] = (\{q_0\}, \{1\} \times \mathcal{A}_1 \cup \{2\} \times \mathcal{A}_2, (\mathcal{A}_2, \mathcal{A}_1), next, out, q_0)$ employs the trivial state transition function

$$next(q_0, (i, x)) \;=\; q_0 \tag{8.13}$$

and the symmetric output function

$$out(q_0, (1, x)) \;=\; (\langle\rangle, \langle x\rangle) \tag{8.14}$$
$$out(q_0, (2, y)) \;=\; (\langle y\rangle, \langle\rangle)\,. \tag{8.15}$$

The cross component is history independent, because it does not need any information from previous input histories to compute further output. In particular, it does not arrange any synchronization between its input channels. □

The following example shows the systematic introduction of states for a component which synchronizes its input streams.

Example 8.8 (synchronization barrier)
A synchronization barrier $syn : \mathcal{A}_1^\star \times \mathcal{A}_2^\star \to \mathcal{A}_1^\star \times A_2^\star$ lets an element on one input channel pass iff there is also an element on the other input channel:

$$syn(X,Y) \;=\; (take(|Y|)(X), take(|X|)(Y)) \tag{8.16}$$

$take(n)(X)$ takes the first $n \in \mathbb{N}$ elements of the stream X as far as they exist, cf. Equations (9.68)–(9.70) in Subsection 9.4.4. The output extension of the synchronization barrier

$$|X| = |Y_1| \implies \varepsilon(X, Y_1 \& \langle y \rangle \& Y_2)(1, x) = (\langle x \rangle, \langle y \rangle) \tag{8.17}$$
$$|X| \geq |Y| \implies \varepsilon(X, Y)(1, x) = (\langle \rangle, \langle \rangle) \tag{8.18}$$
$$|X_1| = |Y| \implies \varepsilon(X_1 \& \langle x \rangle \& X_2, Y)(2, y) = (\langle x \rangle, \langle y \rangle) \tag{8.19}$$
$$|X| \leq |Y| \implies \varepsilon(X, Y)(2, y) = (\langle \rangle, \langle \rangle) \tag{8.20}$$

depends on the final segment of the longer input stream.

The history abstraction $\alpha : \mathcal{A}_1^\star \times \mathcal{A}_2^\star \to (\mathcal{A}_1^\star \times \{\langle \rangle\} \cup \{\langle \rangle\} \times \mathcal{A}_2^\star)$ retains a final segment of the longer output stream:

$$|X_1| = |Y| \implies \alpha(X_1 \& X_2, Y) = (X_2, \langle \rangle) \tag{8.21}$$
$$|X| = |Y_1| \implies \alpha(X, Y_1 \& Y_2) = (\langle \rangle, Y_2) \tag{8.22}$$

The history abstraction leads to the state refinement $M[syn, \alpha] = (\mathcal{A}_1^\star \times \{\langle \rangle\} \cup \{\langle \rangle\} \times \mathcal{A}_2^\star, \{1\} \times \mathcal{A}_1 \cup \{2\} \times \mathcal{A}_2, (\mathcal{A}_1, \mathcal{A}_2), next, out, (\langle \rangle, \langle \rangle))$ with the state transition function

$$next((X, \langle \rangle), (1, x)) = (X \triangleright x, \langle \rangle) \tag{8.23}$$
$$next((\langle \rangle, y \triangleleft Y), (1, x)) = (\langle \rangle, Y) \tag{8.24}$$
$$next((\langle \rangle, Y), (2, y)) = (\langle \rangle, Y \triangleright y) \tag{8.25}$$
$$next((x \triangleleft X, \langle \rangle), (2, y)) = (X, \langle \rangle) \tag{8.26}$$

and the output function

$$out((X, \langle \rangle), (1, x)) = (\langle \rangle, \langle \rangle) \tag{8.27}$$
$$out((\langle \rangle, y \triangleleft Y), (1, x)) = (\langle x \rangle, \langle y \rangle) \tag{8.28}$$
$$out((\langle \rangle, Y), (2, y)) = (\langle \rangle, \langle \rangle) \tag{8.29}$$
$$out((x \triangleleft X, \langle \rangle), (2, y)) = (\langle x \rangle, \langle y \rangle). \tag{8.30}$$

The synchronization barrier retains the final segment of its longer input stream as far as the corresponding data on the other input stream have not arrived yet. Therefore it is called a *buffering* component. □

The next example shows the effect on the state if we consider only one of the two output streams of the synchronization barrier.

Example 8.9 (projected synchronization)
The projected synchronization $\Pi_1(syn(X, Y)) = take(|Y|)(X)$ outputs each element on the first channel if there is a synchronization element on the second channel, the control channel.

The output extension

$$|X| = |Y_1| \implies \varepsilon(X, Y_1 \& \langle y \rangle \& Y_2)(1, x) = \langle x \rangle \tag{8.31}$$
$$|X| \geq |Y| \implies \varepsilon(X, Y)(1, x) = \langle \rangle \tag{8.32}$$
$$|X_1| = |Y| \implies \varepsilon(X_1 \& \langle x \rangle \& X_2, Y)(2, y) = \langle x \rangle \tag{8.33}$$
$$|X| \leq |Y| \implies \varepsilon(X, Y)(2, y) = \langle \rangle, \tag{8.34}$$

which is obtained as a projection on the first component of the output extension of the synchronization barrier (8.17)–(8.20), does not depend on the data on the control channel but only on the length of the control stream. Hence the history abstraction $\alpha : \mathcal{A}_1^* \times \mathcal{A}_2^* \to (\mathcal{A}_1^* \cup \mathbb{P})$ records only the length of the surplus on the second input channel instead of its content:

$$|X_1| = |Y| \implies \alpha(X_1 \& X_2, Y) = X_2 \tag{8.35}$$
$$|X| = |Y_1| \implies \alpha(X, Y_1 \& \langle y \rangle \& Y_2) = |y \triangleleft Y_2| \tag{8.36}$$

The state refinement $M[\Pi_1 \circ syn, \alpha] = (\mathcal{A}_1^* \cup \mathbb{P}, \{1\} \times \mathcal{A}_1 \cup \{2\} \times \mathcal{A}_2, \mathcal{A}_1, next, out, \langle \rangle)$ employs the state transition function ($m > 1$, $n \geq 1$)

$$next(X, (1, x)) = X \triangleright x \tag{8.37}$$
$$next(1, (1, x)) = \langle \rangle \tag{8.38}$$
$$next(m, (1, x)) = m - 1 \tag{8.39}$$
$$next(\langle \rangle, (2, y)) = 1 \tag{8.40}$$
$$next(x \triangleleft X, (2, y)) = X \tag{8.41}$$
$$next(n, (2, y)) = n + 1 \tag{8.42}$$

and the output function

$$out(X, (1, x)) = \langle \rangle \tag{8.43}$$
$$out(n, (1, x)) = \langle x \rangle \tag{8.44}$$
$$out(\langle \rangle, (2, y)) = \langle \rangle \tag{8.45}$$
$$out(x \triangleleft X, (2, y)) = \langle x \rangle \tag{8.46}$$
$$out(n, (2, y)) = \langle \rangle. \tag{8.47}$$

The projected synchronization needs no buffer for the control channel. Instead it only records the number of pending control commands.   □

The states in the previous examples comprise only information for the synchronization of data on the input channels, whereas the component in the following example needs to retain information from the previous input histories apart from buffering due to synchronization.

Example 8.10 (memory cell with command and data channels)
This example *memsep* : $\mathcal{C}^* \times \mathcal{D}^* \to \mathcal{D}^*$ is adapted from the memory with
separate command and data channel in Example 10.17 which is the result of
an interface refinement step of the ordinary memory cell from Example 6.6.
$\mathcal{C} = \{\mathsf{r}, \mathsf{w}\}$ constitutes the set of commands and $\mathcal{D} \neq \emptyset$ the set of data such
that $\mathcal{C} \cap \mathcal{D} = \emptyset$. The specification of the memory cell ($C \in \mathcal{C}^*$, $D \in \mathcal{D}^*$) is:

$$
\begin{align}
memsep(C, \langle\rangle) &= \langle\rangle \tag{8.48}\\
memsep(\langle\rangle, D) &= \langle\rangle \tag{8.49}\\
memsep(\mathsf{r} \triangleleft C, D) &= memsep(C, D) \tag{8.50}\\
memsep(\langle\mathsf{w}\rangle, D) &= \langle\rangle \tag{8.51}\\
memsep(\mathsf{w} \triangleleft \mathsf{w} \triangleleft C, d \triangleleft D) &= memsep(\mathsf{w} \triangleleft C, D) \tag{8.52}\\
memsep(\mathsf{w} \triangleleft \mathsf{r} \triangleleft C, d \triangleleft D) &= d \triangleleft memsep(\mathsf{w} \triangleleft C, d \triangleleft D) \tag{8.53}
\end{align}
$$

Its output extension depends on the balance between the number of write
commands and the number of data. Let $n = ||C||_\mathsf{w}$ denote the number of
write commands in the command stream C:

$$
\begin{align}
\varepsilon(C, D)(1, \mathsf{w}) &= \langle\rangle \tag{8.54}\\
n = 0 \vee n > |D| \implies \varepsilon(C, D)(1, \mathsf{r}) &= \langle\rangle \tag{8.55}\\
n = |D \triangleright d| \implies \varepsilon(C, D\&\langle d\rangle\&D')(1, \mathsf{r}) &= \langle d\rangle \tag{8.56}\\
n = 0 \vee n \leq |D| \implies \varepsilon(C, D)(2, d) &= \langle\rangle \tag{8.57}\\
n = |D| \wedge (C' = \langle\rangle \vee \mathit{first}(C') = \mathsf{w}) \implies & \notag\\
\varepsilon(C\&\langle\mathsf{w}\rangle\&\mathsf{r}^m\&C', D)(2, d) &= d^m \tag{8.58}
\end{align}
$$

The history abstraction $\alpha : \mathcal{C}^* \times \mathcal{D}^* \to (\mathcal{D}^{\leq 1} \times \mathcal{D}^* \cup \mathcal{C}^*)$ collects pending
commands or records the last datum stored combined with pending data,
respectively ($n = ||C||_\mathsf{w}$):

$$
\begin{align}
\alpha(\mathsf{r}^m, D) &= (\langle\rangle, D) \tag{8.59}\\
n = |D \triangleright d| \implies \alpha(C, D\&\langle d\rangle\&D') &= (\langle d\rangle, D') \tag{8.60}\\
n = |D| \implies \alpha(C\&\langle\mathsf{w}\rangle\&C', D) &= C' \tag{8.61}
\end{align}
$$

The state transition function and the output function of the resulting state
refinement $M[memsep, \alpha] = (\mathcal{D}^{\leq 1} \times \mathcal{D}^* \cup \mathcal{C}^*, \{1\} \times \mathcal{C} \cup \{2\} \times \mathcal{D}, \mathcal{D}, next, out,$
$(\langle\rangle, \langle\rangle))$ are given in the following transition table ($S \in \mathcal{D}^{\leq 1}$, $c \in \mathcal{C}$):

Q	x	$next(q,x)$	$out(Q,x)$
$(\langle\rangle, D)$	$(1,r)$	$(\langle\rangle, D)$	$\langle\rangle$
$(\langle d\rangle, D)$	$(1,r)$	$(\langle d\rangle, D)$	$\langle d\rangle$
$(S, \langle\rangle)$	$(1,w)$	$\langle\rangle$	$\langle\rangle$
$(S, d \triangleleft D)$	$(1,w)$	$(\langle d\rangle, D)$	$\langle\rangle$
C	$(1,c)$	$C \triangleright c$	$\langle\rangle$
(S, D)	$(2,d)$	$(S, D \triangleright d)$	$\langle\rangle$
r^n	$(2,d)$	$(\langle d\rangle, \langle\rangle)$	d^n
$r^n \& \langle w\rangle \& C$	$(2,d)$	C	d^n

The example makes clear that the state is often a combination of buffers for the input streams and further history information.   □

The examples confirm that the methodology can naturally be transferred to stream processing functions with several input streams.

Concluding remarks

In this chapter we showed that the restrictions we made in the previous chapters on state refinement can be revoked. We presented the generalizations to infinite output streams, infinite input streams, more than one output stream, and more than one input stream. Although we presented these generalizations independently of each other in separate sections, they can be combined, of course.

Chapter 9

Property Refinement

The state refinement introduced in the previous chapters yields a finer view of a component while preserving the input / output behaviour. In this chapter, we investigate property refinement which constitutes a different notion of refinement. Property refinement restricts the set of possible behaviours of a component which arise by *underspecification*.

Underspecified components often appear during the early phases of a system development, in particular for input which is considered to be unexpected, incomplete, or erroneous. Compared to fully specified components, underspecified components have a broader range of applications because they can be adapted for being reused in other systems.

The characteristic property for underspecified components is that for some input streams the output is not defined uniquely. Stream processing functions uniquely specify the behaviour of a component. Therefore, we need new specification techniques for underspecified components. The techniques for resolving underspecification depend on the specification technique. In this thesis, we concentrate on specifications with partially defined functions, in particular functions which are defined on a prefix closed subset of all input streams and functions which are only specified for infinite input streams, and specifications with parameters.

We introduce each of these specification techniques and specialize the corresponding definition of property refinement. Furthermore, we present systematic methods how to obtain a property refinement.

Underspecification is closely related to *nondeterminism*. Although these concepts are sometimes used synonymously in the literature, they definitely denote different concepts. A nondeterministic component may output different results when provided with the same input several times whereas an underspecified component always emits the same output for each input, but this particular output may not yet be specified uniquely. At the end of the chapter we discuss nondeterminism which is specified with oracles.

9.1   Property Refinement for Underspecified Components

First of all, we give a semantic characterization of underspecified components while leaving open the specification technique. Then we define the property refinement for underspecified components narrowing the set of possible behaviours.

The behaviour of an underspecified component is modelled by a set of possible behaviours.

Definition 9.1 (underspecified component)
An *underspecified component* is described as a set of stream processing functions $\mathcal{F} \subseteq \mathcal{A}_1^{\infty} \times \ldots \times \mathcal{A}_m^{\infty} \to \mathcal{B}_1^{\infty} \times \ldots \times \mathcal{B}_n^{\infty}$ with the same interface. An empty set denotes an *inconsistent* specification. Each function in $\mathcal{F}$ determines a possible behaviour of the component.   □

In contrast to [BS01b] who also include unrealizable behaviours into the underspecification, we consider only continuous functions on streams.

A property refinement for an underspecified component results in restricting the set of possible behaviours.

Definition 9.2 (property refinement of an underspecified component)
An underspecified component $\mathcal{G} \subseteq \mathcal{A}_1^{\infty} \times \ldots \times \mathcal{A}_m^{\infty} \to \mathcal{B}_1^{\infty} \times \ldots \times \mathcal{B}_n^{\infty}$ is a *property refinement* of an underspecified component $\mathcal{F} \subseteq \mathcal{A}_1^{\infty} \times \ldots \times \mathcal{A}_m^{\infty} \to \mathcal{B}_1^{\infty} \times \ldots \times \mathcal{B}_n^{\infty}$ with the same interface, if

$$\mathcal{G} \subseteq \mathcal{F}$$

holds.   □

Property refinement is reflexive, transitive, and antisymmetric. Moreover, property refinement is compositional.

Proposition 9.3
If $\mathcal{G}_1$ is a property refinement of $\mathcal{F}_1$, and $\mathcal{G}_2$ is a property refinement of $\mathcal{F}_2$, then the composition $\mathcal{G}_1 \oplus \mathcal{G}_2$, lifted to sets, refines $\mathcal{F}_1 \oplus F_2$.   □

The techniques for resolving underspecification depend on the nature of underspecification and the corresponding specification techniques. Popular specification techniques for underspecification are partially defined functions, which we deal with in the following three sections, and parameterization, which is the subject of Section 9.5.

9.2 Partially Defined Stream Processing Functions

The behaviour of a component need not be specified for input streams which are not (yet) supposed to appear in the designated environment of the component. *Assumption/commitment* specifications [Bro98b, SDW96] guarantee a correct behaviour only if the input from the environment fulfils the assumption. For describing this form of underspecification, we consider partially defined stream processing functions restricting the domain of the function to the subset of the input streams validating the assumption. In this section, we survey the general considerations for resolving underspecification for invalid input streams.

A partially defined function uniquely determines the behaviour for valid input streams and allows arbitrary behaviour for invalid input streams.

Definition 9.4 (partially defined stream processing function)
A *partially defined* stream processing function is described by a non-empty set $\mathcal{F}|_{\mathcal{D}} \subseteq \mathcal{A}_1^\infty \times \ldots \times \mathcal{A}_m^\infty \to \mathcal{B}_1^\infty \times \ldots \times \mathcal{B}_n^\infty$ of stream processing functions which agree on the set $\mathcal{D} \subseteq \mathcal{A}_1^\infty \times \ldots \times \mathcal{A}_m^\infty$ of *valid* input streams and which make possible any behaviour for *invalid* input streams $\mathcal{U} = (\mathcal{A}_1^\infty \times \ldots \times \mathcal{A}_m^\infty) \setminus \mathcal{D}$:

$$f, g \in \mathcal{F}|_{\mathcal{D}} \quad \implies \quad f|_{\mathcal{D}} = g|_{\mathcal{D}}$$
$$g|_{\mathcal{D}} = f|_{\mathcal{D}} \wedge f \in \mathcal{F}|_{\mathcal{D}} \quad \implies \quad g \in \mathcal{F}|_{\mathcal{D}}$$

The restriction $f|_{\mathcal{D}} : \mathcal{D} \to \mathcal{B}_1^\infty \times \ldots \times \mathcal{B}_n^\infty$ of a possible behaviour $f \in \mathcal{F}|_{\mathcal{D}}$ to valid input streams describes the *partially defined behaviour*. □

A non-empty set $\mathcal{F}|_{\mathcal{D}}$ is uniquely determined by the set $\mathcal{D}$ and a stream processing function $f \in \mathcal{F}|_{\mathcal{D}}$. In terms of assumption/commitment, the set of valid input streams validate the assumption, and the behaviour constitutes the commitment.

Resolving the underspecification for a partially defined component $f : \mathcal{D} \to \mathcal{B}_1^\infty \times \ldots \times \mathcal{B}_n^\infty$ defined on input streams $\mathcal{D} \subseteq \mathcal{A}_1^\infty \times \ldots \times \mathcal{A}_m^\infty$ consists in completing the definition of f to a stream processing function $f' : \mathcal{A}_1^\infty \times \ldots \times \mathcal{A}_m^\infty \to \mathcal{B}_1^\infty \times \ldots \times \mathcal{B}_n^\infty$ such that

$$f'|_\mathcal{D} \;=\; f \tag{9.1}$$

holds.

For the definition of the output of an invalid input stream, valid prefixes as well as valid prolongations of invalid input streams must be taken into account due to the monotonicity and continuity requirement. The output of an invalid input stream is a prolongation of the output of its longest valid prefix. Furthermore, the output of an invalid input stream is a prefix of the maximal common prefix of the output of all its valid prolongations provided they exist: $(X \in \mathcal{U}, \{Y \in \mathcal{D} \mid X \sqsubset Y\} \neq \emptyset)$

$$\bigsqcup_{\substack{Y \sqsubset X \\ Y \in \mathcal{D}}} f(Y) \;\sqsubseteq\; f'(X) \;\sqsubseteq\; \prod_{\substack{X \sqsubset Y \\ Y \in \mathcal{D}}} f(Y) \tag{9.2}$$

In the following two sections, we approach property refinement for partially defined functions from the methodological point of view. We investigate stream processing functions which are defined on a prefix closed subset of input streams, and stream processing functions which are only defined for infinite input streams.

9.3 Property Refinement for Erroneous Input Streams

Many components are not designed to run in an arbitrary environment. A major source for underspecification arises from erroneous input streams, for which the behaviour of the component is undetermined. The behaviour for erroneous input streams can conveniently be resolved after the introduction of states. Therefore we investigate how the systematic introduction of states can be applied to regular behaviours only. For that, we first of all introduce state transition machines which are defined only on regular input, before we transfer our concepts for state refinement to regular behaviours. Finally, we discuss how the underspecification for erroneous input streams can be resolved after the introduction of states.

As in all chapters on state refinement apart from the last one, we restrict ourselves to finite streams and components with one input channel and one output channel. The generalizations proceed as in Chapter 8.

We require that an erroneous input history cannot be corrected by any prolongation and thus remains erroneous. Consequently, prolongations of erroneous input are also erroneous.

Definition 9.5 (regular and erroneous input streams)
A set of input streams $\mathcal{A}^\star$ may be split into disjoint sets of *regular* and *erroneous* input streams:

$$\mathcal{A}^\star = \mathcal{R} \,\dot{\cup}\, \mathcal{E} \tag{9.3}$$

We assume that the set of erroneous input streams is upward closed: $X \in \mathcal{E} \implies X \& Y \in \mathcal{E}$, and that the empty history is regular: $\langle\rangle \in \mathcal{R}$. $\square$

An equivalent requirement to the property "upward closed" for erroneous input streams is that the set of regular input streams is prefix closed. Every erroneous input stream has a unique maximal regular prefix.

Characteristic examples for regular input streams may be ordered streams $\langle x_1, x_2, \ldots, x_n \rangle$, in which the elements $x_1 \leq x_2 \leq \ldots \leq x_n$ occur (ascendingly) ordered provided there is a linear order on the basic set of input data [DS99, DS00]. Characteristic examples for erroneous streams are streams containing illegal requests or streams containing new input data which have been introduced by an input interface refinement step (cf. Section 10.1.2).

Definition 9.6 (regular and erroneous behaviour)
The behaviour of a component $f : \mathcal{A}^\star \to \mathcal{B}^\star$ whose set of input streams $\mathcal{A}^\star$ is split into the set $\mathcal{R}$ of regular input streams and the set $\mathcal{E}$ of erroneous input streams is composed from the *regular behaviour* $f|_\mathcal{R} : \mathcal{R} \to \mathcal{B}^\star$ and the *erroneous behaviour* $f|_\mathcal{E} : \mathcal{E} \to \mathcal{B}^\star$. $\square$

By the monotonicity requirement, the output for an erroneous input stream is a prolongation of the output of its longest regular prefix.

Now we analyse the space of possible resolutions for an erroneous behaviour. Given a set $\mathcal{R}$ of regular input streams of a set of streams $\mathcal{A}^\star$ and a regular behaviour $\tilde{f} : \mathcal{R} \to \mathcal{B}^\star$, the stream processing functions $f : \mathcal{A}^\star \to \mathcal{B}^\star$ with $f|_\mathcal{R} = \tilde{f}$ are the possible resolutions. The *least resolution* yields the output of the longest regular prefix $R \in \mathcal{R}$ of an erroneous input stream $R \& \langle e \rangle \& E \in \mathcal{E}$:

$$f(R \& \langle e \rangle \& E) = f(R) \tag{9.4}$$

where $R \triangleright e \in \mathcal{E}$.

A *maximal resolvation* does not exist in the set of functions with finite output streams, because the set of stream processing functions with finite output streams with the same interface has no maximal elements.

By the way, in the set of stream processing functions with finite and infinite output streams the maximal resolvations are $(R \in \mathcal{R}, R \triangleright e \in \mathcal{E})$

$$f(R \& \langle e \rangle \& E) \;=\; f(R) \& B \tag{9.5}$$

where $B \in \mathcal{B}^\omega$ is a constant infinite stream. Only if the set of output data $\mathcal{B}$ is a singleton set, then the only maximal resolvation is also the *greatest resolvation*.

9.3.1 Partially Defined State Transition Machines

Before we present how to directly obtain a state refinement of a resolvation of the erroneous behaviour without explicitly specifying the erroneous behaviour in advance, we have to provide a model for a state refinement of the regular behaviour only. In this subsection, we introduce state transition machines with partially defined state transition and output functions which are suitable for modelling the behaviour of stream processing functions which are only specified on a non-empty downward closed set of input streams.

If a component is specified in the form of a state transition machine, under-specification arises if the state transition function and/or the output function are not specified completely. We consider the special case where the state transition and the output function are defined on the same subset of pairs of states and inputs.

Definition 9.7 (partially defined state transition machine)
A *partially defined state transition machine* $\widetilde{M}$ is a tuple $(\mathcal{Q}, \mathcal{A}, \mathcal{B}, \mathcal{P}, \widetilde{next},$ $\widetilde{out}, q_0)$ where $\mathcal{Q}$, $\mathcal{A}$, $\mathcal{B}$, and q_0 are as in Definition 3.1 and $\widetilde{next} : \mathcal{P} \to \mathcal{Q}$ and $\widetilde{out} : \mathcal{P} \to \mathcal{B}^\star$ are defined on the same subset $\mathcal{P} \subseteq \mathcal{Q} \times \mathcal{A}$ of pairs of states and inputs.   □

The set $\mathcal{D} \subseteq \mathcal{A}^\star$ of input streams for which the multi-step state transition and the multi-step output function in the initial state are defined is defined inductively as follows:

  (1) $\langle \rangle \in \mathcal{D}$.
  (2)   If $X \in \mathcal{D}$ and $(\widetilde{next}^\star(q_0)(X), x) \in \mathcal{P}$, then $X \triangleright x \in \mathcal{D}$.

The non-empty set $\mathcal{D}$ of defined input streams is prefix closed, and the set $\mathcal{U} = \mathcal{A}^\star \setminus \mathcal{D}$ of undefined input stream is upward closed. Therefore we call streams in the set $\mathcal{D}$ regular and the streams in the set $\mathcal{U}$ erroneous input streams of a partially defined state transition machine. Since a partially defined state transition machine splits its input streams into a non-empty, downward closed set of input streams for which the output is defined and an upward closed set of input streams for which the output is not defined, it represents an abstract machine model for stream transformers with erroneous input streams.

We briefly discuss state transition machines whose state transition function $\widetilde{next}$ and output function $\widetilde{out}$ are defined on different subsets of $\mathcal{Q} \times \mathcal{A}$ and may be defined arbitrarily otherwise. If $\widetilde{next}(q, x)$ is defined whereas $\widetilde{out}(q, x)$ is not defined, then the transition from the state q with the input datum d inserts an arbitrary substream into the output stream. The future behaviour remains uninfluenced by the underspecified transition. If $\widetilde{out}(q, x)$ is defined whereas $\widetilde{next}(q, x)$ is not defined, then the behavior after the output $\widetilde{out}(q, x)$ can be the behaviour from any arbitrary state of the state transition machine. In general, in that case nothing much can be said about the future behaviour of the state transition machine.

9.3.2 State Refinement for Regular Behaviours

The property "prefix-closed" of regular input streams allows to construct a state refinement for a regular behaviour as described in the chapters on state refinement, such that for regular input streams the output of the refining partially defined state transition machine agrees with the regular behaviour.

Definition 9.8 (regular history abstraction)
The restriction $\widetilde{\alpha} = \alpha|_{\mathcal{R}}$ of a history abstraction $\alpha : \mathcal{A}^* \to \mathcal{Q}$ for the stream transformer $f : \mathcal{A}^* \to \mathcal{B}^*$ is a *regular history abstraction* for the regular behaviour $f|_{\mathcal{R}}$. □

A regular history abstraction for a regular behaviour $\widetilde{f}$ cannot be extended to a history abstraction for every resolvation of the underspecification of $\widetilde{f}$. The reaction to errors cannot employ more information from the previous input history than the information which is provided for the reaction to regular input. As a consequence for example, if the the history abstraction identifies at least two prefixes of erroneous input streams, then the reaction to an error cannot be a complete error log which outputs the complete prehistory which has lead to the error.

Theorem 9.9
A regular history abstraction $\widetilde{\alpha} : \mathcal{R} \to \mathcal{Q}$ of a regular behaviour $\widetilde{f} : \mathcal{R} \to \mathcal{B}^*$ determines a partially defined state transition machine $\widetilde{M}[\widetilde{f}, \widetilde{\alpha}] = (\mathcal{Q}, \mathcal{A}, \mathcal{B}, \mathcal{P},$

$\widetilde{next}, \widetilde{out}, \widetilde{\alpha}(\langle\rangle))$ where $\widetilde{next}(\widetilde{\alpha}(X), x) = \widetilde{\alpha}(X \triangleright x)$ and $\widetilde{out}(\widetilde{\alpha}(X), x) = \varepsilon(X, x)$ are defined on $\mathcal{P} = \{(\widetilde{\alpha}(X), x) \mid X \triangleright x \in \mathcal{R}\}$.

The set $\mathcal{D}$ on which the multi-step transition functions are defined covers the set $\mathcal{R}$ of regular input streams:

$$\mathcal{R} \subseteq \mathcal{D} \tag{9.6}$$

A resolution M of the partially defined state transition machine $\widetilde{M}[\widetilde{f}, \widetilde{\alpha}]$ is a state refinement of a resolution f of the regular behaviour $\widetilde{f}$

$$f \rightsquigarrow_{state} M$$

because the multi-step output function of the partially defined state transition machine extends the regular behaviour of the stream transformer: $(R \& X \in \mathcal{R})$

$$f(R) \,\&\, \widetilde{out}^{*}(\widetilde{\alpha}(R))(X) \;=\; f(R \& X) \qquad \qquad \square$$

Given a regular behaviour, we can apply the same construction for a state refinement as in Theorem 4.9 and as in Lemma 6.5.

In Equation (9.6), $\mathcal{D}$ is a proper superset of $\mathcal{R}$, if regular input streams X and Y are abstracted to the same state $\widetilde{\alpha}(X) = \widetilde{\alpha}(Y)$ and the extension $X \triangleright x \in \mathcal{E}$ is erroneous while the corresponding extension $Y \triangleright x \in \mathcal{R}$ is regular.

Characteristic applications are memory components with bounded resources or components which need an appropriate initializing input stream before operating properly. We now demonstrate the state introduction for a bounded stack whose behaviour is not specified in case of stack underflow and stack overflow.

Example 9.10 (interactive bounded stack)
An interactive bounded stack with $n > 0$ places receives push commands with a datum and pop commands. A pop command outputs the last datum pushed onto the stack which has not been requested yet. The set $\mathcal{I}$ of input commands is $push(\mathcal{D}) \cup \{pop\}$ where $\mathcal{D} \neq \emptyset$ is the non-empty set of data. The set of output data is $\mathcal{D}$.

The regular input streams $X \in \mathcal{R}_n$ are characterized by the property

$$||Y||_{pop} \leq ||Y||_{push(\mathcal{D})} \leq n + ||Y||_{pop} \tag{9.7}$$

for all prefixes $Y \sqsubseteq X$. The number of pop commands must not exceed the number of push commands, and the number of push commands must not exceed the stack capacity plus the number of pop commands.

The specification $istack : \mathcal{R}_n \to \mathcal{D}^\star$ on regular input streams follows the recursion scheme

(1) $push(\mathcal{D})^{\leq n} \in \mathcal{R}_n$.

(2) If $Q \& X \in \mathcal{R}_n$, $Q \in push(\mathcal{D})^{<n}$, then $Q \& \langle push(d), pop \rangle \& X \in \mathcal{R}_n$.

which constitutes an inductive definition of the regular input streams $\mathcal{R}_n$.

Push commands do not produce output. A regular pop command outputs the last datum that has been pushed onto the stack and has not been requested yet: $(P \in push(\mathcal{D})^{\leq n}, Q \in push(\mathcal{D})^{<n})$

$$istack(P) = \langle \rangle \tag{9.8}$$

$$istack(Q \& \langle push(d), pop \rangle \& X) = d \triangleleft istack(Q \& X) \tag{9.9}$$

The function $istack$ validates a decomposition property by Theorem 2.15 for $X \& Y \in \mathcal{R}_n$:

$$istack(X \& Y) = istack(X) \& istack(lifo(X) \& Y) \tag{9.10}$$

where the auxiliary function $lifo : \mathcal{R}_n \to push(\mathcal{D})^{\leq n}$ follows from the recursion structure of $istack$:

$$lifo(P) = P \tag{9.11}$$

$$lifo(Q \& \langle push(d), pop \rangle \& X) = lifo(Q \& X) \tag{9.12}$$

The choice of the history abstraction according to Lemma 6.5 restricts the possible behaviour in case of erroneous input. We assume that the reaction to erroneous input does not employ more information from the history than is necessary for the reaction to regular input.

By Theorem 6.4, the set of states is $\mathcal{Q} = push(\mathcal{D})^{\leq n}$. We drop the constructors $push$ in the state and determine the partially defined state transition function from $\widetilde{next}(Q, x) = (push^\star)^{-1}(lifo(push^\star(Q) \triangleright x))$ where $push^\star = map(push)$ applies the constructor $push$ to every element in a stream and $(push^\star)^{-1} : push(\mathcal{D})^\star \to \mathcal{D}^\star$ drops the constructors $push$ in a stream. We assume $|D| < n$:

$$
\begin{aligned}
\widetilde{next}(D, push(d)) &= (push^\star)^{-1}(lifo(push^\star(D) \triangleright push(d))) \\
&= D \triangleright d \tag{9.13} \\
\widetilde{next}(D \triangleright d, pop) &= (push^\star)^{-1}(lifo(push^\star(D) \& \langle push(d), pop \rangle)) \\
&= (push^\star)^{-1}(lifo(push^\star(D))) \\
&= D \tag{9.14}
\end{aligned}
$$

Under the same assumption, we determine the partially defined output function from $\widetilde{out}(Q, x) = istack(push^\star(Q) \rhd x)$:

$$
\begin{aligned}
\widetilde{out}(D, push(d)) &= istack(push^\star(D) \rhd push(d)) \\
&= \langle\rangle & (9.15) \\
\widetilde{out}(D \rhd d, pop) &= istack(push^\star(D) \& \langle push(d), pop\rangle) \\
&= d \lhd istack(push^\star(D)) \\
&= \langle d\rangle & (9.16)
\end{aligned}
$$

In summary, the refining partially defined state transition machine on regular input histories is $\widetilde{M} = (\mathcal{D}^{\leq n}, \mathcal{I}, \mathcal{D}, (\mathcal{D}^{\leq n} \setminus \{\langle\rangle\}) \times \{pop\} \cup \mathcal{D}^{<n} \times push(\mathcal{D}), \widetilde{next}, \widetilde{out}, \langle\rangle)$ through the regular history abstraction $\widetilde{\alpha} = (push^\star)^{-1} \circ lifo$. □

The behaviour of the state transition machine is completely defined for regular input streams. The state transition machine is not defined for *stack overflow* – when a push command encounters a full stack – and for *stack underflow* – when a pop command encounters an empty stack. We discuss the behaviour for erroneous input streams in Example 9.11.

9.3.3   Resolving the Underspecification

In general, the behaviour for erroneous input streams is resolved in late phases of the design, for example after the introduction of states. In the previous subsection, we showed how to obtain a partially defined state refinement for a regular behaviour. In this section, we discuss how the behaviour for erroneous input streams can be resolved after the state introduction by defining abstractions of erroneous input streams or by completing the definition of the state transition function and the output function.

For the specification of the erroneous behaviour it is sometimes necessary to *extend the set of output data*, for example with messages for error or recovery reports. The extension of the set of output data by new output symbols constitutes an output interface refinement step, cf. Subsection 10.3.1. Furthermore, a resolution of the underspecification for the state transition function may require *abstractions of erroneous input histories* which are not necessary for the regular behaviour and therefore have not been considered for the set of states of the partially defined state transition machine $\widetilde{M} = (\mathcal{Q}, \mathcal{A}, \mathcal{B}, \mathcal{P}, \widetilde{next}, \widetilde{out}, q_0)$ refining the regular behaviour. A partially defined state transition machine $\widetilde{M'} = (\mathcal{Q} \cup \mathcal{Q'}, \mathcal{A}, \mathcal{B} \cup \mathcal{B'}, \mathcal{P}, \widetilde{next}, \widetilde{out}, q_0)$ with more states $\mathcal{Q'}$ and more output data $\mathcal{B'}$ shows the same behaviour on regular input streams. Of course, for resolving the underspecification, the state transition function and the output function must also be defined for new states.

The strategies for error recovery can be adopted from parser recovery techniques [Cie79, HRS84]. When encountering an erroneous input datum, the component may ignore it, it may break, it may insert a substream before the erroneous input so that the input becomes correct, or it may postpone a substream until its insertion does not invalidate the input stream.

In the following, we assume that the regular input stream $R \in \mathcal{R}$ has been processed, that means that the machine is in the state $q = \widetilde{\alpha}(R)$, when an element e which invalidates the input stream $R \triangleright e \in \mathcal{E}$ is detected and $next(q, e)$ and $out(q, e)$ are not defined.

Fault tolerant behaviour

A fault tolerant component ignores unexpected input. In that case we complete the definition of the state transition function by the equation

$$next(q, e) \;=\; q\,. \tag{9.17}$$

If this equation is chosen for all unspecified transitions and we define $out(q, e) = \langle \rangle$, then we obviously have

$$f(R \& \langle e \rangle \& E) \;=\; f(R \& E) \tag{9.18}$$

for a regular input stream $R \in \mathcal{R}$ and an erroneous input stream $R \triangleright e \in \mathcal{E}$.

Fault sensitive behaviour

A fault sensitive component breaks on unexpected input. In that case we introduce a new absorbing state *fail* and complete the definition of the state transition function by the equations

$$next(q, e) \;=\; fail \tag{9.19}$$
$$next(fail, x) \;=\; fail\,. \tag{9.20}$$

If we take these equations for all unspecified transitions and define $out(q, e) = \langle \rangle$ and $out(fail, x) = \langle \rangle$ for all $x \in \mathcal{A}$, then we obviously have

$$f(R \& \langle e \rangle \& E) \;=\; f(R) \tag{9.21}$$

for a regular input stream $R \in \mathcal{R}$ and an erroneous input stream $R \triangleright e \in \mathcal{E}$.

Error correcting behaviour by insertion

An error correcting component may try inserting an imaginary substream in front of a datum which invalidates a regular input stream, thereby ensuring that the input stream becomes regular.

The state $next(\widetilde{\alpha}(R), e)$, which is reached from the state $\widetilde{\alpha}(R)$ $(R \in \mathcal{R})$ with the invalidating element $e \in \mathcal{A}$ $(R \triangleright e \in \mathcal{E})$, is the state which would be reached when the error correcting substream $C \in \mathcal{A}^\star$ $(R \& C \triangleright e \in \mathcal{R})$ were processed before e:

$$next(\widetilde{\alpha}(R), e) \;=\; \widetilde{\alpha}(R \& C \triangleright e) \tag{9.22}$$

If we define $out(\widetilde{\alpha}(R), e) = out^\star(\widetilde{\alpha}(R))(C \triangleright e)$, so that the output of the imaginarily inserted substream is also inserted, then we obviously have

$$f(R \& \langle e \rangle \& E) \;=\; f(R \& C \& \langle e \rangle \& E) \,. \tag{9.23}$$

This strategy is only applicable for situations in which such a correcting substream exists.

Error correcting behaviour by postponement

An error correcting component may try postponing a substream invalidating an input stream, until its insertion does not invalidate the input stream so far. For that we introduce new states $(\widetilde{\alpha}(\mathcal{R}), \mathcal{A}^+)$ accumulating the postponed input in their second component: $(R \in \mathcal{R}, \; R \triangleright e \in \mathcal{E})$

$$next(\widetilde{\alpha}(R), e) \;=\; (\widetilde{\alpha}(R), \langle e \rangle) \tag{9.24}$$

$$next((\widetilde{\alpha}(R), E), x) \;= \tag{9.25}$$
$$\begin{cases} (\widetilde{\alpha}(R), E \triangleright x) & \text{if } R \& \langle x \rangle \in \mathcal{E} \\ (\widetilde{\alpha}(R \& \langle x \rangle \& E_1), e \triangleleft E_2) & \text{if } E = E_1 \& \langle e \rangle \& E_2, \\ & \quad R \& \langle x \rangle \& E_1 \in \mathcal{R}, \text{ and} \\ & \quad R \& \langle x \rangle \& E_1 \& \langle e \rangle \in \mathcal{E} \\ \widetilde{\alpha}(R \& \langle x \rangle \& E) & \text{if } R \& \langle x \rangle \& E \in \mathcal{R} \end{cases}$$

A new state $(\widetilde{\alpha}(R), \langle e \rangle)$ is reached as soon as an element e invalidates an input stream R (9.24). Further input data which also invalidate the input stream are appended to the postponed input in the second component E of the state. Otherwise, the maximal prefix E_1 of the postponed input E or E itself respectively is appended to the regular input $R \triangleright x$ so that $R \& \langle x \rangle \& E_1$ or $R \& \langle x \rangle \& E$ are regular.

If we define the output function

$$out(\widetilde{\alpha}(R), e) \;=\; \langle\rangle \tag{9.26}$$

$$out((\widetilde{\alpha}(R), E), x) \;=\; \begin{cases} \langle\rangle & \text{if } R\&\langle x\rangle \in \mathcal{E} \\ out^\star(\widetilde{\alpha}(R))(x \lhd E_1) & \text{if } E = E_1\&\langle e\rangle\&E_2, \\ & \quad R\&\langle x\rangle\&E_1 \in \mathcal{R}, \text{ and} \\ & \quad R\&\langle x\rangle\&E_1\&\langle e\rangle \in \mathcal{E} \\ out^\star(\widetilde{\alpha}(R))(x \lhd E) & \text{if } R\&\langle x\rangle\&E \in \mathcal{R} \end{cases} \tag{9.27}$$

so that substreams which are removed from the second component of the state provide the corresponding output, then we have

$$f(R\&\langle e\rangle\&E) \;=\; \begin{cases} f(R\&\langle d, e\rangle\&E_1\&E_2) & \text{if } E = E_1\&\langle d\rangle\&E_2 \text{ with} \\ & \quad R \rhd d \in \mathcal{R} \text{ and} \\ & \quad E_1 = \langle e_1, \dots, e_n\rangle \text{ and} \\ & \quad R \rhd e_i \in \mathcal{E} \text{ for } 1 \le i \le n \\ f(R) & \text{else}. \end{cases} \tag{9.28}$$

The invalidating data are postponed until their insertion is possible. The last case shows that the correction of an error by postponing input is not always possible. As a modification, postponed input can be discarded if it gets too long.

Of course, there are further possibilities how to resolve the underspecification. In particular error and recovery report streams should be taken into account for the underspecified output function.

The presented strategies for the resolution are demonstrated by the following example.

Example 9.11 (interactive bounded stack — revisited)
In Example 9.10 we derived a partially defined state transition machine for the regular behaviour of an interactive bounded stack. Now we discuss how to resolve the missing transitions for the state $Q \in \mathcal{D}^n$ and the current input $push(d)$, and for the state $\langle\rangle$ and the current input pop. First we propose two completions of the state transition function each for stack overflow and for stack underflow, thereby possibly introducing new states. Then we also suggest two completions for the output function each for stack overflow and for stack underflow, and discuss the output function on the new states which may be introduced by the completion of the state transition function.

In case of stack overflow, the state transition function may, for example, ignore an illegal push command according to Equation (9.17):

$$next(Q, push(d)) \;=\; Q \tag{9.29}$$

Alternatively, an imaginary pop command is inserted in front of the illegal push command according to Equation (9.22):

$$next(Q, push(d)) \;=\; lead(Q) \triangleright d \tag{9.30}$$

In case of stack underflow, the interactive bounded stack may break according to Equations (9.19) and (9.20) for a new state *fail*:

$$next(\langle\rangle, pop) \;=\; fail \tag{9.31}$$
$$next(fail, x) \;=\; fail \tag{9.32}$$

Alternatively, it may store illegal pop commands until a datum is pushed onto the stack according to Equations (9.24) and (9.25) representing the states $(\langle\rangle, pop^m)$ by $m > 0$:

$$next(\langle\rangle, pop) \;=\; 1 \tag{9.33}$$
$$next(m, pop) \;=\; m + 1 \tag{9.34}$$
$$next(1, push(d)) \;=\; \langle\rangle \tag{9.35}$$
$$next(m + 1, push(d)) \;=\; m \tag{9.36}$$

Now we discuss the completion of the output function. An illegal push command may produce no output:

$$out(Q, push(d)) \;=\; \langle\rangle \tag{9.37}$$

Alternatively, the set of output data is extended with a new error symbol $\circledast_{\text{overflow}}$ reporting a stack overflow:

$$out(Q, push(d)) \;=\; \langle \circledast_{\text{overflow}} \rangle \tag{9.38}$$

An illegal pop command may also produce no output

$$out(\langle\rangle, pop) \;=\; \langle\rangle \,, \tag{9.39}$$

or may emit an error symbol reporting a stack underflow:

$$out(\langle\rangle, pop) \;=\; \langle \circledast_{\text{underflow}} \rangle \tag{9.40}$$

If a new failure state *fail* has been introduced to resolve the underspecification for stack underflow, there may be no reaction to any input in this state

$$out(fail, x) \;=\; \langle\rangle \,, \tag{9.41}$$

or an error message ⊛ is emitted on a pop command:

$$out(fail, pop) \;\; = \;\; \langle \circledast \rangle \tag{9.42}$$

If new states have been introduced for the accumulation of illegal pop commands, then the output function may be defined according to Equations (9.26) and (9.27):

$$out(\langle \rangle, pop) \;\; = \;\; \langle \rangle \tag{9.43}$$
$$out(m, pop) \;\; = \;\; \langle \rangle \tag{9.44}$$
$$out(m, push(d)) \;\; = \;\; \langle d \rangle \tag{9.45}$$

$\square$

In this section we showed how the introduction of states can well be carried out before resolving the underspecification for a given regular behaviour. We presented important strategies for resolving the underspecification on the level of a state transition machine.

9.4   Refining Infinite to Finite Behaviour

We often specify the behaviour of a component on finite streams and extend it to infinite streams by continuity. The other way round, it is occasionally easy to specify a component only for infinite input streams, and it requires care to define the behaviour for finite input, which is considered to be incomplete.

Stream processing functions which are only defined on infinite streams cause problems even in networks with only infinite communication histories, because infinite streams do not form a complete partial order. Therefore, fixpoints, which are necessary for the feedback operator, need not exist. Even if fixpoints exist, there may be several incomparable fixpoints. If a least fixpoint exists, it cannot be approximated.

In this section, we show how to extend a given infinite behaviour to a behaviour on finite streams so that the behaviour on finite streams approximates the given infinite behaviour. First, we investigate the order theoretic aspects of finite behaviours approximating the infinite behaviours. Then we present a method how to derive the maximally defined finite behaviour provided it exists, and indicate further fields of application for this method. Finally, we show how to obtain a weaker defined behaviour of a finite refinement.

9.4.1   Finite Refinement

Before we present a method for obtaining a finite behaviour for a given
infinite behaviour in the following section, we analyse the set of possible
finite behaviours for an infinite behaviour. In general there exists more than
one finite behaviour that approximates the given infinite behaviour. In some
cases however, there is no such finite behaviour.

We concentrate on stream processing functions with a single input stream and
a single output stream. The generalization to stream processing functions
with more input or output streams causes no problems.

Definition 9.12 (finite refinement)
A stream processing function $f : \mathcal{A}^\star \to \mathcal{B}^\infty$ on finite streams is called a *finite
refinement* of a function $F : \mathcal{A}^\omega \to \mathcal{B}^\infty$ on infinite streams, if F coincides
with the unique continuous extension $\widehat{f}|_{\mathcal{A}^\omega}$ of f on infinite streams. The set

$$Fin(F) \;=\; \{f : \mathcal{A}^\star \to \mathcal{B}^\infty \mid \widehat{f}|_{\mathcal{A}^\omega} = F\}$$

contains the finite refinements of F.   □

Not every function which is defined on infinite streams has a finite refinement.
Since an arbitrary subset of the algebraic cpo of input streams need not be an
algebraic cpo, it may contain infinite streams which cannot be approximated
by finite streams.

Definition 9.13 (approximable)
The function $F : \mathcal{A}^\omega \to \mathcal{B}^\infty$ on infinite streams is called *approximable* if it
has a finite refinement, that is $Fin(F) \neq \emptyset$.   □

Non-approximable functions need to inspect a complete infinite input history in order to determine a non-empty suffix of the output. The following
example specifies a function on infinite streams which is not approximable.

Example 9.14 (inspection of an infinite input stream)
A function $F : \mathcal{A}^\omega \to \mathcal{A}^\star$ indicating whether an infinite input stream does
not contain the particular element $d \in \mathcal{A}$ is not approximable, if $|\mathcal{A}| > 1$:

$$F(X) \;=\; \begin{cases} \langle\rangle & \text{if } X \text{ contains the element } d \\ \langle d \rangle & \text{if } X \in (\mathcal{A} \setminus \{d\})^\omega \end{cases} \tag{9.46}$$

If $\widehat{f} : \mathcal{A}^\infty \to \mathcal{A}^\star$ were the unique continuous extension of a finite approximation f of F, then we would have $\widehat{f}(X) = \langle d \rangle$ for $X \in (\mathcal{A} \setminus \{d\})^\omega$. Since $\langle d \rangle$ is
a finite element, there is a finite stream $Y \sqsubseteq X$ with $\widehat{f}(Y) = \langle d \rangle$. However,
$\widehat{f}(Y \& d^\omega) = F(Y \& d^\omega) = \langle\rangle$ is not a prefix of $\widehat{f}(Y)$.   □

If F is approximable, then $Fin(F)$ forms a partial order with a maximal element, which is the subject of the following subsection. $Fin(F)$ does not possess a least element, provided F is not the constant function yielding the empty stream, because for each function $f \in Fin(F)$ there is a stream processing function $g \sqsubseteq f$ in $Fin(F)$ which coincides with f for all but at least one input stream X which only yields a prefix of $f(X)$.

In summary, not every function on infinite streams has a finite refinement. In general, the finite refinement is not unique, and there is not a least defined refinement. The following subsection searches for the greatest finite refinement.

9.4.2 Maximal Common Prefix Technique

After discussing the existence of a finite refinement for a function on infinite streams, we now introduce a systematic method how to derive a finite refinement by order-theoretic reasoning. The presented method yields the greatest finite behaviour provided it exists.

The output for a finite input stream must be a prefix of the output of all the infinite streams prolonging the finite input. Therefore, the basis for our refinement technique is the greatest lower bound of streams with respect to the prefix order, which is the maximal common prefix. An operational specification of the maximal common prefix operator for two streams can be found in [Dos01b].

Lemma 9.15
Let $\mathcal{S} \neq \emptyset$ be a non-empty set of streams. The greatest lower bound $\bigsqcap \mathcal{S}$ exists, because the complete partial order of streams is consistently complete. Common prefixes can be extracted, and if the maximal common prefix is the empty stream, then $\bigsqcap \mathcal{S}$ is the empty stream:

$$\bigsqcap_{X \in \mathcal{S}} (A \& X) \;=\; A \& \bigsqcap \mathcal{S}$$

$$x \triangleleft X, y \triangleleft Y \in \mathcal{S}, x \neq y \;\implies\; \bigsqcap \mathcal{S} \;=\; \langle \rangle \qquad\qquad \square$$

The following theorem is the key for the refinement of infinite to finite behaviours.

Theorem 9.16
The infinite behaviour $F : \mathcal{A}^\omega \to \mathcal{B}^\infty$ has the greatest finite approximation $f : \mathcal{A}^\star \to \mathcal{B}^\infty$ defined by

$$f(X) \;=\; \bigsqcap F(X \& \mathcal{A}^\omega).$$

If F is approximable, then f is a finite refinement of F.

If F is not approximable, then we have $\widehat{f}(X) \sqsubset F(X)$ for an $X \in \mathcal{A}^\omega$.   □

Proof: f is an upper bound for $g \in Fin(F)$, because $g(X) \sqsubseteq \bigsqcap F(X\&\mathcal{A}^\omega)$
for $X \in \mathcal{A}^\star$. Moreover we have $\widehat{f}|_{\mathcal{A}^\omega} \sqsubseteq F$.

If F is approximable, then there is a finite refinement $h \in Fin(F)$,
for which $F = \widehat{h}|_{\mathcal{A}^\omega} \sqsubseteq \widehat{f}|_{\mathcal{A}^\omega} \sqsubseteq F$. Consequently, $\widehat{f}_{\mathcal{A}^\omega} = F$.   □

With this theorem we obtain the maximally defined finite refinement of a stream processing function which is only defined for infinite streams, provided there exists a finite refinement at all. A weaker defined behaviour can be obtained from the maximally defined finite behaviour by retaining a suffix of the output, cf. Subsection 9.4.4.

We demonstrate the application of the theorem with two examples. They show that the result of the maximal common prefix technique indeed is the maximally defined finite refinement which need not coincide with the intuitive finite refinement. This phenomenon arises, for example, when a non-strict operation, whose arguments need not necessarily all be known for delivering the result, is repeatedly applied to input which either arrives in sequence on a single channel or in parallel on different channels.

We investigate components which repeatedly apply the if-then-else operation $ite : \mathbb{B} \times \mathcal{D} \times \mathcal{D} \to \mathcal{D}$ $(\mathcal{D} \neq \emptyset)$ defined by

$$ite(b,t,e) \;=\; \left\{ \begin{array}{ll} t & \text{if } b = \mathbf{T} \\ e & \text{if } b = \mathbf{F} \end{array} \right. \tag{9.47}$$

to its inputs.

Example 9.17 (serial if-then-else)
In the first example we assume that the input of the serial if-then-else component $Ite_-^\omega : \mathbb{B}^\omega \to \mathbb{B}^\omega$ is transmitted in sequence. The serial if-then-else component is only specified on infinite streams:

$$Ite_-^\omega(b \triangleleft t \triangleleft e \triangleleft X) \;=\; ite(b,t,e) \triangleleft Ite_-^\omega(X) \tag{9.48}$$

A specification of the serial if-then-else component on finite streams $ite_-^\star :$ $\mathbb{B}^\star \to \mathbb{B}^\infty$ is obtained through the maximal common prefix operator:

$$ite_-^\star(X) \;=\; \bigsqcap Ite_-^\omega(X\&\mathbb{B}^\omega) \tag{9.49}$$

The derivation of the direct recursive equations proceeds by a case analysis concerning the length of the input stream. We present characteristic cases of the derivation:

$ite^{\star}_{-}(\langle \mathbf{F}, x \rangle)$

$= \quad \bigcap Ite^{\omega}_{-}(\mathbf{F} \triangleleft x \triangleleft \mathbb{B}^{\omega})$

$= \quad \bigcap (Ite^{\omega}_{-}(\mathbf{F} \triangleleft x \triangleleft \mathbf{T} \triangleleft \mathbb{B}^{\omega}) \cup Ite^{\omega}_{-}(\mathbf{F} \triangleleft x \triangleleft \mathbf{F} \triangleleft \mathbb{B}^{\omega}))$

$= \quad \bigcap (\mathbf{T} \triangleleft Ite^{\omega}_{-}(\mathbb{B}^{\omega}) \cup \mathbf{F} \triangleleft Ite^{\omega}_{-}(\mathbb{B}^{\omega}))$

$= \quad \langle \rangle$

$ite^{\star}_{-}(\langle \mathbf{T}, x \rangle)$

$= \quad \bigcap Ite^{\omega}_{-}(\mathbf{T} \triangleleft x \triangleleft \mathbb{B}^{\omega})$

$= \quad \bigcap_{r \in \mathbb{B}} Ite^{\omega}_{-}(\mathbf{T} \triangleleft x \triangleleft r \triangleleft \mathbb{B}^{\omega})$

$= \quad \bigcap (x \triangleleft Ite^{\omega}_{-}(\mathbb{B}^{\omega}))$

$= \quad x \triangleleft \bigcap Ite^{\omega}_{-}(\mathbb{B}^{\omega})$

$= \quad x \triangleleft \langle \rangle$

The remaining cases are derived similarly. We summarize the result:

$$ite^{\star}_{-}(\langle \rangle) \quad = \quad \langle \rangle \tag{9.50}$$

$$ite^{\star}_{-}(\langle b \rangle) \quad = \quad \langle \rangle \tag{9.51}$$

$$ite^{\star}_{-}(\langle \mathbf{F}, x \rangle) \quad = \quad \langle \rangle \tag{9.52}$$

$$ite^{\star}_{-}(\langle \mathbf{T}, x \rangle) \quad = \quad \langle x \rangle \tag{9.53}$$

$$ite^{\star}_{-}(b \triangleleft t \triangleleft e \triangleleft X) \quad = \quad ite(b, t, e) \triangleleft ite^{\star}_{-}(X) \tag{9.54}$$

The serial if-then-else component can deliver output even if the arguments of the if-then-else operation have not arrived yet if the first argument is $\mathbf{T}$ and the second argument has arrived, cf. Equation (9.53). The reason is that these two arguments already determine the value of the if-then-else operation no matter what the third argument is.

In Example 9.22 a weaker defined behaviour of the serial if-then-else component is derived. □

The parallel if-then-else component shows even more situations where output can be computed even if some of the three arguments are not present yet.

Example 9.18 (parallel if-then-else)
Now we investigate a component which applies the if-then-else operation to input which arrives in parallel on three channels. The parallel if-then-else component $Ite^{\omega}_{\equiv} : \mathbb{B}^{\omega} \times \mathbb{B}^{\omega} \times \mathbb{B}^{\omega} \to \mathbb{B}^{\omega}$ is only specified on infinite streams:

$$Ite^{\omega}_{\equiv}(b \triangleleft B, t \triangleleft T, e \triangleleft E) \quad = \quad ite(b, t, e) \triangleleft Ite^{\omega}_{\equiv}(B, T, E) \tag{9.55}$$

A specification of the parallel if-then-else component on finite streams $ite^{\star}_{\equiv} : \mathbb{B}^{\star} \times \mathbb{B}^{\star} \times \mathbb{B}^{\star} \to \mathbb{B}^{\infty}$ is obtained through the maximal common prefix operator:

$$ite^{\star}_{\equiv}(B, T, E) \quad = \quad \bigcap Ite^{\omega}_{\equiv}(B \& \mathbb{B}^{\omega}, T \& \mathbb{B}^{\omega}, E \& \mathbb{B}^{\omega}) \tag{9.56}$$

We present characteristic cases of the derivation:

$$
\begin{aligned}
&ite^{\star}_{\equiv}(\langle\rangle, x \triangleleft T, not(x) \triangleleft E) \\
={}& \textstyle\bigsqcap Ite^{\omega}_{\equiv}(\mathbb{B}^{\omega}, x \triangleleft T \& \mathbb{B}^{\omega}, not(x) \triangleleft E \& \mathbb{B}^{\omega}) \\
={}& \textstyle\bigsqcap (Ite^{\omega}_{\equiv}(\mathbf{T} \triangleleft \mathbb{B}^{\omega}, x \triangleleft T \& \mathbb{B}^{\omega}, not(x) \triangleleft E \& \mathbb{B}^{\omega}) \\
& \quad \cup Ite^{\omega}_{\equiv}(\mathbf{F} \triangleleft \mathbb{B}^{\omega}, x \triangleleft T \& \mathbb{B}^{\omega}, not(x) \triangleleft E \& \mathbb{B}^{\omega})) \\
={}& \textstyle\bigsqcap (ite(\mathbf{T}, x, not(x)) \triangleleft Ite^{\omega}_{\equiv}(\mathbb{B}^{\omega}, T \& \mathbb{B}^{\omega}, E \& \mathbb{B}^{\omega}) \\
& \quad \cup ite(\mathbf{F}, x, not(x)) \triangleleft Ite^{\omega}_{\equiv}(\mathbb{B}^{\omega}, T \& \mathbb{B}^{\omega}, E \& \mathbb{B}^{\omega})) \\
={}& \textstyle\bigsqcap (x \triangleleft Ite^{\omega}_{\equiv}(\mathbb{B}^{\omega}, T \& \mathbb{B}^{\omega}, E \& \mathbb{B}^{\omega}) \cup not(x) \triangleleft Ite^{\omega}_{\equiv}(\mathbb{B}^{\omega}, T \& \mathbb{B}^{\omega}, E \& \mathbb{B}^{\omega})) \\
={}& \langle\rangle
\end{aligned}
$$

$$
\begin{aligned}
&ite^{\star}_{\equiv}(\langle\rangle, x \triangleleft T, x \triangleleft E) \\
={}& \textstyle\bigsqcap Ite^{\omega}_{\equiv}(\mathbb{B}^{\omega}, x \triangleleft T \& \mathbb{B}^{\omega}, x \triangleleft E \& \mathbb{B}^{\omega}) \\
={}& \textstyle\bigsqcap \bigcup_{b \in \mathbb{B}} Ite^{\omega}_{\equiv}(b \triangleleft \mathbb{B}^{\omega}, x \triangleleft T \& \mathbb{B}^{\omega}, x \triangleleft E \& \mathbb{B}^{\omega}) \\
={}& \textstyle\bigsqcap \bigcup_{b \in \mathbb{B}} (ite(b, x, x) \triangleleft Ite^{\omega}_{\equiv}(\mathbb{B}^{\omega}, T \& \mathbb{B}^{\omega}, E \& \mathbb{B}^{\omega})) \\
={}& \textstyle\bigsqcap (x \triangleleft Ite^{\omega}_{\equiv}(\mathbb{B}^{\omega}, T \& \mathbb{B}^{\omega}, E \& \mathbb{B}^{\omega})) \\
={}& x \triangleleft \textstyle\bigsqcap Ite^{\omega}_{\equiv}(\mathbb{B}^{\omega}, T \& \mathbb{B}^{\omega}, E \& \mathbb{B}^{\omega}) \\
={}& x \triangleleft ite^{\star}_{\equiv}(\langle\rangle, T, E)
\end{aligned}
$$

The remaining cases are derived similarly or follow directly by monotonicity.

The result is:

$$
\begin{aligned}
ite^{\star}_{\equiv}(\langle\rangle, \langle\rangle, E) &= \langle\rangle & (9.57) \\
ite^{\star}_{\equiv}(\langle\rangle, T, \langle\rangle) &= \langle\rangle & (9.58) \\
ite^{\star}_{\equiv}(\langle\rangle, x \triangleleft T, x \triangleleft E) &= x \triangleleft ite^{\star}_{\equiv}(\langle\rangle, T, E) & (9.59) \\
ite^{\star}_{\equiv}(\langle\rangle, x \triangleleft T, not(x) \triangleleft E) &= \langle\rangle & (9.60) \\
ite^{\star}_{\equiv}(\mathbf{T} \triangleleft B, \langle\rangle, E) &= \langle\rangle & (9.61) \\
ite^{\star}_{\equiv}(\mathbf{F} \triangleleft B, T, \langle\rangle) &= \langle\rangle & (9.62) \\
ite^{\star}_{\equiv}(\mathbf{T} \triangleleft B, t \triangleleft T, \langle\rangle) &= t \triangleleft ite^{\star}_{\equiv}(B, T, \langle\rangle) & (9.63) \\
ite^{\star}_{\equiv}(\mathbf{F} \triangleleft B, \langle\rangle, e \triangleleft E) &= e \triangleleft ite^{\star}_{\equiv}(B, \langle\rangle, E) & (9.64) \\
ite^{\star}_{\equiv}(b \triangleleft B, t \triangleleft T, e \triangleleft E) &= ite(b, t, e) \triangleleft ite^{\star}_{\equiv}(B, T, E) & (9.65)
\end{aligned}
$$

Equations (9.59), (9.63), and (9.64) point out that the maximal common prefix technique yields the maximally defined finite behaviour. Equation (9.63) corresponds to Equation (9.53) from the serial if-then-else. Equation (9.64) is the analogous case to Equation (9.63). If the arguments on the second and the third channel agree (9.59), then they already determine the output even if the condition on the first channel has not arrived. □

9.4.3 More Fields of Application for the Maximal Common Prefix Technique

We touch on two further fields of application of the maximal common prefix technique.

If for an invalid input stream of a partially defined stream processing function some prolongations are valid, yet prefixes may be invalid, then the maximal common prefix technique can also be applied to obtain a maximally defined resolution of the underspecification. For a partially defined function f : $\mathcal{D} \to \mathcal{B}^\infty$, which is undefined on the set $\mathcal{U} = \mathcal{A}^* \setminus \mathcal{D}$, the result $\tilde{f}(X)$ for an invalid input stream $X \in \mathcal{U}$ can be defined as the maximal common prefix of the output streams of all valid extensions of the input stream:

$$\tilde{f}(X) \;\; = \;\; \prod_{\substack{X \sqsubseteq Y \\ Y \in \mathcal{D}}} f(Y) \qquad (9.66)$$

The maximal common prefix technique can also be applied to obtain a stronger, in particular the maximally defined finite behaviour for a fully specified component. A stronger behaviour of a stream transformer agrees with the original stream transformer on infinite input streams and, possibly, yields a prolongation of the behaviour on finite streams.

For a stream transformer $f : \mathcal{A}^\infty \to \mathcal{B}^\infty$, the maximal behaviour f_{max} : $\mathcal{A}^\infty \to \mathcal{B}^\infty$ is obtained with the maximal common prefix technique:

$$f_{max}(X) \;\; = \;\; \prod f(X \& \mathcal{A}^\omega) \qquad (9.67)$$

f_{max} is the greatest finite refinement of $f|_{\mathcal{A}^\omega}$. In the following subsection we show how a weaker defined behaviour can be obtained for a given finite behaviour.

9.4.4 Refining Behaviours with Bound Functions

The maximal common prefix technique yields the greatest finite refinement of an infinite behaviour, provided it exists. Sometimes, we are aiming at a weaker defined behaviour, for example for obtaining an io-synchronous function or for allowing an easier implementation. We apply bound functions which retain a final segment of the output, in order to obtain a weaker defined behaviour of a finite behaviour.

For a weaker defined behaviour, the behaviour on infinite streams remains the same, whereas the behaviour on finite streams may carefully be bounded.

Definition 9.19 (weaker defined behaviour)
A stream processing function $g : \mathcal{A}^\infty \to \mathcal{B}^\infty$ is called a *(finitely) weaker defined behaviour* of $f : \mathcal{A}^\infty \to \mathcal{B}^\infty$, if g approximates f

$$g \sqsubseteq f$$

and they agree on infinite input streams:

$$f|_{\mathcal{A}^\omega} = g|_{\mathcal{A}^\omega} \qquad\qquad \square$$

A given stream processing function can be weakened by bound functions [Dos00b, Dos01a] allowing a component to retain a suffix of the output for a finite input history, but which also guarantee that the retained output appears sometime if the input is continued with an infinite input stream.

We present a bound function which takes a prefix of the input with a given length and another bound function which cuts off a suffix of the input of a given length.

The bound function $take : \mathbb{N} \to (\mathcal{A}^\star \to \mathcal{A}^\star)$ takes a fixed number of elements at the beginning of an input stream and retains the rest:

$$take(0)(X) = \langle\rangle \qquad\qquad (9.68)$$
$$take(n)(\langle\rangle) = \langle\rangle \qquad\qquad (9.69)$$
$$take(n+1)(x \triangleleft X) = x \triangleleft take(n)(X) \qquad\qquad (9.70)$$

$take(n)$ is monotonic for every $n \in \mathbb{N}$. If the bound function $take$ outputs unbounded increasing prefixes of a finite behaviour applied to increasing finite input streams, then the infinite behaviour remains unchanged.

Proposition 9.20
Let the stream processing function $f : \mathcal{A}^\star \to \mathcal{B}^\infty$ describe a finite behaviour and $N : \mathcal{A}^\star \to \mathbb{N}$ be a monotonic size function. If for every infinite input stream $X \in \mathcal{A}^\omega$, the function N is not bounded by f, which means that $\bigsqcup_{Z \sqsubseteq X} N(Z) \geq |\widehat{f}(X)|$ (with respect to the usual complete partial order on $\mathbb{N} \cup \{\infty\}$), then the function $g : \mathcal{A}^\star \to \mathcal{B}^\infty$ defined by

$$g(X) = take(N(X))(f(X))$$

is a weaker defined behaviour of f. $\qquad\qquad \square$

Proof: g is monotonic because N and f are monotonic.
    We have $g \sqsubseteq f$ because $take(m)(Y) \sqsubseteq Y$.
    We have $\widehat{f} = \widehat{g}$ because

$$\bigsqcup take(n_i)(Y_i) = \bigsqcup Y_i$$

if $(Y_i)_{i \in \mathbb{N}}$ is a weakly ascending infinite sequence of streams and $(n_i)_{i \in \mathbb{N}}$ is a weakly ascending infinite sequence of natural numbers with $\bigsqcup n_i \geq \bigsqcup |Y_i|$. $\qquad\square$

For applications of this proposition, the size function often depends on the length of the input.

In order to obtain a weaker defined behaviour it is sometimes more intuitive to specify the number of elements which are retained instead of the number of elements which are output. Therefore we provide another bound function $cut : \mathbb{N} \rightarrow (\mathcal{A}^\star \rightarrow \mathcal{A}^\star)$ cutting off a fixed number of elements at the rear of the input stream:

$$
\begin{align}
cut(0)(X) &= X \tag{9.71}\\
cut(n)(\langle\rangle) &= \langle\rangle \tag{9.72}\\
cut(n+1)(X \triangleright x) &= cut(n)(X) \tag{9.73}
\end{align}
$$

For infinite input streams, $cut(n)$ is the identity.

For obtaining a weaker defined behaviour, the bound function cut is often preferred if the size function for cut is a constant function. For finite input streams $X \in \mathcal{A}^\star$, cut and $take$ are related by the equation

$$
cut(n)(X) = take(|X| \div n)(X). \tag{9.74}
$$

Above $\div$ denotes subtraction in the natural numbers. By rewriting a bound function cut into the bound function $take$, we can apply the above proposition to obtain a weaker defined behaviour.

We demonstrate the application of the proposition with two examples.

Example 9.21 (shift register — revisited)
We can specify the shift register $shift(n) : \mathcal{A}^\star \rightarrow \mathcal{A}^\infty$ from Example 2.16 with $n > 0$ places by

$$
shift(n)(X) = cut(n)(X) \tag{9.75}
$$

or with $take$ by

$$
shift(n)(X) = take(|X| \div n)(X). \tag{9.76}
$$

The size function $N(X) = |X| \div n$ is monotonic and unbounded for the finite prefixes of an infinite input stream. By Proposition 9.20, a shift register is a weaker defined behaviour of the identity. $\qquad\square$

Now we take up the serial if-then-else component from Example 9.17. There we derived the maximally defined finite behaviour of a given infinite behaviour. Here we derive the intuitive finite behaviour with the bound function *take*.

Example 9.22 (serial if-then-else — revisited)

The serial if-then-else component outputs as much as possible depending on the value of the next inputs. Here we specify a weaker defined if-then-else component $ite^\star : \mathbb{B}^\star \to \mathbb{B}^\infty$ whose length of the output stream is independent of the values of the next input:

$$ite^\star(X) \quad = \quad take(|X| \operatorname{div} 3)(ite^\star_-(X)) \qquad (9.77)$$

By Proposition 9.20 this equation indeed specifies a weaker defined behaviour of the serial if-then-else component. The short derivation

$$
\begin{aligned}
|X| < 3 \implies \quad & ite^\star(X) \\
= \quad & take(|X| \operatorname{div} 3)(ite^\star_-(X)) \\
= \quad & take(0)(ite^\star_-(X)) \\
= \quad & \langle\rangle \\[4pt]
& ite^\star(x_1 \lhd x_2 \lhd x_3 \lhd X) \\
= \quad & take(|x_1 \lhd x_2 \lhd x_3 \lhd X| \operatorname{div} 3)(ite^\star_-(x_1 \lhd x_2 \lhd x_3 \lhd X)) \\
= \quad & take(1 + |X| \operatorname{div} 3)(\textstyle\bigcap Ite^\omega_-(x_1 \lhd x_2 \lhd x_3 \lhd X \& \mathbb{B}^\omega)) \\
= \quad & take(1 + |X| \operatorname{div} 3)(ite(x_1, x_2, x_3) \lhd \textstyle\bigcap Ite^\omega_-(X \& \mathbb{B}^\omega)) \\
= \quad & ite(x_1, x_2, x_3) \lhd take(|X| \operatorname{div} 3)(\textstyle\bigcap Ite^\omega_-(X \& \mathbb{B}^\omega)) \\
= \quad & ite(x_1, x_2, x_3) \lhd ite^\star(X)
\end{aligned}
$$

yields

$$
\begin{aligned}
|X| < 3 \implies ite^\star(X) \quad &= \quad \langle\rangle & (9.78) \\
ite^\star(x_1 \lhd x_2 \lhd x_3 \lhd X) \quad &= \quad ite(x_1, x_2, x_3) \lhd ite^\star(X) . & (9.79)
\end{aligned}
$$

The weaker defined if-then-else component waits for at least three elements in the input stream before it produces its output.   □

This example pointed out that a weaker defined finite behaviour can in general be derived from the infinite behaviour with a bound function without deriving the maximally defined behaviour before.

In this section, we presented the maximal common prefix technique which yields the maximally defined finite behaviour for a function which is specified only for infinite input streams provided it exists. With bound functions we can obtain a weaker defined finite behaviour.

9.5 Property Refinement for Parameterized Specifications

Occasionally, underspecification can be described by a parameterization. Characteristic examples are components with bounded resources such as a shift register or a buffer with unspecified capacity, or a merge component with an unspecified merge strategy, or components with an unspecified initialization.

We first of all demonstrate the specification of components with parameterization. Then we concentrate on the relationship between state transition machines and components with an unspecified initialization.

Definition 9.23 (underspecification with parameterization)
Given the specification of a stream processing function $f : \mathcal{P} \to (\mathcal{A}_1^\infty \times \ldots \times \mathcal{A}_m^\infty \to \mathcal{B}_1^\infty \times \ldots \times \mathcal{B}_n^\infty)$ with parameters $\mathcal{P} \neq \emptyset$, the underspecified component with the behaviour $f(\mathcal{P})$ is underspecified with *parameterization*. □

Since this form of underspecification can be resolved simply by restricting the set of values for the parameter or by instantiating the parameter with a value, respectively, we only discuss property refinement for parameterized specifications with some characteristic examples.

The following example demonstrates how the unspecified parameter of a component can be inspected by the environment to control its interaction.

Example 9.24 (distribution with underspecified strategy)
The component $distr : \{1, \ldots, n\}^\omega \to (\mathcal{A}^\star \to (\mathcal{A}^\infty)^n)$ distributes its input stream to $n > 0$ channels according to a strategy which is its first parameter:

$$distr(S)(\langle\rangle) \;=\; (\langle\rangle, \ldots, \langle\rangle) \tag{9.80}$$

$$distr(i \lhd S)(x \lhd X) \;=\; (\underbrace{\langle\rangle, \ldots, \langle\rangle}_{(i-1)-\text{times}}, \langle x \rangle, \underbrace{\langle\rangle, \ldots, \langle\rangle}_{(n-i)-\text{times}}) \,\&\, distr(S)(X) \tag{9.81}$$

Although the strategy of the underspecified distribution component is left open, we can assume that it is known to the environment – in contrast to nondeterminism, cf. Section 9.6. Thus it can be used by a merge component $merge : \{1, \ldots, n\}^\omega \to ((\mathcal{A}^\star)^n \to \mathcal{A}^\star)$ which merges its n input streams such that the sequential composition of distribution and merge is the identity:

$$distr(S) \,;\, merge(S) \;=\; id_{\mathcal{A}^\star} \tag{9.82}$$

From this equation we derive the output of the merge component for non-empty input streams:

$$merge(i \triangleleft S)((\underbrace{\langle\rangle, \ldots, \langle\rangle}_{(i-1)-\text{times}}, \langle x\rangle, \underbrace{\langle\rangle, \ldots, \langle\rangle}_{(n-i)-\text{times}}) \,\&\, distr(S)(X))$$

$$= \quad merge(i \triangleleft S)(distr(i \triangleleft S)(x \triangleleft X))$$
$$= \quad x \triangleleft X$$
$$= \quad x \triangleleft merge(S)(distr(S)(X))$$

For $(Y_1, \ldots, Y_n) = distr(S)(X)$ we conclude

$$merge(i \triangleleft S)(Y_1, \ldots, Y_{i-1}, y_i \triangleleft Y_i, Y_{i+1}, \ldots, Y_n) \quad = \qquad\qquad (9.83)$$
$$y_i \triangleleft merge(S)(Y_1, \ldots, Y_n) \,.$$

The monotonicity of *merge* requires that Equation (9.83) is also valid for stream tuples which cannot be output of $distr(S)$, in case the data set $\mathcal{A}$ contains more than one element. We also conclude by monotonicity:

$$merge(i \triangleleft S)(Y_1, \ldots, Y_{i-1}, \langle\rangle, Y_{i+1}, \ldots, Y_n) \quad = \quad \langle\rangle \qquad\qquad (9.84)$$

For $n = 2$ output channels and for the strategy $S = \langle 1, 2\rangle^\omega$, we obtain the round robin merge from Example 7.6.   □

The example showed that components with parameterization can be integrated into a system design before instantiating the parameters. In that case, the other components of the system possibly need to be parameterized with the same parameter.

The next example takes up finite refinements with a reordering component. We start with a parameterized specification for infinite streams, derive the maximally defined finite behaviour depending on the parameter, and then discuss instantiations of the parameter.

Example 9.25 (reordering)
We assume that the set Π contains the bijective functions $\pi : \mathbb{N} \to \mathbb{N}$, called *permutations*, on natural numbers. $Reorder : \Pi \to (\mathcal{A}^\omega \to \mathcal{A}^\omega)$ is a parameterized reordering component on infinite input streams. So $Reorder(\pi)(X)$ is a permutation of the elements of the input stream X according to the permutation function π:

$$Reorder(\pi)(X) \;=\; get(\pi^{-1}(0))(X) \,\&\, Reorder(\pi \ominus 1)(del(\pi^{-1}(0))(X)) \quad (9.85)$$

The auxiliary function $get : \mathbb{N} \to (\mathcal{A}^\infty \to \mathcal{A}^\infty)$ defined by $(j > 0)$

$$get(i)(\langle\rangle) \quad = \quad \langle\rangle \qquad\qquad\qquad (9.86)$$
$$get(0)(x \triangleleft X) \quad = \quad \langle x\rangle \qquad\qquad\qquad (9.87)$$
$$get(j)(x \triangleleft X) \quad = \quad get(j-1)(X) \qquad\qquad (9.88)$$

yields the element at a given position provided it exists. The auxiliary function $del : \mathbb{N} \to (\mathcal{A}^\infty \to \mathcal{A}^\infty)$ defined by $(j > 0)$

$$
\begin{align}
del(i)(\langle\rangle) &= \langle\rangle \tag{9.89} \\
del(0)(x \triangleleft X) &= X \tag{9.90} \\
del(j)(x \triangleleft X) &= x \triangleleft del(j-1)(X) \tag{9.91}
\end{align}
$$

deletes the element at a given position in a stream provided it exists. Finally, $(\pi \ominus 1)$ defined by

$$
(\pi \ominus 1)(i) = \begin{cases} \pi(i) - 1 & \text{if } i < \pi^{-1}(0) \\ \pi(i+1) - 1 & \text{if } i \geq \pi^{-1}(0) \end{cases} \tag{9.92}
$$

is the corresponding permutation function for the remaining stream.

If the data set $\mathcal{A}$ of the reordering component on infinite streams is a singleton set, then the maximally defined finite behaviour is the identity for every permutation function. Otherwise, the maximally defined finite refinement $reorder(\pi)(X) = \bigsqcap Reorder(\pi)(X \& \mathcal{A}^\omega)$ is:

$$
\begin{align}
reorder(\pi)(X) &= \tag{9.93} \\
&\begin{cases} \langle\rangle & \text{if } \pi^{-1}(0) \geq |X| \\ get(\pi^{-1}(0))(X) \& reorder(\pi \ominus 1)(del(\pi^{-1}(0))(X)) & \text{if } \pi^{-1}(0) < |X| \end{cases}
\end{align}
$$

We aim at a bounded reordering component $breorder(n)(\pi) : \mathcal{A}^\star \to \mathcal{A}^\infty$ which retains exactly the last $n \in \mathbb{N}$ elements of the reordered input stream, provided the input stream has at least n elements, that means we require:

$$
|breorder(n)(X)| = |X| \div n \tag{9.94}
$$

We first apply the bound function *take* to *reorder* in order to obtain a reordering component $treorder : \mathbb{N} \to (\Pi \to (\mathcal{A}^\star \to \mathcal{A}^\infty))$ whose output does not exceed $|X| \div n$:

$$
treorder(n)(\pi)(X) = take(X \div n)(reorder(\pi)(X)) \tag{9.95}
$$

In the second step, we restrict the set of possible permutation functions Π to those permutations Π_n validating

$$
\pi^{-1}(i) \div i \ \leq \ n \tag{9.96}
$$

so that at least $|X| \div n$ elements of the output can be determined.

In summary, we get the bounded reordering component $breorder(n) = treorder(n)|_{\Pi_n}$.

For $n = 0$, we obtain the reordering component $breorder(0)$ which does not
retain any elements at all:

$$|breorder(0)(\pi)(X)| \;\; = \;\; |X| \qquad\qquad (9.97)$$

In that case, the set of possible permutation functions $\Pi_0 = \{id_\mathbb{N}\}$ contains
only the identity on natural numbers, and $breorder(0)$ is the identity on the
respective streams.   □

The example exemplified the combination of various techniques for property
refinement, such as the most common prefix technique, bound functions, and
the reduction of possible parameters, for obtaining a desired finite refinement.

A frequent case of underspecification with parameters arises for components
which operate properly only after an initialization phase. In the following,
we relate a form of underspecification with parameters with state transition machines with undefined initial state. For that we restrict ourselves to
components with a finite input stream and a finite output stream.

Underspecified initialization

Some components, such as memory components, need an initializing input
stream in order to operate properly. We generalize the notion of a state
transition machine such that it can describe the behaviours of components
whose initialization is coded into a state parameter.

A state transition machine without determined initial state specifies the behaviour of a component whose reaction to initializing input streams is insignificant.

Definition 9.26 (state transition machine with a set of initial states)
Let $\mathcal{Q}' \subseteq \mathcal{Q}$ be a set of initial states. A *state transition machine with a
set of initial states* $\mathcal{M} = \{(\mathcal{Q}, \mathcal{A}, \mathcal{B}, next, out, q_0) \mid q_0 \in \mathcal{Q}'\}$, for short $\mathcal{M} =
(\mathcal{Q}, \mathcal{A}, \mathcal{B}, next, out, \mathcal{Q}')$, is a set of state transition machines which only differ
in their initial state.   □

The set $out^\star(\mathcal{Q}')$ contains the possible behaviours of the state transition
machine with a set of initial states $\mathcal{Q}'$.

The following proposition characterizes some underspecified components
whose state refinement is a state transition machine with a set of initial
states.

Proposition 9.27
For a component $f : \mathcal{A}^\star \to \mathcal{B}^\star$ with the state refinement $M = (\mathcal{Q}, \mathcal{A}, \mathcal{B}, next,$ $out, q_0)$, let $\mathcal{P} \subseteq \mathcal{A}^\star$ be a set of possible *initializing input streams*. The set

$$\mathcal{F} = \{(C\&) \,; f \,; rest^{|f(C)|} \mid C \in \mathcal{P}\}$$

describes an underspecified component with an initialization from the set $\mathcal{P}$. Then the state transition machine $\mathcal{M} = (\mathcal{Q}, \mathcal{A}, \mathcal{B}, next, out, next^\star(q_0)(\mathcal{P}))$ with a set of initial states describes the behaviour of the underspecified component $\mathcal{F}$. $\square$

The behaviour of such an underspecified component is composed of an auxiliary sectioning component $(C\&) : \mathcal{B}^\star \to \mathcal{B}^\star$ – defined by $(C\&)(Y) = C\&Y$ – which prefixes the input stream with an initializing input stream, the main component f, and another auxiliary component $rest^{|f(C)|}$ which removes the reaction of the main component to the initializing input stream from the output.

Initializing input streams often generate no output. If we have $f(C) = \langle\rangle$ for all $C \in \mathcal{P}$, then the underspecified component in the previous proposition simplifies to $\{(C\&) \,; f \mid C \in \mathcal{P}\}$.

Underspecification through leaving open the initial state can easily be reduced by restricting the set of possible initial states.

The input streams which do not completely establish such a proper initialization are in general mapped to "undesired states" by the history abstraction. The choice of a particular initial state can make these states superfluous because they are unreachable from the chosen initial state, as is demonstrated in the following examples.

Example 9.28 (memory cell with unspecified initialization)
The specification of a memory cell with an arbitrary initialization can be based on the specification from Example 6.6 with the state refinement $M = (\mathcal{D}^{\leq 1}, \mathcal{C}, \mathcal{D}, next, out, q_0)$ by considering, for example, the streams with at most one write command and without read commands as initializing input streams: $\mathcal{P} = \{\langle\rangle\} \cup \langle \mathsf{w}(\mathcal{D})\rangle$. The set $\{(C\&) \,; mem \mid C \in \mathcal{P}\}$ specifies these memory components. The state transition machine with a set of initial states $\mathcal{M} = (\mathcal{D}^{\leq 1}, \mathcal{C}, \mathcal{D}, next, out, \mathcal{D}^{\leq 1})$ is their state refinement.

Choosing $q_0 = \langle\rangle$ yields the memory cell from Example 6.6. Choosing $q_0 = \langle c \rangle$ yields a memory cell which has been initialized with the value $c \in \mathcal{D}$. In that case, the state $\langle\rangle$ can be eliminated, because it is unreachable. Since the empty stream is the history abstraction of all the input streams without a write command, the memory cell with such an initialization cannot encounter illegal read commands any more. $\square$

Another characteristic component which previously has been specified with an unsatisfactory initial state is the shift register.

Example 9.29 (shift register with unspecified initialization)
The specification of a shift register with an arbitrary initialization can be based on the specification of the initially empty shift register $shift(n)$ from Example 5.15 with the state refinement $M = (\mathcal{A}^{\leq n}, \mathcal{A}, \mathcal{A}, next, out, \langle\rangle)$ by allowing each state as initializing input: $\mathcal{P} = \mathcal{A}^{\leq n}$.

A generalized specification $\{(C\&); shift(n) \mid C \in \mathcal{A}^{\leq n}\}$ leaves open the initial content of the shift register. It is refined by the state transition machine with a set of initial states $\mathcal{M} = (\mathcal{A}^{\leq n}, \mathcal{A}, \mathcal{A}, next, out, \mathcal{A}^{\leq n})$.

Assuming that the shift register is initially full, we restrict the initial state to $\mathcal{A}^n$: $\mathcal{M} = (\mathcal{A}^n, \mathcal{A}, \mathcal{A}, next, out, \mathcal{A}^n)$ where the unreachable states corresponding to partially filled shift registers are eliminated.   □

The techniques for state refinement cooperate with specifications for components with unspecified initialization by leaving open the initial state. Specifications with infinite stream parameters may serve as auxiliary functions for describing nondeterministic components.

9.6   Nondeterministic Components

Nondeterministic components model real-life components whose behaviour is influenced by some internal or external effects that are abstracted away in the model of real life. The sources of nondeterminism are, for example, irregular events, unreliable network constituents, the relative timing of input "activities" on different input channels [Par83], or chaotic behaviour.

In contrast to underspecification, the environment of a nondeterministic component cannot rely on a certain output for an input stream. A nondeterministic component may deliver different output when provided with a particular input several times whereas the behaviour of an underspecified component is accessible to its environment. Nondeterministic components must be modelled carefully when using stream processing functions due to the well-known merge anomaly [Kel78, BA81, Bro83, Bro88]. It arises when nondeterministic systems are modelled by relating sets of input streams with sets of output streams. In that case the causality between elements in the input stream and elements in the output stream gets lost.

9.6.1 Oracles

According to [BO01, p. 175] "Nondeterminism is underspecification that is resolved by operational means only at the runtime of a system". These resolving decisions at runtime are the hidden effects that affect a nondeterministic component, but are not included in the specification. They can be modelled by oracles. An oracle is a (tuple of) infinite input streams that provide these decisions for resolvations modelling hidden effects at runtime. The behaviour of a nondeterministic component can thus be described by a stream processing function with an oracle stream as additional parameter which is hidden from the environment, cf. Figure 9.1, in contrast to an underspecified component with a parameterization. Underspecification is not resolved at runtime, but externally before running a component.

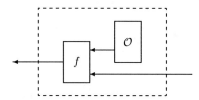

Figure 9.1: Nondeterministic component with an oracle stream

More generally, oracles can be understood as sources that output a decision stream which can neither be determined nor observed by the environment. An oracle can produce decision streams which guarantee a fair behaviour of the component.

If a "nondeterministic" decision of a component depends on its previous input or output respectively, oracles which observe input and output of the component are appropriate, cf. Figure 9.2.

Definition 9.30 (nondeterministic component)
Let $f : \mathcal{B}_1^\infty \times \ldots \times \mathcal{B}_n^\infty \times \mathcal{A}_1^\infty \times \ldots \times \mathcal{A}_m^\infty \to \mathcal{C}_1^\infty \times \ldots \times \mathcal{C}_p^\infty$ be a stream processing function and $\mathcal{O} \subseteq (\mathcal{C}_1^\infty \times \ldots \times \mathcal{C}_p^\infty \times \mathcal{A}_1^\infty \times \ldots \times \mathcal{A}_m^\infty \to \mathcal{B}_1^\infty \times \ldots \times \mathcal{B}_n^\infty)$ be a set of stream processing functions. A *nondeterministic component* $(f, \mathcal{O})$ is the composition of a deterministic component f and an arbitrary oracle $O \in \mathcal{O}$:

$$\circlearrowright_p (\mathsf{X}_{m+p}(\sigma)\,;\,(id_{\mathcal{C}_1^\infty \times \ldots \times \mathcal{C}_p^\infty} \,\|\, copy)\,;\,(O \,\|\, id_{\mathcal{A}_1^\infty \times \ldots \times \mathcal{A}_m^\infty})\,;\,f\,;\,copy)$$

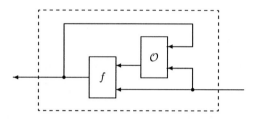

Figure 9.2: Nondeterministic component with an observing oracle

with the permutation function $\sigma_{m+p} : \mathcal{C}_1^\infty \times \ldots \times \mathcal{C}_p^\infty \times \mathcal{A}_1^\infty \times \ldots \times \mathcal{A}_m^\infty \to \mathcal{A}_1^\infty \times \ldots \times \mathcal{A}_m^\infty \times \mathcal{C}_1^\infty \times \ldots \times \mathcal{C}_p^\infty$ defined by

$$\sigma(i) = \begin{cases} i+p & \text{if } 1 \leq i \leq m \\ i-m & \text{if } m < i \leq m+p \end{cases}$$

□

The specification of nondeterministic stream processing functions with oracles suggests a definition for nondeterministic state transition machines with a nondeterministic state transition and a nondeterministic output function. An oracle stream could provide the choices for a particular transition in each nondeterministic state the state transition machine encounters.

9.6.2   Property Refinement for Nondeterministic Components

Property refinement for a nondeterministic component means "reducing the degree of nondeterminism", which amounts to reducing the set of possible oracles.

Definition 9.31 (property refinement of a nondeterministic component) A nondeterministic component $(f, \mathcal{O}_2)$ is a *property refinement of a nondeterministic component* $(f, \mathcal{O}_1)$ if $\mathcal{O}_2 \subseteq \mathcal{O}_1$ holds:

$$(f, \mathcal{O}_1) \ \leadsto_{oracle} \ (f, \mathcal{O}_2)$$

□

We demonstrate property refinement for a nondeterministic merge component, thereby pointing out the differences to underspecification with parameterization.

Example 9.32 (nondeterministic merge component)
A nondeterministic merge component merges two input streams according to a decision stream provided by an oracle. The function $nmerge : \mathcal{A}^\infty \to \mathcal{A}^\infty$ describes a behaviour

$$nmerge = merge(P) \tag{9.98}$$

for every $P \in \{1,2\}^\omega$. The auxiliary function $merge : \{1,2\}^\omega \to (\mathcal{A}^\infty \times \mathcal{A}^\infty \to \mathcal{A}^\infty)$ from Example 9.24 merges two input streams. The arbitrary "strategy" P is hidden from the environment.

This merge component $nmerge$ is not fair. The oracle streams 1^ω and 2^ω ignore one of the input channels for ever. A fair merge $fnmerge(P)$ is obtained by a property refinement step restricting the set of oracles P to $(1^+2 \cup 2^+1)^\omega$ [Möl94]. Then for two infinite input streams each element from an input stream will eventually appear on the output stream.

A further property refinement step leads to a bounded fair merge $bfnmerge(P)$, where $P \in (11^{\leq n}2 \cup 22^{\leq n}1)^\omega$ for $n \geq 0$. Then every channel is omitted at most $n + 2$ times. □

The technique for introducing fairness and bounded fairness explicated in this example generalizes to other components with several input streams.

In contrast to the underspecified merge component from Example 9.24, the oracle can neither be observed nor be influenced by the environment. As a consequence, there is no corresponding distribution component that distributes the input stream into several output streams so that the nondeterministic merge component restores the original stream.

For a nondeterministic distribution component there is a merge component which restores the original stream only if the order of the elements in the original stream is coded into the messages, for example by time stamps.

The following example demonstrates how the environment of nondeterministic components has to take care that the correct behaviour of the overall system is guaranteed for every possible oracle.

Example 9.33 (unreliable transmission)
Communication often suffers from unreliable transmission media. The communicating components must arrange their communication such that every message is eventually transmitted correctly.

First we specify an unreliable transmission medium. The function $transmit :$ $\mathbb{N}^\omega \to (\mathcal{A}^\star \to (\mathcal{A} \cup \{\circledast\})^\infty)$ specifies a transmission medium which discernibly fakes single elements:

$$transmit(N)(\langle\rangle) = \langle\rangle \tag{9.99}$$

$$transmit(0 \triangleleft N)(x \triangleleft X) = x \triangleleft transmit(N)(X) \tag{9.100}$$

$$transmit((n+1) \triangleleft N)(x \triangleleft X) = \circledast \triangleleft transmit(n \triangleleft N)(X) \tag{9.101}$$

A faked datum $\circledast$ may, for example, be detected by a checksum error. For any oracle $N \in \mathbb{N}^\omega$ the transmission medium $ntransmit = transmit(N)$ may not fake an infinite number of input elements in sequence, although the receiver always has to expect a faked datum. If the oracle is $N = 0^\omega$, then the transmission medium is good-natured and transmits the complete input stream correctly.

This component $ntransmit$ is a property refinement of a component with an oracle stream in $(\mathbb{N} \cup \{\infty\})^\omega$, where $transmit(\infty \triangleleft N)(x \triangleleft X) = \circledast \triangleleft transmit(\infty \triangleleft N)(X)$, which does not guarantee a transmission at all. The component $ntransmit$ can be refined by restricting the set of oracles to $\{0, \ldots, n\}^\omega$ which guarantees transmission in at most $n+1$ attempts.

If the unreliable transmission medium $ntransmit$ carries out the transmission of data between a sender and a receiver, the behaviour of sender and receiver must guarantee that each datum is transmitted eventually, whatsoever the oracle of the unreliable transmission is instantiated. Therefore, sender and receiver are connected by a reliable channel reporting acknowledgements @ from the receiver to the sender.

The sender $send : \mathcal{A}^* \times \{@, \circledast\}^* \to \mathcal{A}^\infty$ sends its first datum and afterwards sends the next datum only upon an acknowledgement. If it receives a faked datum on the feedback channel, the previous datum is resent:

$$send(\langle\rangle, A) = \langle\rangle \tag{9.102}$$

$$send(x \triangleleft X, \langle\rangle) = \langle x\rangle \tag{9.103}$$

$$send(x \triangleleft X, @ \triangleleft A) = x \triangleleft send(X, A) \tag{9.104}$$

$$send(x \triangleleft X, \circledast \triangleleft A) = x \triangleleft send(x \triangleleft X, A) \tag{9.105}$$

The receiver $receive : (\mathcal{A} \cup \{\circledast\})^* \to (\mathcal{A}^\infty \times \{@, \circledast\}^\infty)$ reports a faked datum to the sender and acknowledges correct data: $(x \in \mathcal{A})$

$$receive(\langle\rangle) = (\langle\rangle, \langle\rangle) \tag{9.106}$$

$$receive(x \triangleleft X) = (\langle x\rangle, \langle@\rangle) \,\&\, receive(X) \tag{9.107}$$

$$receive(\circledast \triangleleft X) = (\langle\rangle, \langle\circledast\rangle) \,\&\, receive(X) \tag{9.108}$$

For any oracle $N \in \mathbb{N}^\omega$, we have

$$\circlearrowleft_1 (send \,;\, transmit(N) \,;\, receive) = id_{\mathcal{A}^*}. \tag{9.109}$$

This network, cf. Figure 9.3, realizes the identity, which is independent of the oracle, and thus guarantees a correct transmission via an unreliable connection.

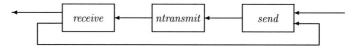

Figure 9.3: Unreliable transmission medium

In order to prove Equation (9.109), we first explicate the sequential composition $g(N) = send \ ; transmit(N) \ ; receive$:

$$
\begin{align*}
g(N)(\langle\rangle, A) &= (\langle\rangle, \langle\rangle) &\text{(9.110)} \\
g(0 \triangleleft N)(x \triangleleft X, \langle\rangle) &= (\langle x \rangle, \langle @ \rangle) &\text{(9.111)} \\
g(0 \triangleleft N)(x \triangleleft X, @ \triangleleft A) &= (\langle x \rangle, \langle @ \rangle) \,\&\, g(N)(X, A) &\text{(9.112)} \\
g(0 \triangleleft N)(x \triangleleft X, \circledast \triangleleft A) &= (\langle x \rangle, \langle @ \rangle) \,\&\, g(N)(x \triangleleft X, A) &\text{(9.113)} \\
g((n+1) \triangleleft N)(x \triangleleft X, \langle\rangle) &= (\langle\rangle, \langle \circledast \rangle) &\text{(9.114)} \\
g((n+1) \triangleleft N)(x \triangleleft X, @ \triangleleft A) &= (\langle\rangle, \langle \circledast \rangle) \,\&\, g(n \triangleleft N)(X, A) &\text{(9.115)} \\
g((n+1) \triangleleft N)(x \triangleleft X, \circledast \triangleleft A) &= (\langle\rangle, \langle \circledast \rangle) \,\&\, g(n \triangleleft N)(x \triangleleft X, A) &\text{(9.116)}
\end{align*}
$$

For the proof of Equation (9.109) we need a lemma relating the number of faked messages and the oracle.

Lemma 9.34

$$
\begin{align*}
0 \leq m < n \implies g(n \triangleleft N)(x \triangleleft X, \circledast^m) &= (\langle\rangle, \circledast^{m+1}) \\
g(n \triangleleft N)(x \triangleleft X, \circledast^n) &= (\langle x \rangle, \circledast^n \& \langle @ \rangle) \\
g(n \triangleleft N)(x \triangleleft X, \circledast^n \& \langle @ \rangle \& A) &= (\langle x \rangle, \circledast^n \& \langle @ \rangle) \,\&\, g(N)(X, A)
\end{align*}
$$

$\square$

The proofs proceed by induction on n.

We now define $f(N) = \circlearrowright_1(g(N))$, and then compute f by fixpoint iteration:

$$
f(N)(X) \;=\; \Pi_1(\bigsqcup_{i \geq 0} g(N)(X, A^i(N, X))) \tag{9.117}
$$

where

$$
\begin{align*}
A^0(N, X) &= \langle\rangle &\text{(9.118)} \\
A^{i+1}(N, X) &= \Pi_2(g(N)(X, A^i(N, X))) . &\text{(9.119)}
\end{align*}
$$

A direct recursive characterization of the feedback channel A after i iterations is:

$$A^i(N, \langle \rangle) \;=\; \langle \rangle \tag{9.120}$$

$$A^i(n \triangleleft N, x \triangleleft X) \;=\; \begin{cases} \circledast^i & \text{if } i \leq n \\ \circledast^n \& \langle @ \rangle \& A^{i-n-1}(N, X) & \text{if } i > n \end{cases} \tag{9.121}$$

The proof proceeds by induction on i.
Therewith we get

$$f(N)(\langle \rangle) \;=\; \langle \rangle \tag{9.122}$$

$$f(n \triangleleft N)(x \triangleleft X) \;=\; x \triangleleft f(N)(X) \tag{9.123}$$

which is the identity for every oracle $N \in \mathbb{N}^\omega$.   □

The specification of nondeterministic components with oracles whose instantiation is hidden from the environment with parameterized functions allows for a specification of the environment guaranteeing that the network with the nondeterministic component behaves correctly for every possible instantiation of the oracle. With a suitable choice for the set of possible oracles we can enforce nice properties such as fairness and bounded fairness.

Concluding remarks

In this chapter we showed how underspecified components can be described. We investigated the resolation of underspecification depending on the specification technique. The state transition machine model was extended so that it can describe the regular behaviour of components or components with an initialization. We presented how to obtain a maximally defined finite behaviour of components which are only specified on infinite streams. Finite behaviours with the same infinite behaviour form a partial order. We discussed how weaker and stronger defined behaviours can be derived.

Underspecification with parameters, in particular parameter streams, serve as auxiliary functions for the specification of nondeterministic components. The environment of a nondeterministic component has to cope with every instantiation of the oracle.

Chapter 10

Interface Refinement

The composition of components and the reuse of components by integrating them into varying environments is occasionally hindered by interfaces which do not fit. In particular for embedded systems, the interface is determined by the environment. With a suitable adaptation of the interfaces, components can be integrated and combined more liberally.

Interface refinement allows, for example, to change the representation of messages, to extend the data set for input and output streams by new symbols, and to change the numbers of input and output channels as well as the arrangement of the input or output streams.

We adapt much of the theory from ordinary data refinement, which changes the representation of data for programs. Interface refinement changes the representation of the input and of the output of an interactive component by relating the input and output on different levels of abstraction. Since our components are interactive, however, we must turn our attention to the monotonicity of the involved functions.

We separately deal with the refinement of the input interface and of the output interface. In particular, we investigate how interface refinement cooperates with state refinement and show prominent applications.

10.1 Introduction to Interface Refinement

The origins of interface refinement lie in the field of data refinement [Hoa72, dRE98]. An abstraction relation establishes a correspondence between the representation of data for an abstract and a concrete program. In our setting, the representation and abstraction functions relate the input and output streams of a component on an abstract and a more concrete level [Bro93b].

In contrast to data refinement, we may consider different correspondences for input and output streams even if the input interface and the output interface of a component coincide.

In this section we present interface refinement for interactive components, transfer the compositions of data refinement to interface refinement and analyse decomposition properties.

We define interface refinement as a U-simulation, cf. Figure 10.1. The vertical arrows relate histories with a different degree of abstraction.

Definition 10.1 (interface refinement)
A stream processing function $g : C_1^\infty \times \ldots \times C_p^\infty \to \mathcal{D}_1^\infty \times \ldots \times \mathcal{D}_q^\infty$ is an *interface refinement* of a stream processing function $f : \mathcal{A}_1^\infty \times \ldots \times \mathcal{A}_m^\infty \to \mathcal{B}_1^\infty \times \ldots \times \mathcal{B}_n^\infty$ through the *input representation* $i\rho : \mathcal{A}_1^\infty \times \ldots \times \mathcal{A}_m^\infty \to C_1^\infty \times \ldots \times C_p^\infty$ and the *output abstraction* $o\alpha : \mathcal{D}_1^\infty \times \ldots \times \mathcal{D}_q^\infty \to \mathcal{B}_1^\infty \times \ldots \times \mathcal{B}_n^\infty$, if

$$f \;=\; o\alpha \circ g \circ i\rho$$

holds. We call f the *refined* or *abstract* function and g the *refining* or *concrete* function, and notate

$$f \;_{i\rho}\!\rightsquigarrow_{o\alpha}\; g \,. \qquad\qquad \square$$

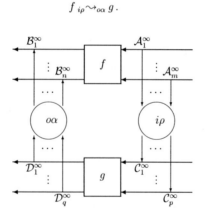

Figure 10.1: Interface refinement

Other notions of interface refinement [dRE98] can be defined analogously. Figure 10.2, which abstracts from the arity of the components and leaves out function names, sketches these notions of refinement.

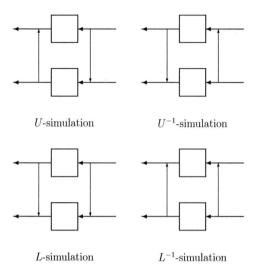

U-simulation   U^{-1}-simulation

L-simulation   L^{-1}-simulation

Figure 10.2: U-, U^{-1}-, L-, and L^{-1}-simulations

A transformation between these notions of refinement is possible if the sequential composition of representation and abstraction functions in the respective order yields the identity [dRE98, BS01b].

We continue with U-simulation using a continuous input representation and a continuous output abstraction. In that case the interface refinement is in fact a sequential decomposition of the abstract component into three components.

In the following, we investigate the composition of interface refinements and the decomposition of an interface refinement.

10.1.1   Composition

We adapt vertical and horizontal composition of data refinements [dRE98] to interface refinement. We start with the *vertical composition*, cf. Figure 10.3.

Proposition 10.2

Let f $_{i\rho_1}\leadsto_{o\alpha_1} g_1$ and g_1 $_{i\rho_2}\leadsto_{o\alpha_2} g_2$. Then g_2 is an interface refinement of f

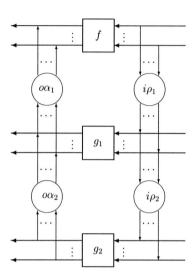

Figure 10.3: Vertical composition of interface refinements

through the input representation $i\rho_2 \circ i\rho_1$ and the output abstraction $o\alpha_1 \circ o\alpha_2$:

$$f \; {}_{i\rho_2 \circ i\rho_1} \rightsquigarrow_{o\alpha_1 \circ o\alpha_2} \; g_2$$

If the representation and abstraction functions are continuous, then the composed input representation function $i\rho_1 \; ; \; i\rho_2$ and the composed output abstraction function $o\alpha_2 \; ; \; o\alpha_1$ are also continuous. □

Figure 10.4 illustrates the *horizontal composition* of interface refinements.

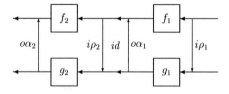

Figure 10.4: Horizontal composition of interface refinements

Proposition 10.3

Let f_1 $_{i\rho_1}\rightsquigarrow_{o\alpha_1}$ g_1 and f_2 $_{i\rho_2}\rightsquigarrow_{o\alpha_2}$ g_2. The sequential composition g_1 ; g_2 is an interface refinement of f_1 ; f_2 through the input representation $i\rho_1$ and the output abstraction $o\alpha_2$

$$f_1 \; ; f_2 \;\; _{i\rho_1}\rightsquigarrow_{o\alpha_2} \;\; g_1 \; ; g_2$$

if $i\rho_2 \circ o\alpha_1 = id$ holds.   □

This subsection showed how interface refinements can be composed.

10.1.2 Decomposition

We decompose an interface refinement into the refinement of the input interface and of the output interface. This decomposition possibility does not arise for data refinement, because data refinement does not distinguish between input and output data.

Assuming that the output abstraction and the input representation respectively are identity functions, input interface refinement and output interface refinement become specializations of interface refinement.

Definition 10.4 (input and output interface refinement)

A stream processing function $g : \mathcal{C}_1^\infty \times \ldots \times \mathcal{C}_p^\infty \rightarrow \mathcal{B}_1^\infty \times \ldots \times \mathcal{B}_n^\infty$ is called an *input interface refinement* of a stream processing function $f : \mathcal{A}_1^\infty \times \ldots \times \mathcal{A}_m^\infty \rightarrow \mathcal{B}_1^\infty \times \ldots \times \mathcal{B}_n^\infty$ through the input representation $\rho : \mathcal{A}_1^\infty \times \ldots \times \mathcal{A}_m^\infty \rightarrow \mathcal{C}_1^\infty \times \ldots \times \mathcal{C}_p^\infty$, notated $f \; _\rho\rightsquigarrow g$, if

$$f \;\; = \;\; g \circ \rho$$

holds.

A stream processing function $g : \mathcal{A}_1^\infty \times \ldots \times \mathcal{A}_m^\infty \rightarrow \mathcal{C}_1^\infty \times \ldots \times \mathcal{C}_p^\infty$ is called an *output interface refinement* of a stream processing function $f : \mathcal{A}_1^\infty \times \ldots \times \mathcal{A}_m^\infty \rightarrow \mathcal{B}_1^\infty \times \ldots \times \mathcal{B}_n^\infty$ through the output abstraction $\alpha : \mathcal{C}_1^\infty \times \ldots \times \mathcal{C}_p^\infty \rightarrow \mathcal{B}_1^\infty \times \ldots \times \mathcal{B}_n^\infty$, notated $f \rightsquigarrow_\alpha g$, if

$$f \;\; = \;\; \alpha \circ g$$

holds.   □

Any interface refinement is the composition of an input interface refinement and an output interface refinement, cf. Figure 10.5.

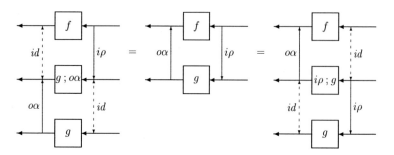

Figure 10.5: Decompositions of an interface refinement into input interface refinement and output interface refinement

Proposition 10.5

The interface refinement f $_{ip}\leadsto_{o\alpha}$ g with a continuous input representation ip and a continuous output abstraction $o\alpha$ can be decomposed into

$$f \; _{ip}\leadsto \; g \; ; o\alpha \; \leadsto_{o\alpha} \; g$$

or

$$f \; \leadsto_{o\alpha} \; ip \; ; g \; _{ip}\leadsto \; g \, . \qquad\qquad \square$$

As every interface refinement can be decomposed into an input interface refinement and an output interface refinement, we can restrict ourselves to the special cases input interface refinement and output interface refinement only. We investigate input interface refinement and output interface refinement separately. We analyse the existence of a concrete function for a given abstract function and a given transformation of the input and output streams respectively. In fact, we investigate, how a given stream processing function can be decomposed into the sequential composition of another given and an unknown stream processing function, cf. Subsection 11.1.2.

10.2 Input Interface Refinement

Input interface refinement changes the representation of the input streams of a component while leaving the output streams unchanged. In this section, we develop concepts for input interface refinement based on stream processing functions which serve as input representations. First, we characterize the stream processing functions which are suitable input representations for an input interface refinement of a given abstract component. Then we generalize the characterization towards input representations for arbitrary abstract functions.

Given an abstract stream processing function and an input representation, a concrete monotonic function exists, if the input representation is suitably defined.

Proposition 10.6

Let $f : \mathcal{A}_1^\infty \times \ldots \times \mathcal{A}_m^\infty \to \mathcal{B}_1^\infty \times \ldots \times \mathcal{B}_n^\infty$ and $\rho : \mathcal{A}_1^\infty \times \ldots \times \mathcal{A}_n^\infty \to \mathcal{C}_1^\infty \times \ldots \times \mathcal{C}_p^\infty$ be stream processing functions validating

$$\rho(X) = \rho(Y) \quad \Longrightarrow \quad f(X) = f(Y).$$

i) Then there exists a function $g : \mathcal{C}_1^\infty \times \ldots \times \mathcal{C}_p^\infty \to \mathcal{B}_1^\infty \times \ldots \times \mathcal{B}_n^\infty$ on streams such that $f = g \circ \rho$ holds. The function g is uniquely determined on the image $\rho(\mathcal{A}_1^\infty \times \ldots \times \mathcal{A}_n^\infty)$ of ρ.

ii) g is monotonic on $\rho(\mathcal{A}_1^\infty \times \ldots \times \mathcal{A}_n^\infty)$ iff ρ validates the stronger condition

$$\rho(X) \sqsubseteq \rho(Y) \quad \Longrightarrow \quad f(X) \sqsubseteq f(Y).$$

iii) g can be completed to a monotonic function, iff for every set $\rho(\mathcal{A})$ $(\mathcal{A} \subseteq \mathcal{A}_1^\infty \times \ldots \times \mathcal{A}_m^\infty)$ which has an upper bound, the set $f(\mathcal{A})$ also has an upper bound. □

Proof: i) g is uniquely defined for $\rho(X)$ by $g(\rho(X)) = f(X)$.

ii) Let $\rho(X) \sqsubseteq \rho(Y)$. Then $g(\rho(X)) \sqsubseteq g(\rho(Y))$ iff $f(X) \sqsubseteq f(Y)$.

iii) For $Z \notin \rho(\mathcal{A}_1^\infty \times \ldots \times \mathcal{A}_m^\infty)$, g can be defined as $g(Z) = \bigsqcup \{f(X) \mid X \in \mathcal{A}_1^\infty \times \ldots \times \mathcal{A}_m^\infty, \rho(X) \sqsubset Z\}$. □

The proposition guarantees that g can be defined so that it is monotonic. It does not guarantee that g is continuous. If f and ρ yield finite output streams for finite input streams, then g can be defined so that it is continuous.

From this proposition we can distil a property for an input representation which is suitable for an input interface refinement of every abstract function.

Proposition 10.7

A stream processing function $\rho : \mathcal{A}_1^\star \times \ldots \times \mathcal{A}_m^\star \to \mathcal{C}_1^\star \times \ldots \times \mathcal{C}_p^\star$ on finite streams is an input representation for input interface refinements of an arbitrary stream processing function $f : \mathcal{A}_1^\star \times \ldots \times \mathcal{A}_m^\star \to \mathcal{B}_1^\star \times \ldots \times \mathcal{B}_n^\star$ on finite streams iff if it validates

$$\rho(X) \sqsubseteq \rho(Y) \quad \Longrightarrow \quad X \sqsubseteq Y ,$$

and for every subset $\mathcal{A} \subseteq \mathcal{A}_1^\star \times \ldots \times \mathcal{A}_m^\star$

$\rho(\mathcal{A})$ has an upper bound $\quad \Longrightarrow \quad \mathcal{A}$ has an upper bound. □

This proposition gives rise to the definition of a universal input representation.

Definition 10.8 (universal input representation)
A stream processing function $\rho : \mathcal{A}_1^\star \times \ldots \times \mathcal{A}_m^\star \to \mathcal{C}_1^\star \times \ldots \times \mathcal{C}_p^\star$ is called a *universal input representation* if

$$\rho(X) \sqsubseteq \rho(Y) \quad \Longrightarrow \quad X \sqsubseteq Y$$

holds for all input streams $X, Y \in \mathcal{A}_1^\star \times \ldots \times \mathcal{A}_m^\star$, and

$$\rho(\mathcal{A}) \text{ has an upper bound} \quad \Longrightarrow \quad \mathcal{A} \text{ has an upper bound}$$

holds for every subset $\mathcal{A} \subseteq \mathcal{A}_1^\star \times \ldots \times \mathcal{A}_m^\star$. □

If $\rho : \mathcal{A}^\star \to \mathcal{C}^\star$ has a single input stream and a single output stream, then the two requirements for a universal input representation coincide.

A universal input representation uniquely determines the concrete function on its image, and it possibly offers freedom for design decisions concerning the behaviour on the other input streams, though respecting monotonicity, cf. Section 9.2.

In the following subsections, we investigate some universal input representations, their influence on the concrete function, and present applications. In each subsection, we concentrate on the construction of a state refinement for a concrete function from a state refinement of the abstract function.

10.2.1   Extension of the Set of Input Data

The stepwise design of a component sometimes requires to extend the basic type of an input channel by additional elements. The component's extended behaviour must agree with the original behaviour on input streams not containing new symbols. Characteristic cases are, for example, additional service request symbols or symbols that evoke the output of new elements of a previous extension of the set of output data, cf. Subsection 10.3.1.

The extension of the set of input data can be recorded by an input interface refinement. The corresponding universal input representation is the inclusion $incl : \mathcal{A}^\star \rightarrow (\mathcal{A} \,\dot{\cup}\, \mathcal{N})^\star$ called *input data extension*, which is the identity on $\mathcal{A}^\star$. The set $\mathcal{A}$ contains the *original* data, and the set $\mathcal{N}$ contains *new* data.

For this input representation, the input interface refinement of the abstract function $f : \mathcal{A}^\star \rightarrow \mathcal{B}^\star$ to a concrete function $g : (\mathcal{A} \,\dot{\cup}\, \mathcal{N})^\star \rightarrow \mathcal{B}^\star$ specializes to

$$f = g|_{\mathcal{A}^\star}. \tag{10.1}$$

The extension of the input data has a close relationship to resolving under-specification for erroneous input streams, cf. Section 9.3.

Proposition 10.9
Let $f : \mathcal{A}^\star \rightarrow \mathcal{B}^\star$ be a stream processing function. The input data extension $\rho : \mathcal{A}^\star \rightarrow (\mathcal{A} \,\dot{\cup}\, \mathcal{N})^\star$ is a universal input representation. The input interface refinement $g : (\mathcal{A} \dot{\cup} \mathcal{N})^\star \rightarrow \mathcal{B}^\star$ through the input representation ρ is uniquely determined on $\mathcal{A}^\star$ through $g|_{\mathcal{A}^\star} = f$. □

In fact, the domain $(\mathcal{A} \,\dot{\cup}\, \mathcal{N})^\star$ is split into a set of regular input streams $\mathcal{R} = \mathcal{A}^\star$ without new input data and the set $\mathcal{E} = (\mathcal{A}\dot{\cup}\mathcal{N})^\star \setminus \mathcal{A}^\star$ of erroneous input with at least one new datum.

Thus, a state refinement of a concrete function can be obtained from a state refinement of the abstract function by Theorem 9.9. If $M = (\mathcal{Q}, \mathcal{A}, \mathcal{B}, next, out, q_0)$ is a state refinement of the abstract function, then $M' = (\mathcal{Q}, \mathcal{A} \,\dot{\cup}\, \mathcal{N}, \mathcal{B}, next', out', q_0)$ is a state refinement of the concrete function. Hereby, $next'$ and out' agree with $next$ and out for the original input data $\mathcal{A}$. The behaviour of the machine functions for new input data can freely be chosen.

If the reaction to new input data requires new output data, then the extension of the set of input data is preceded with an extension of the set of output data, cf. Subsection 10.3.1.

The following example presents an application of the input data extension for a counter.

Example 10.10 (counter with reset)
We model a counter with reset as an instantiation of an ordinary scan component, cf. Example 5.23. Hence, we extend the set of input data $\mathcal{A}$ by a reset symbol @ and assume that $0 \in \mathcal{B}$ is a designated element. The counting operation is denoted $\oplus : \mathcal{B} \times \mathcal{A} \rightarrow \mathcal{B}$. The counter $count : \mathcal{B} \rightarrow ((\mathcal{A}\dot{\cup}\{@\})^\star \rightarrow \mathcal{B}^\star)$ is partially specified by $count = scan(\oplus)$.

In order to obtain a state refinement of an input interface refinement, the
state-based specification (10.2)–(10.3), which is directly obtained from Equations (5.73)–(5.74), is extended by an arbitrary equation (10.4) for input
streams starting with the reset symbol: $(x \in \mathcal{A})$

$$count(s)(\langle\rangle) = \langle\rangle \tag{10.2}$$
$$count(s)(x \triangleleft X) = (s \oplus x) \triangleleft count(s \oplus x)(X) \tag{10.3}$$
$$count(s)(@ \triangleleft X) = count(\mathbf{0})(X) \tag{10.4}$$

The new reset symbol does not produce any output. The successor state is
chosen as the designated element $\mathbf{0} \in \mathcal{B}$.   □

Characteristic new symbols in the set of input data are *hiatons* [Par83, BD92]
denoting "no datum", "timeout", or "corrupted datum".

Example 10.11 (receiving hiatons)
Hiatons can be inserted into streams in order to make a system io-synchronous
if each component emits at most one proper datum for each element in the
input stream. If hiatons are introduced into a system, then the set of input data and possibly the set of output data of the components must be
extended by the hiaton symbol □. We construct state refinements of two
concrete functions which interpret hiatons differently.

Let $M = (\mathcal{Q}, \mathcal{A}, \mathcal{B}, next, out, q_0)$ be a state refinement of a stream transformer $f : \mathcal{A}^\star \to \mathcal{B}^\star$. The state transition machine M can be extended to a
state refinement $M' = (\mathcal{Q}, \mathcal{A} \cup \{\square\}, \mathcal{B}, next', out', q_0)$ of the concrete function
$dropHiatons : (\mathcal{A} \cup \{\square\})^\star \to \mathcal{B}^\star$ which ignores hiatons by setting $(x \in \mathcal{A})$

$$next'(q, x) = next(q, x) \tag{10.5}$$
$$out'(q, x) = out(q, x) \tag{10.6}$$
$$next'(q, \square) = q \tag{10.7}$$
$$out'(q, \square) = \langle\rangle . \tag{10.8}$$

After an extension of the set of output data by □, cf. Subsection 10.3.1, the
state transition machine M can be extended to a state refinement $M'' =
(\mathcal{Q}, \mathcal{A} \cup \{\square\}, \mathcal{B} \cup \{\square\}, next'', out'', q_0)$ of the concrete function *passHiatons* :
$(\mathcal{A} \cup \{\square\})^\star \to (\mathcal{B} \cup \{\square\})^\star$ which lets hiatons pass by setting $(x \in \mathcal{A})$

$$next''(q, x) = next(q, x) \tag{10.9}$$
$$out''(q, x) = out(q, x) \tag{10.10}$$
$$next''(q, \square) = q \tag{10.11}$$
$$out''(q, \square) = \langle\square\rangle . \tag{10.12}$$

The systematic introduction of hiatons is well compatible with state refinements. The reaction of the system to hiatons can be determined without history information. □

The results in this subsection confirmed that the extension of the input data can easily be carried out after the derivation of a state refinement if the reaction to new data need not employ more information from the history than is provided for the original data.

10.2.2 Data Refinement on the Set of Input Data

Ordinary data refinement changes the representation of the data for noninteractive algorithms. For an interactive component, data refinement on the elements of the basic data set of an input stream allows to change the representation of the single elements which can be received on the input channel. We transfer data refinement to input streams and investigate its cooperation with state refinement.

We assume that the data refinement on the basic set of input data is conducted by an injective representation function. Then data refinement on the basic set cooperates with state refinement.

Proposition 10.12
Let $r : \mathcal{A} \to \mathcal{C}$ be an injective function. Then $map(r) : \mathcal{A}^\star \to \mathcal{C}^\star$ is a universal input representation for input interface refinement.

Let $M = (\mathcal{Q}, \mathcal{A}, \mathcal{B}, next, out, q_0)$ be a state refinement for the abstract function $f : \mathcal{A}^\star \to \mathcal{B}^\star$, and let $M' = (\mathcal{Q}, \mathcal{C}, \mathcal{B}, next', out', q_0)$ be a state transition machine with $next'(q, r(x)) = next(q, x)$ and $out'(q, r(x)) = out(q, x)$. Then M' is a state refinement of a concrete function $g : \mathcal{C}^\star \to \mathcal{B}^\star$ with $g(map(r)(X)) = f(X)$. □

The proof follows from Proposition 10.14.

The proposition not only specifies a state refinement of a concrete function for a state refinement of the given abstract function. It also uniquely determines a state refinement of the abstract function for a given state refinement of a concrete function.

Example 10.25 demonstrates data refinement on the set of input data in combination with data refinement on the set of output data.

10.2.3   IO-Synchronous Universal Input Representation

The universal input representation investigated in the previous subsection was a history independent io-synchronous stream processing function. We generalize this input representation to a state-based io-synchronous universal input representation which transforms the elements from the input stream taking their prehistory into account. As in the previous subsections, we investigate, in particular, how to construct a state refinement of a concrete function from a state refinement of the abstract function.

For the definition of the io-synchronous universal input representation, we employ the operation $\oplus : Q' \times \mathcal{A} \to Q'$, and we assume that $\otimes : Q' \times \mathcal{A} \to \mathcal{C}$ is an operation which is injective in its second argument: $q' \otimes x = q' \otimes y \implies x = y$. The stream processing function $scan''(\otimes, \oplus) : Q' \to (\mathcal{A}^\star \to \mathcal{C}^\star)$, specified by $scan''(\otimes, \oplus) = scan'(\langle \cdot \rangle \circ \otimes, \oplus)$, is io-synchronous.

Proposition 10.13
The stream processing function $scan''(\otimes, \oplus)(q) : \mathcal{A}^\star \to \mathcal{C}^\star$ is a universal input representation for every $q \in Q'$, $\oplus : Q' \times \mathcal{A} \to Q'$, if the operation $\otimes : Q' \times \mathcal{A} \to \mathcal{C}$ is injective in its second argument.   □

Proof: We show $scan''(\otimes, \oplus)(q)(X) \sqsubseteq scan''(\otimes, \oplus)(q)(Y) \implies X \sqsubseteq Y$ for all $q \in Q'$ by induction on X:

IB: $X = \langle \rangle$: $\langle \rangle \sqsubseteq Y$

IS: If $X \neq \langle \rangle$ and $Y = \langle \rangle$, the assumption $scan''(\otimes, \oplus)(q)(X) \sqsubseteq scan''(\otimes, \oplus)(q)(Y)$ is invalid.
For two non-empty input streams we have:

$$scan''(\otimes, \oplus)(q)(x \triangleleft X) \sqsubseteq scan''(\otimes, \oplus)(q)(y \triangleleft Y)$$
$$\implies (q \otimes x) \triangleleft scan''(\otimes, \oplus)(q \oplus x)(X) \sqsubseteq$$
$$(q \otimes y) \triangleleft scan''(\otimes, \oplus)(q \otimes y)(Y)$$
$$\implies q \otimes x = q \otimes y \wedge$$
$$scan''(\otimes, \oplus)(q \oplus x)(X) \sqsubseteq scan''(\otimes, \oplus)(q \oplus y)(Y)$$
$$\implies x = y \wedge scan''(\otimes, \oplus)(q \oplus x)(X) \sqsubseteq scan''(\otimes, \oplus)(q \oplus x)(Y)$$
$$\overset{IH}{\implies} x = y \wedge X \sqsubseteq Y$$
$$\implies x \triangleleft X \sqsubseteq y \triangleleft Y \qquad\qquad \square$$

Input interface refinement with the universal input representation $scan''(\otimes, \oplus)$ cooperates with state refinement.

Proposition 10.14
If $M = (Q, \mathcal{A}, \mathcal{B}, next, out, q_0)$ is a state refinement of a stream processing function $f : \mathcal{A}^\star \to \mathcal{B}^\star$, then the state transition machine $M' = (Q \times$

$\mathcal{Q}', \mathcal{C}, \mathcal{B}, next', out', (q_0, q'_0))$ with

$$next'((q, q'), q' \otimes x) = (next(q, x), q' \oplus x)$$
$$out'((q, q'), q' \otimes x) = out(q, x)$$

is a state refinement of a concrete function $g : \mathcal{C}^* \to \mathcal{B}^*$ of an input interface refinement of f through the universal input representation $scan''(\otimes, \oplus)(q'_0)$ where the operation $\otimes$ must be injective in its second argument. □

The proof proceeds by induction on the input stream. The obtained state refinement for the concrete function can often be reduced. [Dos02] presents the sequential decomposition of an ordinary scan component into two ordinary scan components.

An instantiation of an io-synchronous universal input representation is, for example, a differentiator in integer numbers with $q \oplus x = x$ and $q \otimes x = x - q$, which only records the differences of the values. The differentiator is an appropriate compression for data with high values but small differences.

In the following example, a time-stamping input representation transforms a stream of signals combined with their duration into a stream of signals combined with a time stamp for their arrival and for their end. We demonstrate how a state refinement of a concrete function can be obtained from a state refinement of an abstract function.

Example 10.15 (time dependent filter)
The reaction of a component sometimes depends on the point of time at which a signal arrives. We model a time-dependent filter which lets messages, for example alarm signals, pass if they occur in an interval in which the alarm is active.

We assume that $alarmtime : \mathbb{N} \to \mathbb{B}$ is a predicate which determines whether a point of time lies in an interval when the alarm is active. Furthermore, we assume that the incoming signals are annotated with their duration. The time dependent filter is specified by the function $f : \mathbb{N} \to ((\mathcal{A} \times \mathbb{P})^* \to \mathcal{A}^*)$ which accumulates the durations of the signals in its state in order to record the current point of time:

$$f(t)(\langle\rangle) = \langle\rangle \tag{10.13}$$
$$f(t)((x, d) \triangleleft X) = \begin{cases} f(t + d)(X) & \text{if } alarmtime(t) = \mathbf{F} \\ x \triangleleft f(t + d)(X) & \text{if } alarmtime(t) = \mathbf{T} \end{cases} \tag{10.14}$$

As the syntactic pattern of the specification coincides with a multi-step output function, the state refinement $M = (\mathbb{N}, \mathcal{A} \times \mathbb{P}, \mathcal{A}, next, out, 0)$ with

$$next(t, (x, d)) \quad = \quad t + d \tag{10.15}$$

$$out(t, (x, d)) \quad = \quad \begin{cases} \langle\rangle & \text{if } alarmtime(t) = \mathbf{F} \\ \langle x \rangle & \text{if } alarmtime(t) = \mathbf{T} \end{cases} \tag{10.16}$$

is directly obtained from the specification.

We employ the input representation $timestamp : \mathbb{N} \rightarrow ((\mathcal{A} \times \mathbb{P})^\star \rightarrow (\mathcal{A} \times \mathbb{N} \times \mathbb{P})^\star)$, with $t \oplus (x, d) = t + d$ and $t \otimes (x, d) = (x, t, t + d)$, where $t \in \mathbb{N}$, $d \in \mathbb{P}$, and $x \in \mathcal{A}$. The function $timestamp$ yields a stream in which the time boundaries are strictly ascending and the end time stamp of each element agrees with the arrival time stamp of the subsequent message.

Following Proposition 10.14, we get a state refinement of a concrete function through the input representation $timestamp$ as $M' = (\mathbb{N} \times \mathbb{N}, \mathcal{A} \times \mathbb{N} \times \mathbb{P}, \mathcal{A}, next', out', (0, 0))$ with

$$\begin{aligned} next'((t, t'), (x, t', t' + d)) \quad &= \quad next'((t, t'), t' \otimes (x, d)) \\ &= \quad (next(t, (x, d)), t' \oplus (x, d)) \\ &= \quad (t + d, t' + d) \,. \end{aligned}$$

Since the initial state is $(0, 0)$, the states which are reachable with representations of input streams are pairs of identical time values. For the output function we have:

$$\begin{aligned} out'((t, t'), (x, t', t' + d)) \quad &= \quad out'((t, t'), t' \otimes (x, d)) \\ &= \quad out(t, (x, d)) \\ &= \quad \begin{cases} \langle\rangle & \text{if } alarmtime(t) = \mathbf{F} \\ \langle x \rangle & \text{if } alarmtime(t) = \mathbf{T} \end{cases} \end{aligned}$$

The state transition and the output function do not make use of the state in the cases they are determined, because the state coincides with the second term in the input triple. Therefore, the concrete function g can be defined as a history independent component. Since the third term in the triples of the input stream was only necessary for determining the next state, we can replace the input representation $timestamp$ by an input representation ρ which only records the first and the second term of the triples.

In summary, we obtain the following concrete function $g : (\mathcal{A} \times \mathbb{N})^\star \rightarrow \mathcal{A}^\star$

$$g(\langle\rangle) \quad = \quad \langle\rangle \tag{10.17}$$

$$g((x, t) \triangleleft Y) \quad = \quad \begin{cases} g(Y) & \text{if } alarmtime(t) = \mathbf{F} \\ x \triangleleft g(Y) & \text{if } alarmtime(t) = \mathbf{T} \end{cases} \tag{10.18}$$

through the input representation $\rho : \mathbb{N} \to ((\mathcal{A} \times \mathbb{P})^\star \to (\mathcal{A} \times \mathbb{N})^\star)$:

$$\rho(t)(\langle\rangle) = \langle\rangle \tag{10.19}$$
$$\rho(t)((x,d) \triangleleft X) = (x,t) \triangleleft \rho(t+d)(X) \tag{10.20}$$

$\square$

The example showed that an input interface refinement through an io-synchronous input representation can lead to a better implementation of a component, as does the related promotion technique [PK82, Bir84] in functional programming.

IO-synchronous functions are powerful input representations. They can inject state information into the input data. With this additional information the concrete function may have a more elegant implementation than the abstract function.

10.2.4 Splitting Commands with Several Arguments

For many interactive components, the set of input data represents commands with several arguments. On the specification level it is convenient to consider a command name and the corresponding arguments as a unit. For an implementation it may be advisable to transmit the command name and the arguments on parallel channels. In this subsection we investigate an input representation which splits a command with several arguments onto several parallel channels.

Let the set $\mathcal{C} \neq \emptyset$ contain command names and the function $args : \mathcal{C} \to \{0, \ldots, n\}$ record the number of arguments of a command name where the maximal number of arguments for a command does not exceed n. The set $\mathcal{A} = \{c(d_1, \ldots, d_{args(c)}) \mid c \in \mathcal{C}, d_i \in \mathcal{D}\}$ denotes the set of commands with arguments in the set $\mathcal{D} \neq \emptyset$. For each command name $c \in \mathcal{C}$, the injective function $split(c) : \{1, \ldots, args(c)\} \to \{1, \ldots, n\}$ describes the distribution of each argument to one of n channels. For reasons of notational simplicity we assumed that all arguments have the same type. The distribution function can distribute the arguments to several channels so that each channel transmits only arguments of the same subtype.

The function $spl(c) : \mathcal{D}^{args(c)} \to \mathcal{C}^\star \times \underbrace{\mathcal{D}^\star \times \ldots \times \mathcal{D}^\star}_{n-\text{times}}$ determines how a single command with its arguments is distributed to a command name channel and n data channels:

$$spl(c)(d_1, \ldots, d_{args(c)}) = (\langle c \rangle, D_1, \ldots, D_n) \tag{10.21}$$

where

$$D_i = \begin{cases} \langle d_j \rangle & \text{if } split(c)(j) = i \text{ for a channel } j \in \{1, \dots, args(c)\} \\ \langle\rangle & \text{otherwise}. \end{cases} \quad (10.22)$$

The function spl is extended from a single command to a stream processing function $spl^\star : \mathcal{A}^\star \to \mathcal{C}^\star \times \underbrace{\mathcal{D}^\star \times \dots, \mathcal{D}^\star}_{n-\text{times}}$ processing a command stream:

$$spl^\star(\langle\rangle) = \langle\rangle \quad (10.23)$$

$$spl^\star(c(d_1, \dots, d_{args(c)}) \triangleleft X) = spl(c)(d_1, \dots, d_{args(c)}) \,\&\, spl^\star(X) \quad (10.24)$$

The following proposition describes how to obtain a concrete function of an input interface refinement of an abstract function with the input representation $spl^\star$.

Proposition 10.16

The function $spl^\star$ is a universal input representation.

If $M = (\mathcal{Q}, \mathcal{A}, \mathcal{B}, next, out, q_0)$ is a state refinement of $f : \mathcal{A}^\star \to \mathcal{B}^\star$, then the function $g : \mathcal{Q} \to (\mathcal{C}^\star \times \underbrace{\mathcal{D}^\star \times \dots, \mathcal{D}^\star}_{n-\text{times}} \to \mathcal{B}^\star)$ with

$$g(q)(Y) = \begin{cases} out(q, c(d_1, \dots, d_{args(c)})) \,\&\, g(next(q, c(d_1, \dots, d_{args(c)})))(X) \\ \qquad \text{if } Y \text{ falls into } Y = spl(c)(d_1, \dots, d_{args(c)}) \,\&\, X \\ \langle\rangle \qquad \text{otherwise} \end{cases}$$

is a concrete function of an input interface refinement of f through the input representation $spl^\star$.   □

The concrete function in the proposition does not always yield the maximally defined concrete function. If the reaction to a command can be computed even if not all its arguments are present, then there is a stronger defined concrete function.

We apply the proposition to the memory cell. It has two commands: a read command without arguments and a write command with one argument.

Example 10.17 (memory cell — revisited)

We aim at refining the state-based memory cell $cell : \mathcal{D}^{\leq 1} \to (\mathcal{C}^\star \to \mathcal{D}^\star)$ from Example 6.6 such that it receives the commands and the data on separate channels. For the input representation $spl^\star : ((\{r\} \cup w(\mathcal{D}))^\star) \to \{r, w\}^\star \times \mathcal{D}^\star$, there is no choice how to distribute the datum for the write command:

$$spl^\star(\langle\rangle) = (\langle\rangle, \langle\rangle) \quad (10.25)$$

$$spl^\star(r \triangleleft X) = (\langle r \rangle, \langle\rangle) \,\&\, spl^\star(X) \quad (10.26)$$

$$spl^\star(w(d) \triangleleft X) = (\langle w \rangle, \langle d \rangle) \,\&\, spl^\star(X) \quad (10.27)$$

With the above proposition we immediately get the concrete function *cellsep*:

$$cellsep(Q)(\langle\rangle, Y) = \langle\rangle \tag{10.28}$$
$$cellsep(Q)(\mathsf{w} \triangleleft X, \langle\rangle) = \langle\rangle \tag{10.29}$$
$$cellsep(Q)(\mathsf{r} \triangleleft X, Y) = Q \,\&\, cellsep(Q)(X, Y) \tag{10.30}$$
$$cellsep(Q)(\mathsf{w} \triangleleft X, d \triangleleft Y) = cellsep(\langle d\rangle)(X, Y) \tag{10.31}$$

If the data set $\mathcal{D}$ contains more than one element, then *cellsep* is the maximally defined concrete behaviour for the abstract function *cell* through the input representation $spl^\star$. □

Splitting a stream of pairs into a pair of streams can also be captured with the splitting input representation.

Example 10.18 (unzip)
A stream of pairs can be considered to be a stream of commands each combined with exactly one argument. That way, the stream processing function $unzip : (\mathcal{A} \times \mathcal{B})^\star \to (\mathcal{A}^\star \times \mathcal{B}^\star)$

$$unzip(\langle\rangle) = (\langle\rangle, \langle\rangle) \tag{10.32}$$
$$unzip((a, b) \triangleleft X) = (\langle a\rangle, \langle b\rangle) \,\&\, unzip(X) \tag{10.33}$$

which turns a stream of tuples into a tuple of streams, is a splitting universal input representation. By Proposition 10.16, it refines the identity function with the concrete function $zip : (\mathcal{A}^\star \times \mathcal{B}^\star) \to (\mathcal{A} \times \mathcal{B})^\star$ defined by:

$$zip(\langle\rangle, B) = \langle\rangle \tag{10.34}$$
$$zip(A, \langle\rangle) = \langle\rangle \tag{10.35}$$
$$zip(a \triangleleft A, b \triangleleft B) = (a, b) \triangleleft zip(A, B) \tag{10.36}$$

The other way round, *zip* is not a universal input representation, because there is no concrete function g such that $zip \,;\, g = id_{\mathcal{A}^\star \times \mathcal{B}^\star}$. We can only achieve a prefix of the identity

$$zip \,;\, g \;\sqsubseteq\; id_{\mathcal{A}^\star \times \mathcal{B}^\star} \tag{10.37}$$

with $g = unzip$. □

Input interface refinement with such a splitting universal input representation lays the basis for splitting input streams more liberally.

Further common universal input representations are a multiplexer, cf. Example 9.24, or the transformation of an input stream of natural numbers in a given interval to binary numbers [BS01b], or channel permutation with the cross operator.

10.2.5   Further Input Representations

In this subsection, we take a look at stream processing functions which occur in common input interface refinements, and which are not universal input representations, though.

Example 10.19 (unpack)

Packing streams is a suitable compression for input streams in which the same element often occurs several times in a row. This is the case, for example, if the basic data set is very small. Unpacking $unpack : (\mathcal{A} \times \mathbb{P})^* \to \mathcal{A}^*$ specified by

$$unpack(\langle\rangle) \;=\; \langle\rangle \tag{10.38}$$
$$unpack((x, n) \lhd X) \;=\; x^n \,\&\, unpack(X) \tag{10.39}$$

is an input representation for components whose behaviour does not depend on the formation of packages.

$unpack$ is not a universal input representation. It cannot refine the identity, because there is no monotonic function $pack$ such that $unpack \,;\, pack = id_{(\mathcal{A} \times \mathbb{P})^*}$, even not for infinite streams and even not for packed streams in which no packages with the same datum occur in a row. The reason is that a monotonic pack function retains the suffix of identical data.

For the same reason, $unpack$ is also unsuitable as an output abstraction for an output interface refinement of the identity: the only monotonic function $pack$ such that $pack \,;\, unpack = id_{\mathcal{A}^*}$ forms singleton packages in $\{(x, 1) \mid x \in \mathcal{A}\}$.
□

Further examples for common input representations are data refinements on the basic set of input data and io-synchronous functions with a non-injective representation function on the basic set of data. Eliminating input streams which do not contribute to the output of the abstract component, cf. Subsection 11.1.2, is also an input interface refinement. More liberal splitting functions can serve as input representations for particular components. For io-synchronous components, it is possible to consider a stream of tuples as input history instead of a tuple of input streams by an input interface refinement through the zip function.

Universal input representations can refine any abstract stream processing function with the same input interface, independent of its behaviour. In this section, we showed how a state refinement of a concrete function can be derived from a state refinement of the abstract function. We also touched input representations whose applicability not only depends on the domain of the abstract function, but also on its behaviour.

10.3 Output Interface Refinement

Output interface refinement changes the representation of the output streams of a component while leaving the input streams unchanged. In this section, we present concepts for output interface refinement based on output abstractions. We concentrate on history independent output abstractions which guarantee the existence of a monotonic concrete function for a given abstract function.

First we analyse the possible concrete functions which are offered by a given output abstraction and a given abstract function. Given an abstraction function $\alpha : C_1^\infty \times \ldots \times C_p^\infty \to B_1^\infty \times \ldots \times B_n^\infty$ and an abstract stream processing function $f : A_1^\infty \times \ldots \times A_m^\infty \to B_1^\infty \times \ldots \times B_n^\infty$, a concrete function $g : A_1^\infty \times \ldots \times A_m^\infty \to C_1^\infty \times \ldots \times C_p^\infty$ can be derived, if the abstraction function is suitably defined, that is its image comprises the image of the abstract function:

$$\alpha(g(A_1^\infty \times \ldots \times A_m^\infty)) = f(A_1^\infty \times \ldots \times A_m^\infty) \qquad (10.40)$$

Such an abstraction function requires a design decision: the result for an input of the concrete function can be chosen among the input stream tuples of the abstraction function which are mapped to the corresponding value in the image of the abstract function:

$$g(X_1, \ldots, X_m) \in \{(Y_1, \ldots, Y_p) \mid \alpha(Y_1, \ldots, Y_p) = f(X_1, \ldots, X_m)\} \quad (10.41)$$

A surjective abstraction function guarantees that the sets for the choices are not empty. An injective abstraction function offers no choice, because the sets contain at most one element. As a consequence, a bijective abstraction function uniquely determines the function $g = \alpha^{-1} \circ f$.

However, there is no guarantee that a monotonic concrete function exists even if the abstraction function is surjective and monotonic, as the following counter example shows.

Example 10.20 (output abstraction *lead*)
We consider the surjective and monotonic abstraction function *lead* and the identity $id : \{0,1\}^\infty \to \{0,1\}^\infty$ as the monotonic abstract function. For the concrete function $g : \{0,1\}^\infty \to \{0,1\}^\infty$, we can choose

$$g(\langle 1 \rangle) \in \{\langle 1, 1 \rangle, \langle 1, 0 \rangle\}. \qquad (10.42)$$

Either choice makes the concrete function g non-monotonic, because for the prolongations of this input the concrete function g can be chosen as follows:

$$g(\langle 1, 1 \rangle) \in \{\langle 1, 1, 1 \rangle, \langle 1, 1, 0 \rangle\} \qquad (10.43)$$
$$g(\langle 1, 0 \rangle) \in \{\langle 1, 0, 1 \rangle, \langle 1, 0, 0 \rangle\} \qquad (10.44)$$

There is no choice for the definition of g on $\langle 1 \rangle$, $\langle 1,1 \rangle$, and $\langle 1,0 \rangle$ such that g is monotonic. $\square$

If we obtain a specification of a concrete function in the form of a state transition machine, its monotonicity is guaranteed. Therefore, we concentrate on history independent output abstractions which abstract the segments of which the output stream is composed. In particular, we characterize the relationship between a state refinement of the concrete and of the abstract function.

Proposition 10.21
Let $f : \mathcal{A}^\star \to \mathcal{B}^\star$ be a stream transformer and $\alpha : \mathcal{C}^\star \to \mathcal{B}^\star$ define a history independent stream transformer, and let $M = (\mathcal{Q}, \mathcal{A}, \mathcal{B}, next, out, q_0)$ be a state refinement of f. The state transition machine $M' = (\mathcal{Q}, \mathcal{A}, \mathcal{C}, next, out', q_0)$ is a state refinement of a function $g : \mathcal{A}^\star \to \mathcal{C}^\star$ such that g is an output interface refinement of the abstract function f through the output abstraction $\alpha : \mathcal{C}^\star \to \mathcal{B}^\star$, iff $\alpha(g(\langle \rangle)) = f(\langle \rangle)$ and $\alpha(out'(q,x)) = out(q,x)$ for reachable states q. $\square$

Proof: The proof proceeds by induction on X:

    IB: $X = \langle \rangle$: $\alpha(g(\langle \rangle)) = f(\langle \rangle)$

    IS: We assume $f(X) = \alpha(g(X))$:

$$
\begin{aligned}
& \alpha(g(X \rhd x)) \\
= \; & \alpha(g(X) \& out'(next^\star(q_0)(X),x)) \\
= \; & \alpha(g(X)) \& \alpha(out'(next^\star(q_0)(X),x)) \\
\overset{IH}{=} \; & f(X) \& \alpha(out'(next^\star(q_0)(X),x)) \\
= \; & f(X) \& out(next^\star(q_0)(X),x) \\
= \; & f(X \rhd x) \qquad\qquad\qquad\qquad\qquad\qquad \square
\end{aligned}
$$

A history independent output abstraction α is only suitable for an output interface refinement of f if its image is diverse enough: $\alpha(\mathcal{C}^\star) \supseteq \{f(\langle \rangle)\} \cup \{out(next^\star(q_0)(X),x),x) \mid X \in \mathcal{A}^\star, x \in \mathcal{A}\}$.

The proposition not only characterizes a state refinement of a concrete function for a given state refinement of an abstract function. It also determines a state refinement of the abstract function for a given concrete function.

In the remainder of the section, we investigate some candidates for history independent output abstractions and show how to obtain a concrete function with an interface refinement step. In particular, for each of the selected output abstractions, we reveal the relationship between a state refinement of an abstract function and a state refinement of a concrete function.

10.3.1 Extension of the Set of Output Data

A preparatory step for further refinements may consist in adding new elements to the basic type of an output channel, for example error symbols or acknowledgements. This step can be conducted by an output interface refinement. Thereby, deleting the new elements from an output stream of the concrete component must yield the corresponding output stream of the abstract component. Such an extension of the set of output data can be modelled by an output interface refinement with an output abstraction deleting the additional symbols from the output stream.

We assume that the set $\mathcal{N}$ contains the *new* output data and that the set $\mathcal{B}$ contains the *original* output data. The function $filter(\mathcal{B}) : (\mathcal{B} \dot{\cup} \mathcal{N})^\star \to \mathcal{B}^\star$ is the monotonic output abstraction filtering the new elements from an output stream. *filter* has an obvious extension to several output streams:

$$filter(\mathcal{B}_1, \ldots, \mathcal{B}_n) = filter(\mathcal{B}_1) \parallel \ldots \parallel filter(\mathcal{B}_n) \qquad (10.45)$$

The function $g : \mathcal{A}^\star \to (\mathcal{B} \dot{\cup} \mathcal{N})^\star$ is an output interface refinement of the abstract function $f : \mathcal{A}^\star \to \mathcal{B}^\star$ through the output abstraction $filter(\mathcal{B})$, if

$$f = g \,; filter(\mathcal{B}) \qquad (10.46)$$

holds. A concrete stream processing function g may deliberately insert new output symbols into the corresponding output streams of the abstract stream processing function f. From a state refinement of an abstract function we can easily obtain a state refinement for a concrete function with Proposition 10.21.

Proposition 10.22
Let $M = (\mathcal{Q}, \mathcal{A}, \mathcal{B}, next, out, q_0)$ be a state refinement of the abstract function $f : \mathcal{A}^\star \to \mathcal{B}^\star$. Then $M' = (\mathcal{Q}, \mathcal{A}, \mathcal{B} \dot{\cup} \mathcal{N}, next, out', q_0)$ is a state refinement of a concrete function of an output interface refinement with the output abstraction $filter(\mathcal{B})$, if

$$out(q, x) = filter(\mathcal{B})(out'(q, x)) \qquad (10.47)$$

holds. □

The following example demonstrates an application of an output data extension.

Example 10.23 (memory cell with acknowledgement)
We refine the ordinary memory cell from Example 6.6 into an io-synchronous memory cell $memack : \mathcal{D}^{\leq 1} \to (\mathsf{w}(\mathcal{D}) \cup \{\mathsf{r}\})^\star \to (\mathcal{D} \cup \{@\} \times \mathcal{D} \cup \{\circledast\})^\star$ which

renders an acknowledgement symbol @ with the datum on a successful write
command and an error symbol $\circledast \notin \mathcal{D}$ on an unsuccessful read command.

The output abstraction $filter(\mathcal{D})$ deletes acknowledgements and error symbols. We adopt Equations (6.24)–(6.28) from Example 6.6 and insert an
acknowledgement (10.49) or an error symbol (10.51) in the cases in which
the ordinary memory cell does not emit output:

$$memack(D)(\langle\rangle) = \langle\rangle \tag{10.48}$$

$$memack(D)(\mathsf{w}(d) \lhd X) = (@, d) \lhd memack(\langle d\rangle)(X) \tag{10.49}$$

$$memack(\langle d\rangle)(\mathsf{r} \lhd X) = d \lhd memack(\langle d\rangle)(X) \tag{10.50}$$

$$memack(\langle\rangle)(\mathsf{r} \lhd X) = \circledast \lhd memack(\langle\rangle)(X) \tag{10.51}$$

That way, the memory cell becomes io-synchronous.   □

Another important application is the output data extension with hiatons. If
each datum from the input stream causes at most one datum on an output
stream, then a system can be made io-synchronous by inserting a hiaton into
the output stream whenever an input datum does not evoke output.

The investigations showed that the introduction of new output data cooperates well with state refinement.

10.3.2 Data Refinement on the Set of Output Data

As with input interface refinement, an ordinary data refinement on the basic
set of an output stream changes the representation of data on a stream. In
the following, we analyse the relationship of data refinement on the set of
output data to state refinement.

Proposition 10.24
Let $M = (\mathcal{Q}, \mathcal{A}, \mathcal{B}, next, out, q_0)$ be a state refinement of the abstract function
$f : \mathcal{A}^\star \to \mathcal{B}^\star$, and let $a : \mathcal{C} \to \mathcal{B}$ be a surjective function. Then the state
transition machine $M' = (\mathcal{Q}, \mathcal{A}, \mathcal{C}, next, out', q_0)$ where

$$out(q, x) = map(a)(out'(q, x)) \tag{10.52}$$

is a state refinement of a concrete function of an output interface refinement
$g : \mathcal{C}^\star \to \mathcal{B}^\star$ of f with the output abstraction $map(a)$.   □

The proof follows from Proposition 10.21.

The following example combines data refinement on the set of input data, cf.
Subsection 10.2.2, with data refinement on the set of output data.

Example 10.25 (converter)
A converter is a crucial io-synchronous component in a control system. It transforms input with hiatons into output without hiatons with the same length. The converter $conv : (\mathcal{D} \cup \{\Box\})^{\star} \to \mathcal{D}^{\star}$ receives a stream of switch control commands and "holes" and always outputs the current switch position. It is a generalization of the converter in [BS01b, p. 106].

The ith output datum is the ith input datum provided it is a switch control command. Otherwise it is the last switch control command prior to the ith datum. If no switch control command has occurred before, then a designated initial switch position $init \in \mathcal{D}$ is emitted. In fact, the converter converts an asynchronous stream of switch control commands into a synchronous command stream. Let $init \in \mathcal{D}$ be a designated element and $d, e \in \mathcal{D}$:

$$conv(\langle\rangle) = \langle\rangle \tag{10.53}$$
$$conv(\langle d\rangle) = \langle d\rangle \tag{10.54}$$
$$conv(d \triangleleft \Box \triangleleft X) = d \triangleleft conv(d \triangleleft X) \tag{10.55}$$
$$conv(d \triangleleft e \triangleleft X) = d \triangleleft conv(e \triangleleft X) \tag{10.56}$$
$$conv(\Box \triangleleft X) = init \triangleleft conv(X) \tag{10.57}$$

The memory cell with acknowledgements on successful writes $memack(\langle\rangle)$ storing elements from the set $\mathcal{D}$, cf. Example 10.23, is an interface refinement of the converter $conv$ through the injective input representation $i\rho : (\mathcal{D} \ \dot\cup \{\Box\})^{\star} \to (\mathsf{w}(\mathcal{D}) \cup \{\mathsf{r}\})^{\star}$ defined by $i\rho = map(r)$ where $r : (\mathcal{D} \ \dot\cup \{\Box\}) \to (\mathsf{w}(\mathcal{D}) \cup \{\mathsf{r}\})$ $(d \in \mathcal{D})$

$$r(d) = \mathsf{w}(d) \tag{10.58}$$
$$r(\Box) = \mathsf{r} \tag{10.59}$$

and the surjective output abstraction $o\alpha : (\mathcal{D} \cup \{@\} \times \mathcal{D} \cup \{\circledast\})^{\star} \to \mathcal{D}^{\star}$ defined by $o\rho = map(a)$ where $a : \mathcal{D} \cup \{@\} \times \mathcal{D} \cup \{\circledast\} \to \mathcal{D}$ $(d \in \mathcal{D})$

$$a(d) = d \tag{10.60}$$
$$a((@, d)) = d \tag{10.61}$$
$$a(\circledast) = init. \tag{10.62}$$

With Propositions 10.12 and 10.24, we get a state refinement $M = (\mathcal{D}^{\leq 1}, \mathcal{D} \ \dot\cup \{\Box\}, \mathcal{D}, next', out', \langle\rangle)$ of the converter from the state refinement $M' = (\mathcal{D}^{\leq 1}, \mathsf{w}(\mathcal{D}) \cup \{\mathsf{r}\}, \mathcal{D} \cup \{@\} \times \mathcal{D} \cup \{\circledast\}, next, out, \langle\rangle)$ of $memack$ with

$next(D, x) = next'(D, r(x))$ and $out(D, x) = map(a)(out'(D, r(x)))$:

$$
\begin{aligned}
next(D, \square) &= next'(D, r(\square)) = next'(D, \mathsf{r}) = D & (10.63)\\
next(D, d) &= next'(D, r(d)) = next'(D, \mathsf{w}(d)) = \langle d\rangle & (10.64)\\
out(\langle\rangle, \square) &= map(a)(out'(\langle\rangle, r(\square))) = map(a)(out'(\langle\rangle, \mathsf{r}))\\
&= map(a)(\langle \circledast \rangle) = \langle init\rangle & (10.65)\\
out(\langle q\rangle, \square) &= map(a)(out'(\langle q\rangle, r(\square))) = map(a)(out'(\langle q\rangle, \mathsf{r}))\\
&= map(a)(\langle q\rangle) = \langle q\rangle & (10.66)\\
out(D, d) &= map(a)(out'(D, r(d))) = map(a)(out'(D, \mathsf{w}(d)))\\
&= map(a)(\langle(d, @)\rangle) = \langle d\rangle & (10.67)
\end{aligned}
$$

Since the states $\langle\rangle$ and $\langle init\rangle$ are output equivalent, we identify them with a state homomorphism mapping $\langle q\rangle$ to q and $\langle\rangle$ to $init$. The function $c(init)(X) = conv(X)$ summarizes the state-based behaviour of the converter:

$$
\begin{aligned}
c(q)(\langle\rangle) &= \langle\rangle & (10.68)\\
c(q)(\square \triangleleft X) &= q \triangleleft c(q)(X) & (10.69)\\
c(q)(d \triangleleft X) &= d \triangleleft c(d)(X) & (10.70)
\end{aligned}
$$

By the way, the converter is not an interface refinement of the memory cell because the consumption of a hiaton cannot be distinguished from "switching" to the current switch position.

A converter with unit delay is described by

$$
conv_{delay}(X) = lead(init \triangleleft conv(X)). \qquad (10.71)
$$

$\square$

The example showed that data refinement on the input as well as data refinement on the output stream is supported by the proposed input representation and output abstraction functions, and that it corresponds to a refinement of the interface of a state transition machine.

In summary, data refinement on the set of output data cooperates well with state refinement.

10.3.3 Grouping Streams

In clocked systems, the components operate io-synchronously. In order to embed an arbitrary component into a clocked system, its output must be synchronized with the input. We present an output abstraction which allows to transform a stream transformer into an instantaneous component by grouping the data of the output stream.

The transformation of a stream transformer $f : \mathcal{A}^\star \to \mathcal{B}^\star$ into an io-synchronous function is based on the assumption that exactly one input element is consumed in each interval and that a group of output data, which means a (sub-)stream, is emitted in each interval. The output timed version $f_{group} :$ $\mathcal{Q} \to (\mathcal{A}^\star \to (\mathcal{B}^\star)^\star)$ groups the output of the transitions of a state refinement $M = (\mathcal{Q}, \mathcal{A}, \mathcal{B}, next, out, q_0)$ of f:

$$f_{group}(q)(\langle\rangle) \;=\; \langle\rangle \tag{10.72}$$
$$f_{group}(q)(x \triangleleft X) \;=\; out(q,x) \triangleleft f_{group}(next(q,x))(X) \tag{10.73}$$

The output timed version f_{group} is instantaneous.

The function $ungroup : (\mathcal{B}^\star)^\star \to \mathcal{B}^\star$ specified by $ungroup = red(\&)(\langle\rangle)$ is the output abstraction for the output interface refinement f_{group} of the abstract function f.

Proposition 10.26
The instantaneous function f_{group} is an output interface refinement of the function f through the output abstraction $ungroup$:

$$f \;=\; f_{group} \;;\; ungroup \qquad\qquad \square$$

The proof follows from Proposition 10.21.

The output timed version is the basis for *retimings*. Retimings can postpone output into later intervals for example by inserting empty intervals or dividing intervals. If several input messages are grouped into an interval, then the corresponding output intervals can also be combined.

In addition to the insertion of hiatons, another formalism for modelling clocked systems is to consider particular messages, called time ticks [Bro90a, Bro93a]. They are not real messages, but denote the end of an interval. In this model, infinite streams are supposed to contain an infinite number of time ticks. Consequently, only a finite number of data can be transmitted during an interval [Bro91].

Further prominent output abstractions are, for example, channel crossing, demultiplexing, or the transformation of the encoding of binary numbers in a given interval by decimal natural numbers.

Output abstractions must carefully be chosen in order not only to guarantee the existence of a concrete function, but also its monotonicity. Output interface refinement with history independent output abstractions cooperates

well with state refinements. An output interface refinement need not affect
the state transitions of state refinements. It has only an effect on the output
function.

Concluding remarks

In this chapter we transferred the notion of data refinement from programs to
interactive components. Representation and abstraction functions relate the
behaviour of components on an abstract and on a concrete level. Since each
interface refinement can be split into input interface refinement and output
interface refinement, we investigated the concepts separately.

Universal input representations guarantee the existence of an input interface
refinement. For some universally applicable input representations we showed
how a concrete function can systematically be obtained from an abstract
function. Thereby, a state refinement of the abstract function can be the key
to a state refinement of the concrete function. Also history independent output abstractions relate state refinements of the concrete and of the abstract
function.

Among other applications, the presented concepts for input and output interface refinement support the extension of the set of input and output data,
and cooperate with data refinement on the set of input and output data.

Chapter 11

Further Refinements

The preceding chapters treated state refinement, property refinement, and interface refinement. Among the notions of refinement for distributed systems are also architecture refinement and communication refinement. In this chapter we survey these two refinements on account of completeness. In the setting of stream processing, communication refinement is an application of architecture refinement.

11.1 Architecture Refinement

The architecture comprises the components of a system and the communication connections between them. The composition operators and basic routing components, such as identity, copy and cross components, sinks and sources, determine the architecture. *Architecture refinement* changes the layout of the system, that means the basic network construction around the system's components, or it decomposes a component of the system into a subsystem of several communicating components. Before discussing possibilities for the decomposition of a component, we briefly touch layout transformations.

11.1.1 Layout Transformation

Layout transformations change the network description of a system layout with the composition operators by inserting basic components like identities, or copy components, or by duplicating components, thereby preserving the behaviour of the system. Algebraic laws for the composition operators are fundamental for this kind of architecture refinement. A calculus for layout transformations for an agent language has been established in [DDM86], and later in [Şte94], see [BŞ01a, Şte00] for revised and extended versions. Figure 11.1 shows an example from [Şte94].

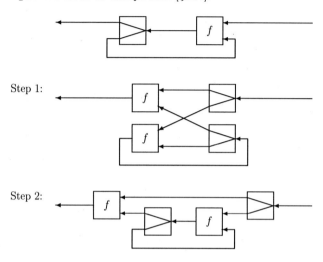

Step 1:

Step 2:

Figure 11.1: Example for layout transformation

11.1.2   Decomposition Refinement

Decomposing a component into communicating subcomponents is an architecture refinement step which goes along with a finer view of a component. A finer view of a component either reveals the state behaviour or it decomposes a component into several components. As with the composition of a network, each decomposition of a system can be obtained by a sequence of sequential, parallel, and feedback decomposition steps.

We discuss the decomposition of a component into two sequentially composed components and into components combined in parallel before concentrating on the relationship between the introduction of a feedback and state refinement.

A *sequential decomposition* is in fact an input or output interface refinement step with a continuous representation or abstraction function respectively, cf. Sections 10.2 and 10.3.

A *parallel decomposition* of a component $f : \mathcal{A}_1^\infty \times \ldots \times \mathcal{A}_m^\infty \to \mathcal{B}_1^\infty \times \ldots \times \mathcal{B}_n^\infty$ with more than one output channel ($n > 1$) can be obtained by splitting it into subcomponents ($1 \leq i \leq n$)

$$f_i = \Pi_i \circ f. \tag{11.1}$$

Each subcomponent f_i is provided with all input streams and computes the respective output stream, cf. Figure 11.2, first step:

$$f = copy_n \, ; (f_1 \parallel \ldots \parallel f_n) \tag{11.2}$$

The function $copy_n : \mathcal{A}_1^\infty \times \ldots \times \mathcal{A}_m^\infty \to (\mathcal{A}_1^\infty \times \ldots \times \mathcal{A}_m^\infty)^n$ is specified by

$$copy_n(X_1, \ldots, X_m) = \underbrace{(\underbrace{X_1, \ldots, X_m}, \ldots, \underbrace{X_1, \ldots, X_m})}_{n-\text{times}}. \tag{11.3}$$

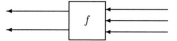

Step 1:

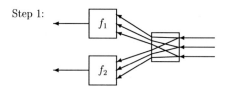

Step 2:

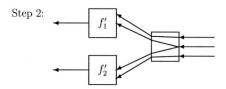

Figure 11.2: Parallel decomposition with elimination of superfluous input channels

If the behaviour of a subcomponent does not depend on all input streams, that means if a subcomponent $f_i : \mathcal{A}_1^\infty \times \ldots \times \mathcal{A}_m^\infty \to \mathcal{B}_i^\infty$ validates

$$f_i(X_1, \ldots, X_{j-1}, X_j, X_{j+1}, \ldots, X_m) = \tag{11.4}$$
$$f_i(X_1, \ldots, X_{j-1}, Y_j, X_{j+1}, \ldots, X_m)$$

for all $X_k \in \mathcal{A}_k^\infty, k \neq j, Y_j \in \mathcal{A}_j^\infty$, then the input channel j can be dropped with an interface refinement step, cf. Figure 11.2, second step.

With the *introduction of feedback*, output information can be reused as input. By feeding back the information which determines the future behaviour of a component, we establish a close relationship between states as history abstractions and feedback.

State and feedback

Each stream processing function can be implemented by a network of two history independent components with a feedback loop. Instead of operating on a local state, the component emits the current state on an additional output port and receives the current state in the next computation step on an additional input port, cf. Figure 11.3.

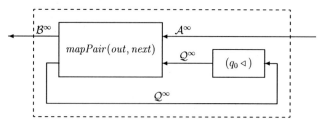

Figure 11.3: Eliminating the state by feedback

The sectioning component $(q_0 \vartriangleleft) : \mathcal{Q}^\star \to \mathcal{Q}^\star$, $q_0 \in \mathcal{Q}$, in the feedback loop first provides the initial state q_0 of a state refinement and then forwards each input unchanged:

$$(q_0 \vartriangleleft)(X) = q_0 \vartriangleleft X \tag{11.5}$$

The stream processing function $mapPair(\otimes, \oplus) : \mathcal{A}^\star \times \mathcal{Q}^\star \to \mathcal{B}^\star \times \mathcal{Q}^\star$ maps the dyadic operations $\otimes : \mathcal{Q} \times \mathcal{A} \to \mathcal{B}^\star$ and $\oplus : \mathcal{Q} \times \mathcal{A} \to \mathcal{Q}$ to the first elements of the two input streams. With the operation $\otimes$ it determines the current output. The operation $\oplus$ yields the next state to be fed back via the prefixing component:

$$mapPair(\otimes, \oplus)(\langle \rangle, Y) = (\langle \rangle, \langle \rangle) \qquad (11.6)$$

$$mapPair(\otimes, \oplus)(X, \langle \rangle) = (\langle \rangle, \langle \rangle) \qquad (11.7)$$

$$mapPair(\otimes, \oplus)(x \triangleleft X, y \triangleleft Y) = \qquad (11.8)$$
$$(y \otimes x, \langle y \oplus x \rangle) \,\&\, mapPair(\otimes, \oplus)(X, Y)$$

The following proposition describes the network with feedback which implements each stream transformer without internal states based on a state refinement.

Proposition 11.1
The behaviour of the state transition machine $M = (\mathcal{Q}, \mathcal{A}, \mathcal{B}, next, out, q_0)$ can be implemented by the network in Figure 11.3:

$$out^\star(q_0) = \circlearrowleft_1 ((id_{\mathcal{A}^\star} \| (q_0 \triangleleft)) \,;\, mapPair(out, next)) \qquad \square$$

Proof: The proof follows from the auxiliary equation

$$((id_{\mathcal{A}^\star} \| (q \triangleleft)) \,;\, mapPair(out, next))(X, states(q)(take(i)(X))) =$$
$$(out^\star(q)(take(i+1)(X)), states(q)(take(i+1)(X)))$$

where $states : \mathcal{Q} \to (\mathcal{A}^\star \to \mathcal{Q}^\star)$ defined by $states(q) = scan(next)(q)$ records the sequence of states.

The proof of the auxiliary equation proceeds by induction on the length i of the feedback stream. $\square$

The new main component $mapPair$ need not be implemented with an internal state and can be further refined.

With this principle, every system as well as every component can be implemented as a feedback network with two simple components. Only the size of the transmitted data on the feedback channel and the cost of the simple components' operations may be unsatisfactory.

This section showed that architecture refinement can be based on the algebraic laws of the composition operators, on interface refinement, and on state refinement. We presented the basic ideas. Powerful concepts for the systematic refinement still need to be explored.

11.2   Communication Refinement

The ISO/OSI layer model describes the communication between components from different levels of abstraction, called layers. The communication between the components on each layer is captured by protocols dedicated to the characteristic tasks originating in the respective view of the communication. *Communication refinement* changes the level of abstraction for the view on the communication between two components, called sender and receiver.

As the transmission requires that all data are transmitted in the correct order without getting into a deadlock, refinements of identity functions on streams play a significant role in the refinement of a communication. In this section, we present a basic concept for communication refinement between two components based on decompositions of the identity.

The following example emphasizes that a proper communication is not only concerned with a properly specified sender and a properly specified receiver. In particular, sender and receiver must fit together.

Example 11.2 (deadlock)
A sender $send : (\mathcal{A}^\star \times \{@\}^\star) \to \mathcal{A}^\star$ sends data to a receiver whenever it receives an acknowledgement from the receiver. The receiver $receive : \mathcal{A}^\star \to (\mathcal{A}^\star \times \{@\}^\star)$ acknowledges each message received:

$$send(X, A) = take(|A|)(X) \tag{11.9}$$
$$receive(Y) = (Y, @^{|Y|}) \tag{11.10}$$

The sender and receiver specified cannot communicate with each other,

$$\circlearrowleft_1 (send \,;\, receive)(X) = \langle\rangle \tag{11.11}$$

because they pursue a different mode of communication. The sender is demand driven whereas the receiver is acknowledgement driven. □

The concept for communication refinement presented in the following is adapted from [Stø96] who takes this idea into consideration for specializing asynchronous to synchronous communication. Communication refinement between two asynchronously communicating components, cf. Figure 11.4, can be based on three architecture refinement steps.

First, an identity component is inserted through a trivial layout transformation, cf. Figure 11.5.

The decisive architecture refinement step consists in the decomposition of the identity component. The identity component is decomposed into two communicating components so that the new components communicate according

Figure 11.4: Components communicating via asynchronous communication

Figure 11.5: Inserting an identity component between the communicating components

to the desired communication protocol, cf. Figure 11.6. Thus, refinements of the identity are fundamental for communication refinement.

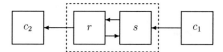

Figure 11.6: Refining the identity component according to a communication protocol

Then the subsystem structure of the overall system is changed through a hierarchical architecture refinement, cf. Figure 11.7, integrating the transmission components as communication stubs into the original communicating components. This step also makes use of a layout transformation extending the feedback to the communicating components and of the associativity of the sequential composition. Only this last step involves the particular communicating components.

Instantiations which can be found in the thesis are, for example,

- input and output interface refinements of the identity, cf. Chapter 10,
- the decomposition of the identity into a multiplexer and a demultiplexer which allow the parallel transmission of data, cf. Examples 7.6 and 9.24,
- the communication via the Alternating Bit Protocol in Example 7.5,

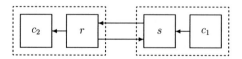

Figure 11.7: Components communicate via a protocol

- the demand driven synchronous communication with the sender from Example 11.2 and the receiver $receive : \mathcal{A}^\star \rightarrow (\mathcal{A}^\star \times \{@\}^\star)$ with an initial request

$$receive(Y) = (Y, @ \lhd @^{|Y|}) \,, \tag{11.12}$$

- the acknowledgement driven synchronous communication via a faking transmission medium, cf. Example 9.33.

We presented a basic concept for communication refinement based on architecture refinement steps. For elaborating the concepts for communication refinement, we need specifying more communications on different levels of abstraction. Then we can explore the decompositions of the identity and investigate how communication protocols can arise from the identity.

Chapter 12

Case Study: Bounded Buffer

In the previous chapters we introduced various specification techniques and refinement concepts for components in distributed systems. In this chapter, we demonstrate with a case study how these refinement concepts can be applied in order to refine the behaviour of a component from an abstract incomplete specification to an implementation as a state transition machine.

We specify a bounded buffer and carefully discriminate between regular and erroneous input histories. First we define the behaviour for regular input histories. Then we introduce a state space such that the transitions of a state transition machine reflect the behaviour of the bounded buffer for regular input histories. In the next step we modify the interface by introducing constructors for the single types of commands. At the end we resolve the underspecification for erroneous input histories such that the sequential composition of bounded buffers leads to a bounded buffer with higher capacity.

12.1 Interface

A bounded buffer stores and retrieves data upon request following a first-in first-out strategy, cf. Figure 12.1.

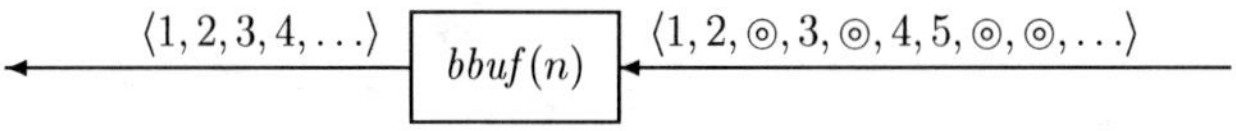

$$\langle 1, 2, 3, 4, \ldots \rangle \quad \boxed{bbuf(n)} \quad \langle 1, 2, \odot, 3, \odot, 4, 5, \odot, \odot, \ldots \rangle$$

Figure 12.1: Bounded buffer with capacity $n \geq 3$

First we decide on the interface of the bounded buffer. The input

$$\mathcal{I} \;=\; \mathcal{D} \,\dot{\cup}\, \{\circledcirc\} \tag{12.1}$$

of the bounded buffer are data $\mathcal{D} \neq \emptyset$ and requests, the output $\mathcal{O} = \mathcal{D}$ are data. Bounded buffers with different capacities are uniformly described by the parameterized stream processing function

$$bbuf : \mathbb{P} \to (\mathcal{I}^\star \to \mathcal{O}^\star)\,. \tag{12.2}$$

We consider only bounded buffers with a positive capacity because a bounded buffer with capacity 0 cannot respond properly neither to data nor to requests.

12.2   Regular Input

In this section we separate the set of all input streams into the sets of regular and erroneous input streams.

In regular input streams, the number of requests does not exceed the number of data and the number of data does not exceed the number of requests and the capacity. The set $\mathcal{R}_n$ of regular input streams for a buffer with capacity n is characterized by:

$$X \in \mathcal{R}_n \quad \Longleftrightarrow \quad ||X||_{\circledcirc} \leq ||X||_{\mathcal{D}} \leq ||X||_{\circledcirc} + n \tag{12.3}$$

An inductive characterization of regular input is:

(1) $\mathcal{D}^{\leq n} \subseteq \mathcal{R}_n$.
(2)   If $d \triangleleft D \in \mathcal{D}^{\leq n}$ and $D\&X \in \mathcal{R}_n$, then $d \triangleleft D\&\langle\circledcirc\rangle\&X \in \mathcal{R}_n$.

Hence, an inductive characterization of erroneous input is:

(1) $\circledcirc \triangleleft \mathcal{I}^\star \subseteq \mathcal{E}_n$.
(2) $\mathcal{D}^{n+1}\&\mathcal{I}^\star \in \mathcal{E}_n$.
(3)   If $d \triangleleft D \in \mathcal{D}^{\leq n}$ and $D\&X \in \mathcal{E}_n$, then $d \triangleleft D\&\langle\circledcirc\rangle\&X \in \mathcal{E}_n$.

Since the set of regular input histories is non-empty and prefix closed, we can apply the concepts from Section 9.3 in order to find a state refinement for the regular behaviour.

12.3   Specification of the Regular Behaviour

In this section, we specify the behaviour of the bounded buffer for regular input streams.

The regular behaviour is specified following the recursion scheme for regular input histories: $(D \in \mathcal{D}^{\leq n},\, d \triangleleft D' \in \mathcal{D}^{\leq n},\, D' \& X \in \mathcal{R}_n)$

$$bbuf(n)(D) \;=\; \langle\rangle \tag{12.4}$$
$$bbuf(n)(d \triangleleft D' \& \langle \odot \rangle \& X) \;=\; d \triangleleft bbuf(n)(D' \& X) \tag{12.5}$$

Data do not evoke output (12.4). For a regular request, the bounded buffer outputs the first datum which has been stored but not requested yet (12.5). $bbuf$ is underspecified concerning buffer underflow and buffer overflow.

By Theorem 2.15, the bounded buffer is monotonic and, in particular, validates the decomposition property for regular input histories $X \& Y \in \mathcal{R}_n$:

$$bbuf(n)(X \& Y) \;=\; bbuf(n)(X) \,\&\, bbuf(n)(queue_n(X) \& Y) \tag{12.6}$$

where the auxiliary function $queue_n : \mathcal{R}_n \to \mathcal{D}^{\leq n}$ on regular input streams retains the input data as far as they have not been requested yet: $(D \in \mathcal{D}^{\leq n},\, d \triangleleft D' \in \mathcal{D}^{\leq n},\, D' \& X \in \mathcal{R}_n)$

$$queue_n(D) \;=\; D \tag{12.7}$$
$$queue_n(d \triangleleft D' \& \langle \odot \rangle \& X) \;=\; queue_n(D' \& X) \tag{12.8}$$

Thus, $bbuf$ validates the assumptions for the state introduction according to Chapter 6.

12.4 State Introduction

Before resolving the underspecification, we aim at a state-based specification of the regular behaviour of the bounded buffer. The introduction of a state into the specification for the regular behaviour of the bounded buffer is based on Theorem 6.4 and Lemma 6.5.

Following Lemma 6.5, $queue_n$ is a suitable history abstraction for the regular behaviour of the bounded buffer.

The state-based bounded buffer $bbuf'(n) : \mathcal{D}^{\leq n} \to (\mathcal{I}^\star \to \mathcal{O}^\star)$ with capacity $n > 0$ is the multi-step output function of the restricted state transition machine $\widetilde{M} = (\mathcal{D}^{\leq n}, \mathcal{I}, \mathcal{O}, (\mathcal{D}^{\leq n} \setminus \{\langle\rangle\}) \times \{\odot\} \cup \mathcal{D}^{<n} \times \mathcal{D}, \widetilde{next}, \widetilde{out}, \langle\rangle)$ by Theorems 6.4 and 9.9. We obtain the single-step functions from $\widetilde{next}(D,x) = queue_n(D \triangleright x)$ and $\widetilde{out}(D,x) = bbuf(D \triangleright x)$: $(d \in \mathcal{D},\, D \in \mathcal{D}^{<n})$

$$\widetilde{next}(d \triangleleft D, \odot) \;=\; D \tag{12.9}$$
$$\widetilde{next}(D, d) \;=\; D \triangleright d \tag{12.10}$$
$$\widetilde{out}(d \triangleleft D, \odot) \;=\; \langle d \rangle \tag{12.11}$$
$$\widetilde{out}(D, d) \;=\; \langle\rangle \tag{12.12}$$

The state transition function and the output function are not specified on $(queue_n(X), x)$ where $X \in \mathcal{R}_n$ and $X \rhd x \in \mathcal{E}_n$. These are the cases when the state is empty and the input is a request (*buffer underflow*) or when the state is full and the input is a datum (*buffer overflow*).

In summary, we get the following state-based regular behaviour of the bounded buffer: $(Q' \in \mathcal{D}^{\le n}, Q \in \mathcal{D}^{<n}, d, q \in \mathcal{D})$

$$bbuf'(n)(Q')(\langle\rangle) = \langle\rangle \tag{12.13}$$
$$bbuf'(n)(q \lhd Q)(\odot \lhd X) = d \lhd bbuf'(n)(Q)(X) \tag{12.14}$$
$$bbuf'(n)(Q)(d \lhd X) = bbuf(n)(Q \rhd d)(X) \tag{12.15}$$

Resolving the underspecification for the erroneous cases, we get a fault tolerant buffer, if the state transition machine remains in one of the existing data states. Introducing new absorbing (control) states for erroneous input leads to a fault sensitive buffer, which breaks on irregular input. We base the resolution of underspecification on an additional property for the composition of bounded buffers. Our design decision will avoid the enlargement of the set of states in order to cope with erroneous input.

12.5 Interface Adaptation

Our aim is to resolve the underspecification for erroneous input streams so that bounded buffers can sequentially be composed to buffers with higher capacity. By now, bounded buffers cannot be sequentially composed because the interfaces do not match. For the sequential composition, the set of output data must be a subset of the set of input data.

In the next step, we introduce constructors for the commands through an input interface refinement. Then we extend the set of output data by data which may occur in the input, and afterwards extend the set of input data by messages which may occur in the output.

In order to equalize input and output sets of the bounded buffer while distinguishing output data from input data, we introduce constructors for inputs and outputs by data refinements on the set of input data following Subsection 10.2.2 and on the set of output data following Subsection 10.3.2. We introduce two constructors for the input:

$$\mathcal{I}' = \{deq\} \cup enq(\mathcal{D}) \tag{12.16}$$

The bijective input representation $i\rho = map(wrap)$ wraps the original request or command into a constructor with $wrap : \mathcal{I} \to \mathcal{I}'$ $(d \in \mathcal{D})$:

$$wrap(\circledcirc) \;=\; deq \qquad\qquad (12.17)$$
$$wrap(d) \;=\; enq(d) \qquad\qquad (12.18)$$

We introduce a single constructor for the output:

$$\mathcal{O}' \;=\; pass(\mathcal{D}) \qquad\qquad (12.19)$$

The bijective output abstraction $o\alpha = map(extract)$ with

$$extract(pass(d)) \;=\; d \qquad\qquad (12.20)$$

extracts the datum from the constructor.

The concrete function $bbuf''(n)$, which is still underspecified, is the result of the data refinement of the sets of input and output data $(Q' \in \mathcal{D}^{\leq n}$, $Q \in \mathcal{D}^{<n})$:

$$bbuf''(n)(Q')(\langle\rangle) \;=\; \langle\rangle \qquad\qquad (12.21)$$
$$bbuf''(n)(q \triangleleft Q)(deq \triangleleft X) \;=\; pass(q) \triangleleft bbuf''(n)(Q)(X) \qquad (12.22)$$
$$bbuf''(n)(Q)(enq(d) \triangleleft X) \;=\; bbuf''(n)(Q \triangleright d)(X) \qquad (12.23)$$

In the next output interface refinement step, the set of output data is extended by the set of input data, cf. Subsection 10.3.1:

$$\mathcal{O}'' \;=\; \mathcal{O}' \cup \mathcal{I}' \qquad\qquad (12.24)$$

We do not employ the new symbols for the reaction to regular input streams.

In the next input interface refinement step, the set of input data is extended, cf. Subsection 10.2.1, so that the sets for input and output agree:

$$\mathcal{I}'' \;=\; \mathcal{O}'' \qquad\qquad (12.25)$$

pass is a new input command for which the behaviour of the bounded buffer is also underspecified in each state.

The result of the interface adaptation is the function $bbuf''(n) : \mathcal{D}^{\leq n} \to (\mathcal{I}''^* \to \mathcal{O}''^*)$, whose output data can serve as input data. It is underspecified for buffer underflow, buffer overflow, and for pass commands in the input.

12.6   Resolution of the Underspecification

We resolve the underspecification with an additional requirement for the composition of bounded buffers. First, we specify the behaviour of the bounded buffer for the new input commands introduced in the previous section. Finally, we resolve the underspecification for buffer underflow and buffer overflow.

We can now add an additional requirement to the specification which allows to compose bounded buffers to buffers with a higher capacity ($Q_1 \in \mathcal{D}^{\leq m}$, $Q_2 \in \mathcal{D}^{\leq n}$):

$$bbuf''(m+n)(Q_2 \& Q_1) \;=\; bbuf''(m)(Q_1)\,;\,bbuf''(n)(Q_2) \quad (12.26)$$

Furthermore, we require that no new states need to be introduced for the implementation of $bbuf''$, which means that the next output can be determined from the current input and the current state. It is not guaranteed that there exists a bounded buffer which validates this additional requirement.

Resolving underspecification for the new command

We derive the behaviour of the bounded buffer for the current input $pass(d)$ in the empty and the non-empty state:

Let $|Q| < m$:

$$
\begin{aligned}
&bbuf''(n)(\langle\rangle)(pass(q) \triangleleft bbuf''(m)(Q)(X)) \\
=\;&bbuf''(n)(\langle\rangle)(bbuf''(m)(q \triangleleft Q)(deq \triangleleft X)) \\
=\;&bbuf''(m+n)(\langle\rangle \& (q \triangleleft Q))(deq \triangleleft X) \\
=\;&pass(q) \triangleleft bbuf''(m+n)(Q)(X) \\
=\;&pass(q) \triangleleft bbuf''(n)(\langle\rangle)(bbuf''(m)(Q)(X))
\end{aligned}
$$

Let $|Q_1| < m$, $|q_2 \triangleleft Q_2| \leq n$:

$$
\begin{aligned}
&bbuf''(n)(q_2 \triangleleft Q_2)(pass(q_1) \triangleleft bbuf''(m)(Q_1)(X)) \\
=\;&bbuf''(n)(q_2 \triangleleft Q_2)(bbuf''(m)(q_1 \triangleleft Q_1)(deq \triangleleft X)) \\
=\;&bbuf''(m+n)((q_2 \triangleleft Q_2) \& (q_1 \triangleleft Q_1))(deq \triangleleft X) \\
=\;&pass(q_2) \triangleleft bbuf''(m+n)((Q_2 \triangleright q_1) \& Q_1)(X) \\
=\;&pass(q_2) \triangleleft bbuf''(n)(Q_2 \triangleright q_1)(bbuf''(m)(Q_1)(X))
\end{aligned}
$$

Assuming that $bbuf''$ is in state transition machine form such that the next output depends only on the state and the current input we conclude:

$$bbuf''(n)(\langle\rangle)(pass(d) \triangleleft X) \;=\; pass(d) \triangleleft bbuf''(n)(\langle\rangle)(X) \quad (12.27)$$
$$bbuf''(n)(q \triangleleft Q)(pass(d) \triangleleft X) \;=\; pass(q) \triangleleft bbuf''(n)(Q \triangleright d)(X) \quad (12.28)$$

Each pass command in the input evokes exactly one pass command in the output. Thus a sequence of pass commands can lay open the internal state without getting into a buffer underflow or overflow.

Resolving underspecification for buffer underflow

We feed a bounded buffer of capacity $m + n$ and the state $q \triangleleft Q$, where $|q \triangleleft Q| < n$, with an input stream beginning with a dequeue command followed by enough pass commands with the same datum d such that the start state $q \triangleleft Q$, the state $next_n^\star(q \triangleleft Q)(out_m(\langle\rangle, deq))$ after processing the output of a buffer underflow, and the state $next_m(\langle\rangle, deq)$ after the buffer underflow are laid open.

$$
\begin{aligned}
&pass(q) \triangleleft bbuf''(m+n)(Q)(X) \\
=\ & bbuf''(m+n)(q \triangleleft Q)(deq \triangleleft X) \\
=\ & bbuf''(n)(q \triangleleft Q)(bbuf''(m)(\langle\rangle)(deq \triangleleft X)) \\
=\ & bbuf''(n)(q \triangleleft Q)(out_m(\langle\rangle, deq)\& bbuf''(m)(next_m(\langle\rangle, deq))(X)) \\
=\ & bbuf''(n)(q \triangleleft Q)(out_m(\langle\rangle, deq))\ \& \\
& bbuf''(n)(next_n^\star(q \triangleleft Q)(out_m(\langle\rangle, deq)))(bbuf''(m)(next_m(\langle\rangle, deq))(X)) \\
=\ & bbuf''(n)(q \triangleleft Q)(out_m(\langle\rangle, deq))\ \& \\
& bbuf''(m+n)(next_n^\star(q \triangleleft Q)(out_m(\langle\rangle, deq))\& next_m(\langle\rangle, deq))(X)
\end{aligned}
$$

We insert the input stream $X = pass^\star(d^{|Q\& next_m(\langle\rangle,deq)\& next_n^\star(q \triangleleft Q)(out_m(\langle\rangle,deq))|})$, where $pass^\star(D)$ applies the constructor $pass$ to every datum in the stream $D \in \mathcal{D}^\star$. This input stream reveals the state Q of the bounded buffer from the first line of the above derivation as well as the state $next_n^\star(q \triangleleft Q)(out_m(\langle\rangle, deq))\& next_m(\langle\rangle, deq)$ of the bounded buffer from the last line. We get:

$$
\begin{aligned}
&pass(q) \triangleleft pass^\star(Q\& d^{|next_m(\langle\rangle,deq)\& next_n^\star(q \triangleleft Q)(out_m(\langle\rangle,deq))|}) \\
=\ & bbuf''(n)(q \triangleleft Q)(out_m(\langle\rangle, deq))\ \& \\
& pass^\star(next_n^\star(q \triangleleft Q)(out_m(\langle\rangle, deq))\& next_m(\langle\rangle, deq)\& d^{|Q|})
\end{aligned}
$$

Considering the length of both streams, we conclude

$$
bbuf''(n)(q \triangleleft Q)(out_m(\langle\rangle, deq)) \quad = \quad \langle pass(q)\rangle \tag{12.29}
$$

and

$$
\begin{aligned}
Q\ \&\ d^{|next_m(\langle\rangle,deq)\& next_n^\star(q \triangleleft Q)(out_m(\langle\rangle,deq))|} \quad &= \tag{12.30} \\
next_n^\star(q \triangleleft Q)(out_m(\langle\rangle, deq))\ \&\ next_m(\langle\rangle, deq)\ \&\ d^{|Q|}\ .
\end{aligned}
$$

For $|\mathcal{D}| > 1$ we conclude $next_m(\langle\rangle, deq) = \langle\rangle$ and $next_n^\star(q \triangleleft Q)(out_m(\langle\rangle, deq)) = Q$. This implies that $out_m(\langle\rangle, deq) = \langle deq\rangle$.

Resolving underspecification for buffer overflow

In the end, we consider buffer overflow. Let $|q \triangleleft Q| = m$.

$$bbuf''(m+n)(q \triangleleft Q \triangleright e)(X)$$
$$= \quad bbuf''(m+n)(q \triangleleft Q)(enq(e) \triangleleft X)$$
$$= \quad bbuf''(n)(\langle\rangle)(bbuf''(m)(q \triangleleft Q)(enq(e) \triangleleft X))$$
$$= \quad bbuf''(n)(\langle\rangle)(out_m(q \triangleleft Q, enq(e))\&bbuf''(m)(next_m(q \triangleleft Q, enq(e)))(X))$$
$$= \quad bbuf''(n)(\langle\rangle)(out_m(q \triangleleft Q, enq(e))) \, \&$$
$$\qquad bbuf''(n)(next_n^\star(\langle\rangle)(out_m(q \triangleleft Q, enq(e))))$$
$$\qquad\qquad\qquad\qquad\qquad\qquad (bbuf''(m)(next_m(q \triangleleft Q, enq(e)))(X))$$
$$= \quad bbuf''(n)(\langle\rangle)(out_m(q \triangleleft Q, enq(e))) \, \&$$
$$\qquad bbuf''(m+n)(next_n^\star(\langle\rangle)(out_m(q \triangleleft Q, enq(e)))\&next_m(q \triangleleft Q, enq(e)))(X)$$

We insert the input stream
$$X = pass^\star(d^{|q \triangleleft Q \triangleright e \& next_m(q \triangleleft Q, enq(e)) \& next_n^\star(\langle\rangle)(out_m(q \triangleleft Q, enq(e)))|}) \text{ and get:}$$

$$pass^\star(q \triangleleft Q \triangleright e \& d^{|next_m(q \triangleleft Q, enq(e)) \& next_n^\star(\langle\rangle)(out_m(q \triangleleft Q, enq(e)))|})$$
$$= \quad bbuf''(n)(\langle\rangle)(out_m(q \triangleleft Q, enq(e))) \, \&$$
$$\qquad pass^\star(next_n^\star(\langle\rangle)(out_m(q \triangleleft Q, enq(e)))\&next_m(q \triangleleft Q, enq(e)) \& d^{|q \triangleleft Q \triangleright e|})$$

Considering the length of both streams, we conclude

$$bbuf''(n)(\langle\rangle)(out_m(q \triangleleft Q, enq(e))) \quad = \quad \langle\rangle \qquad\qquad (12.31)$$

and

$$q \triangleleft Q \triangleright e \, \& \, d^{|next_m(q \triangleleft Q, enq(e)) \& next_n^\star(\langle\rangle)(out_m(q \triangleleft Q, enq(e)))|} \quad = \qquad\qquad (12.32)$$
$$next_n^\star(\langle\rangle)(out_m(q \triangleleft Q, enq(e))) \, \& \, next_m(q \triangleleft Q, enq(e)) \, \& \, d^{|q \triangleleft Q \triangleright e|} \, .$$

For $|\mathcal{D}| > 1$ we conclude $next_n^\star(\langle\rangle)(out_m(q \triangleleft Q, enq(e))) = \langle q \rangle$ by $Q \in \mathcal{D}^{m-1}$ and $next_n^\star(Q')(X') \in \mathcal{D}^{\leq n}$ for all $Q' \in \mathcal{D}^{\leq n}$, $X' \in \mathcal{I}''^\star$, and $next_m(q \triangleleft Q, enq(e)) = Q \triangleright e$. This implies that $out_m(q \triangleleft Q, enq(e)) = \langle enq(q) \rangle$.

For $|\mathcal{D}| = 1$ the underspecifications of the bounded buffer $bbuf''$ can for example be resolved by setting

$$bbuf''(n)(Q)(enq(d) \triangleleft X) \quad = \quad bbuf''(n)(Q)(X) \qquad\qquad (12.33)$$
$$bbuf''(n)(Q)(deq \triangleleft X) \quad = \quad pass(d) \triangleleft bbuf''(n)(Q)(X) \qquad (12.34)$$

In summary, we now know that there is at most one resolution for the underspecification that allows for the composition of bounded buffers as specified above. Since it was not guaranteed that there exists such a specification at all, a proof is still required that $bbuf''(m)(Q_1) \, ; \, bbuf''(n)(Q_2) = bbuf''(m+n)(Q_2\&Q_1)$. (The proof proceeds by induction on the input stream.)

The resulting state refinement of the completely specified bounded buffer for regular inputs, pass commands, buffer overflow, and buffer underflow is:

$$(Q' \in \mathcal{D}^{\leq n}, Q \in \mathcal{D}^{<n}, q \triangleleft Q'' \in \mathcal{D}^n)$$

$$
\begin{align}
bbuf''(n)(Q')(\langle\rangle) &= \langle\rangle && (12.35) \\
bbuf''(n)(q \triangleleft Q)(deq \triangleleft X) &= pass(q) \triangleleft bbuf''(n)(Q)(X) && (12.36) \\
bbuf''(n)(Q)(enq(d) \triangleleft X) &= bbuf''(n)(Q \triangleright d)(X) && (12.37) \\
bbuf''(n)(\langle\rangle)(pass(d) \triangleleft X) &= pass(d) \triangleleft bbuf''(n)(\langle\rangle)(X) && (12.38) \\
bbuf''(n)(q \triangleleft Q)(pass(d) \triangleleft X) &= pass(q) \triangleleft bbuf''(n)(Q \triangleright d)(X) && (12.39) \\
bbuf''(n)(q \triangleleft Q'')(enq(d) \triangleleft X) &= enq(q) \triangleleft bbuf''(n)(Q'' \triangleright d)(X) && (12.40) \\
bbuf''(n)(\langle\rangle)(deq \triangleleft X) &= deq \triangleleft bbuf''(n)(\langle\rangle)(X) && (12.41)
\end{align}
$$

In [Bro90b], bounded buffers are specified without a state and are then extended such that they can be composed sequentially. The specification distinguishes between exceptional and reliable input streams. In contrast to our development, which is correct by construction, the refinement steps in [Bro90b] and also in [BS01b] are a combination of intuition and verification.

The systematic development of the bounded buffer guided by design decisions showed that the introduced concepts for refinement are indeed suitable for a stream based system design.

Chapter 13

Conclusion

At the end of the thesis, we review its goals and summarize and evaluate the obtained results. Thereby, we highlight the contribution of the thesis. We then show perspectives for future work and discuss our results in the field of related work.

13.1 Topics and Results of the Thesis

This work was driven by the idea of working out definitions and concepts for the development of components in distributed systems through refinement steps. The specification of the behaviour of a distributed system and the refinement steps were carried out in the setting of stream processing functions. The book [BS01b] summarizing the progress made in the last years in the field of stream processing served as the starting point for the thesis. The main goal was to develop concepts for a systematic introduction of states.

The major contribution of the thesis lies in the field of state refinement. We established a formal framework for transforming the input / output behaviour of asynchronously communicating components into a state-based description. For this purpose we defined a state transition machine model whose transitions are triggered by the consumption of input and which may emit output. We related state transition machines with the same behaviour by state homomorphisms. Then we provided a formal definition of state refinements guaranteeing the existence of a state refinement for every stream transformer. Our investigations on state homomorphisms and history abstractions gave rise to a constructive method how to obtain a state refinement. The design decision concentrates on the choice of the history abstraction, which establishes a relationship between input histories and states. In our approach, the states are abstractions of the input histories.

The key idea for the systematic introduction of states was the observation that the previous input history completely determines the future behaviour of a deterministic component. A history-based input / output description of a component's behaviour implicitly induces a state-based description. The naïve approach was to retain the complete previous input history as the current state. With different history abstractions, we obtain state refinements of the same stream transformer varying in the type of their state space. A history abstraction is in fact a state homomorphism from the naïve solution to a more elaborate one.

After presenting the concepts for a systematic introduction of states, we dealt with the methodology for state refinement. Here we investigated classes of stream processing functions with significant history abstractions and the corresponding state refinements.

For a large group of stream processing functions the history abstraction can be obtained from a decomposition property with a history condensing function mapping each input stream to an input stream which contains the necessary information for the future behaviour without evoking output. The state refinement can easily be read from the decomposition property. Control states can be extracted from a specification with mutually recursive stream processing functions.

At first, we only dealt with functions on finite streams with exactly one input and one output stream. Then we discussed extensions of the approach. The extensions to infinite input streams and to several output streams arise naturally. Infinite output streams for finite input streams can formally be handled with our framework. Yet such components contradict the idea of a state transition machine processing the input stream element by element and producing the corresponding output in each step. The extension of the presented approach to components with several input ports required considerations concerning the synchronization of the consumption of data from different input channels. Thereby, we found a natural generalization of our approach leading to state transition machines with several input channels which validate independence requirements for the message consumption on different input ports.

We also introduced further notions of refinement concentrating on methodological aspects and the cooperation of these refinements with state refinement.

Property refinement reduces the set of possible behaviours of a component. For a particular form of partially defined stream processing functions, called regular behaviours, we introduced partially defined state transition machines which allow for a systematic property refinement reducing the underspecification of the stream processing function. State transition machines with unspecified initial state were used to refine components whose reaction to initializing input is not fixed. In the field of property refinement, we also provided a technique for refining infinite to finite behaviours.

We separated interface refinement into steps for input interface refinement and for output interface refinement and considered their cooperation with state refinement. Important input interface refinement steps add new input symbols resulting in new transitions and possibly in new states. We also captured the effect of interface refinements with io-synchronous input representations on state refinements. Important output interface refinement steps which cooperate with state refinements transform the output for single input elements. They may extend the set of output data, transform the single elements of the set of output data, or group output streams.

The contribution of the thesis in the field of architecture refinement consists in establishing a relationship between state and feedback. The stream processing approach is based on asynchronous communication via unbounded FiFo channels. With communication refinement we can refine the general communication, for example by enforcing synchronous communication or by imposing bounds for the communication buffers.

In the foundation part, we presented a syntactic criterion for checking the monotonicity of a stream processing function which saves tedious proofs.

The thesis confirmed that stream processing is indeed a suitable semantic basis for the uniform specification of distributed systems and their development through refinement steps. The stream processing approach can bridge system views [BP01]. We showed that input / output descriptions can systematically be transformed into state-based descriptions from which action-based specifications can be generated.

13.2   Fields of Related Work

We address some fields of related work which have not been mentioned in the thesis so far. We concentrate on languages and tools which can serve for rapid prototyping and simulation starting from a stream based specification. Furthermore, we explicate the connection to process algebras and object based approaches.

13.2.1   Stream Processing Functions in Haskell

At a first glance, the functional programming language *Haskell* [Bir98] with lazy evaluation and infinite lists appears suitable for implementing specifications of stream processing functions for rapid prototyping. In contrast to the stream processing framework used in this thesis, Haskell discriminates finite lists, partial lists, and infinite lists. Furthermore a list can contain partial elements. Haskell's infinite lists without partial elements correspond to infinite streams. Finite streams correspond to partial lists because in the setting of stream processing, a component has to cope with immanent prolongations of finite streams.

In general, specifications of stream processing functions cannot straightforwardly be transferred to a Haskell program as the following example shows.

Example 13.1 (stuttering removal — revisited)
The straightforward implementation of the stuttering removal specification from Example 5.16 without state reads:

```
unstutter :: Eq(a) => [a] -> [a]
-- deletes consecutive duplicates in a finite stream
unstutter []        = []
unstutter [x]        = [x]
unstutter (x:y:xx)
          | x==y =    unstutter(y:xx)
          | x/=y = x:unstutter(y:xx)
```

The algorithm `unstutter` works properly on finite lists. However, for a nonempty partial list, the algorithm does not emit the last element of the desired partial result. Also for an infinite list whose elements are equal from a certain position on the algorithm yields the partial list which is the assumed result without the last element.   □

The reason is that stream processing functions are often defined on finite streams with an arbitrary access pattern and the behaviour on infinite streams is approximated by the results on finite streams. In Haskell, we need to approximate the result by partial lists. However, algorithms which are transferred from a state transition machine work for finite and infinite streams, since state transition machines process an input stream element by element.

13.2.2   Further Languages for Components

Among the coordination languages, the language *K2* [Aßm97] for cooperating processes is close to the stream processing approach. *K2* bases the network of components on coloured Petri nets. The communication between processes is realized via bounded buffers.

The functional programming language *Erlang* [AVWW96] was originally designed for telecommunication applications. Concurrent processes each have a mailbox and communicate via asynchronous message passing.

The method FOCUS [BS01b] describes systems as predicates over input and output streams.

13.2.3 Stream Simulator

The stream simulator [Hof01] is a graphical simulation tool for networks of stream processing functions. The *components* run as Java threads which read from and write to *channels* which themselves are implemented as Java threads visualizing the current data on the channels. A component communicates with its input and output channels' threads via methods defined in an interface. It can check whether an input channel is empty, inspect the first element of an input channel, delete the first element from an input channel, and write an element to an output channel.

A *network editor* allows to construct the network structure including the interface of components and to attach a Java method to a component which implements the behaviour. During a *simulation* of the system, the components continuously change the contents of the channels.

13.2.4 Process Algebra

The stream processing approach records the history of input / output activities of a component separately on each channel. In the process algebraic approach the behaviour of a system is specified by a process term describing the causal relationship between input, output and possibly internal activities of a component. Process algebras, such as CSP [Hoa80], CCS [Mil89], ACP [BK84], and LOTOS [BB88], model the possible behaviours of a system for example by traces of events, by labelled transition systems, or by event structures.

In our approach, events naturally evolve from a state refinement. Reading an element from an input stream constitutes an input event, and emitting an element on the output stream is an output event. Further internal events such as state updates can also be considered [DS01b, DS02, Dos03a]. That way, for example the state transition machine of the memory cell from Example 6.6

translates into a CSP process term:

$$\text{MEM}(d) \quad = \quad \text{in?}c \rightarrow$$
$$\text{if} \ \ c = \text{w}(e) \ \text{then} \ \text{MEM}(e)$$
$$\text{else} \ (\text{out!}d \rightarrow \text{MEM}(d))$$

Since process languages comprise external and internal nondeterminism, not every process term corresponds directly to a stream processing function.

13.2.5   Object Based Approaches

The stream processing approach shows a relationship to object based specification techniques [Rum96, Bro98c]. In a rigorous approach, objects, which can considered to be components, communicate only via messages which one object sends to another object. With this assumption, the behaviour of objects can be modelled by stream processing functions.

One crucial difference between objects and stream processing components is that objects have a life cycle. They can be created and destroyed whereas the structure of a system in the stream based approach presented in this thesis cannot be adapted dynamically.

13.3   Future Work

For discovering further advanced concepts for refinement, the stream processing approach needs to be applied to more case studies, in particular to real world developments. Future work will produce methodologies for state introduction into components with several input channels. Furthermore, it prepares the extension of state transition machines to nondeterminism. Future case studies will benefit from more liberal representation and abstraction relations for interface refinement.

Many systems cannot be modelled in the setting of (untimed) stream processing, because specification and refinement techniques for *time* have been left aside in the thesis. The presented stream model abstracts from time. The only time information integrated into the model is the order of transmission of the messages on each channel. Often it is advisable to separate the functional aspects and the timing aspects of a system behaviour, because the abstraction from time makes formal reasoning and transformation easier. Unfortunately the isolation of the functional behaviour from the timing aspects is not always possible.

The deterministic stream processing approach cannot model a component which merges the elements of two or more input streams to a single stream so that the component eventually lets each element of a finite input stream pass, while no further assumptions can be made about the input streams. This concerns components whose behaviour depends on the *relative timing* of the elements on different input channels, such as the interleave function [Hen82] assumed to exist as the basis for modelling operating systems with stream processing functions. [Bro97a, Bro01b, Bro03] present ideas how to integrate *discrete* as well as *continuous time* into stream based specifications.

A common technique for modelling timed systems is to enrich a specification in an untimed framework with time information so that the enriched specification can be adopted to a familiar formalism abstracting from time. For example, a timed automaton is transformed into a region graph [AD94] or a small region graph [FPS01, PF99a, PF99b] which accepts the same language, concentrating on the data part and abstracting from absolute timing. We consider timed components to interpret some of the information of an ordinary stream as time information. Thereby, the environment guarantees that time is progressing. Future work aims at investigating and relating several approaches how to integrate different degrees of timing in order to incorporate as much timing information as necessary, yet not more than necessary.

Well-known concepts for the integration of time information into streams are hiatons [Par83], time stamps [SM94, RS96], timeout messages, and end of transmission symbols for partial streams. Another common approach provides the distributed system with a global clock [Lam78] or at least with a common pulse, in analogy to timed automata where all the local clocks precede at the same rate.

In order to synchronize the consumption of data from different input streams, a weaker form of timing is sufficient recording the relative timing of messages on different input streams. Data which are characterized as *synchronization symbols* can only be processed simultaneously on all input channels of a component. An io-synchronous system is a special case of a system with synchronization symbols by considering all messages as synchronization symbols. Time ticks [Bro90a, Bro93a] are synchronization symbols which do not carry any information apart from the time information.

For putting the approach into practice, we head for improving the *tool support*. By now, most of the refinements can be carried out with the Lübeck Transformation System LTS [Mag03, DM02, DM01]. A translation of LTS output into input for the existing graphical stream simulation tool can be implemented with reasonable effort.

In long term, the specification and development methods for distributed systems will benefit from the elaboration of the relationship between the stream processing approach and other formal methods.

Bibliography

[AAA+91]   Martín Abadi, Bowen Alpern, Krzysztof R. Apt, Nissim Francez, Shmuel Katz, Leslie Lamport, and Fred B. Schneider. Preserving liveness: Comments on "safety and liveness from a methodological point of view". *Information Processing Letters*, 40(3):141–142, 1991.

[AD94]   Rajeev Alur and David L. Dill. A theory of timed automata. *Theoretical Computer Science*, 126:183–235, 1994.

[AH93]   Luca Aceto and Matthew Hennessy. Towards action-refinement in process algebras. *Information and Computation*, 103:204–269, 1993.

[AL91]   Martín Abadi and Leslie Lamport. The existence of refinement mappings. *Theoretical Computer Science*, 82:253–284, 1991.

[Arn94]   André Arnold. *Finite Transition Systems*. Prentice Hall International Series in Computer Science. Prentice-Hall, 1994.

[AS85]   Bowen Alpern and Fred B. Schneider. Defining liveness. *Information Processing Letters*, 21:181–185, 1985.

[Aßm97]   Claus Aßmann. Coordinating functional processes using Petri nets. In W. Kluge, editor, *Implementation of Functional Languages (IFL'96)*, number 1268 in Lecture Notes in Computer Science, pages 162–183. Springer, 1997.

[AVWW96]   Joe Armstrong, Robert Virding, Claes Wikström, and Mike Williams. *Concurrent Programming in Erlang*. Prentice-Hall, 1996.

[BA81]   J. Dean Brock and William B. Ackerman. Scenarios: A model of non-determinate computation. In J. Diaz and I. Ramos, editors,

Formalization of Programming Concepts, number 107 in Lecture Notes in Computer Science, pages 252–259. Springer, 1981.

[Bac90]   Ralph-Johan R. Back. Refinement calculus, part II: Parallel and reactive programs. In de Bakker et al. [dBdRR90], pages 67–93.

[Bar98]   Judith Barnard. COMX: a design methodology using communicating X-machines. *Information and Software Technology*, 40:271–280, 1998.

[BB88]   Tommaso Bolognesi and Ed Brinksma. Introduction to the ISO specification language LOTOS. *Computer Networks and ISDN Systems*, 14(1):25–59, 1988.

[BCG$^+$99] Tudor Bălănescu, Anthony J. Cowling, Horia Georgescu, Marian Gheorghe, Mike Holcombe, and Cristina Vertan. Communicating stream X-machines systems are no more than X-machines. *Journal of Universal Computer Science*, 5(9):494–507, 1999.

[BD92]   Manfred Broy and Claus Dendorfer. Modelling operating system structures by timed stream processing functions. *Journal of Functional Programming*, 2(1):1–21, January 1992.

[BD00]   Eerke Boiten and John Derrick. Liberating data refinement. In R. Backhouse and J.N. Oliveira, editors, *Mathematics of Program Construction (MPC 2000)*, number 1837 in Lecture Notes in Computer Science, pages 144–166. Springer, 2000.

[BFH$^+$98] Eike Best, Wojciech Frączak, Richard P. Hopkins, Hanna Klaudel, and Elisabeth Pelz. M-nets: An algebra of high-level Petri nets, with an application to the semantics of concurrent programming languages. *Acta Informatica*, 35:813–857, 1998.

[Bir84]   Richard S. Bird. The promotion and accumulation strategies in transformational programming. *ACM Transactions on Programming Languages and Systems*, 6(4):487–504, October 1984.

[Bir98]   Richard S. Bird. *Introduction to Functional Programming Using Haskell*. Prentice Hall International Series in Computer Science. Prentice-Hall, 1998.

[BJP91]   Micah Beck, Richard Johnson, and Keshav Pingali. From control flow to dataflow. *Journal of Parallel and Distributed Computing*, 12:118–129, 1991.

[BK84] Jan A. Bergstra and Jan W. Klop. Process algebra for synchronous communication. *Information and Control*, 60:109–137, 1984.

[BL99] Eike Best and Alexander Lavrov. Generalised composition operations for high-level Petri nets. *Fundamenta Informaticae*, 40(2–3):125–163, 1999.

[BN94] I. Babcsányi and A. Nagy. Mealy-automata in which the output-equivalence is a congruence. *Acta Cybernetica*, 11(3):121–126, 1994.

[BO01] Manfred Broy and Ernst-Rüdiger Olderog. Trace-oriented models of concurrency. In J.A. Bergstra, A. Ponse, and S.A. Smolka, editors, *Handbook of Process Algebra*, pages 101–195. Elsevier Science Publishers, 2001.

[BP00a] Max Breitling and Jan Philipps. Diagrams for dataflow. In J. Grabowski and S. Heymer, editors, *Formale Beschreibungstechniken für verteilte Systeme*, pages 101–110. Shaker Verlag, 2000.

[BP00b] Max Breitling and Jan Philipps. Step by step to histories. In T. Rus, editor, *Algebraic Methodology and Software Technology (AMAST'2000)*, number 1816 in Lecture Notes in Computer Science, pages 11–25. Springer, 2000.

[BP01] Max Breitling and Jan Philipps. Bridging system views. In S. Autexier and H. Mantel, editors, *Proceedings of the Verification Workshop (VERIFY'01) (in connection with International Joint Conference on Automated Reasoning, IJCAR'01)*, Technical Report TR DII 08/01. Università degli studi di Siena, 2001.

[Bro83] Jarvis Dean Brock. *A Formal Model of Non-determinate Dataflow Computation*. PhD thesis, Department of Electrical Engineering and Computer Science, Massachusetts Institute of Technology, August 1983.

[Bro86] Manfred Broy. A theory for nondeterminism, parallelism, communication, and concurrency. *Theoretical Computer Science*, 45:1–61, 1986.

[Bro88]   Manfred Broy. Nondeterministic data flow programs: How to
            avoid the merge anomaly. *Science of Computer Programming*,
            10:65–85, 1988.

[Bro90a]   Manfred Broy. Functional specification of time sensitive commu-
            nicating systems. In de Bakker et al. [dBdRR90], pages 153–179.

[Bro90b]   Manfred Broy. On bounded buffers: Modularity, robustness,
            and reliability in reactive systems. In W.H.J. Feijen, A.J.M. van
            Gasteren, D. Gries, and J. Misra, editors, *Beauty is our Busi-
            ness – A Birthday Salute to Edsger W. Dijkstra*, Monographs in
            Computer Science, pages 83–93. Springer, 1990.

[Bro91]   Manfred Broy. Formal modelling of networks of time sensitive
            interactive systems. In *Proceedings of the International Confer-
            ence "Computer Networks '91", Wroclaw, Poland*, pages 19–33.
            Wydawnictwo Politechniki Wroclawskicj, June 1991.

[Bro93a]   Manfred Broy. Functional specification of time sensitive commu-
            nicating systems. *ACM Transactions on Software Engineering
            and Methodology*, 2(1):1–46, January 1993.

[Bro93b]   Manfred Broy. (Inter-)action refinement: The easy way. In
            M. Broy, editor, *Program Design Calculi*, volume 118 of *NATO
            ASI Series F*, pages 121–158. Springer, 1993.

[Bro97a]   Manfred Broy. Refinement of time. In M. Bertram and T. Rus,
            editors, *Transformation-Based Reactive System Development
            (ARTS'97)*, number 1231 in Lecture Notes in Computer Science,
            pages 44–63. Springer, 1997.

[Bro97b]   Manfred Broy. The specification of system components by state
            transition diagrams. Technical Report TUM-I9729, Technische
            Universität München, May 1997.

[Bro98a]   Manfred Broy. Compositional refinement of interactive systems
            modelled by relations. In W.-P. de Roever, H. Langmaack, and
            A. Pnueli, editors, *Compositionality: The Significant Difference*,
            number 1536 in Lecture Notes in Computer Science, pages 130–
            149. Springer, 1998.

[Bro98b]   Manfred Broy. A functional rephrasing of the assum-
            tion/commitment specification style. *Formal Methods in System
            Design*, 13(1):87–119, May 1998.

[Bro98c] Manfred Broy. A uniform mathematical concept of a component – Appendix to M. Broy et al.: What characterizes a (software) component? *Software — Concepts & Tools*, 19:57–59, 1998.

[Bro00] Manfred Broy. From states to histories. In D. Bert, C. Choppy, and P. Mosses, editors, *Recent Trends in Algebraic Development Techniques (WADT'99)*, number 1827 in Lecture Notes in Computer Science, pages 22–36. Springer, 2000.

[Bro01a] Manfred Broy. From states to histories: Relating state and history views onto systems. In T. Hoare, M. Broy, and R. Steinbrüggen, editors, *Engineering Theories of Software Construction*, volume 180 of *Series III: Computer and System Sciences*, pages 149–186. IOS Press, 2001.

[Bro01b] Manfred Broy. Refinement of time. *Theoretical Computer Science*, 253(1):3–26, 2001.

[Bro03] Manfred Broy. Abstractions from time. In A. McIver and C. Morgan, editors, *Programming Methodology*, Monographs in Computer Science, chapter 5, pages 95–107. Springer, 2003.

[BŞ01a] Manfred Broy and Gheorghe Ştefănescu. The algebra of stream processing functions. *Theoretical Computer Science*, 258:99–129, 2001.

[BS01b] Manfred Broy and Ketil Stølen. *Specification and Development of Interactive Systems: Focus on Streams, Interfaces, and Refinement*. Monographs in Computer Science. Springer, 2001.

[Bur75] William H. Burge. Stream processing functions. *IBM Journal of Research and Development*, 19(1):12–25, January 1975.

[BvW90] Ralph-Johan R. Back and Joakim von Wright. Refinement calculus, part I: Sequential nondeterministic programs. In de Bakker et al. [dBdRR90], pages 42–66.

[BvW98] Ralph-Johan Back and Joakim von Wright. *Refinement Calculus: a Systematic Introduction*. Graduate Texts in Computer Science. Springer, 1998.

[BWW96] Judith Barnard, J. Whitworth, and M. Woodward. Communicating X-machines. *Information and Software Technology*, 38:401–407, 1996.

[Cie79]   Joachim Ciesinger. A bibliography of error-handling. *ACM SIG-PLAN Notices*, 14(1):16–26, 1979.

[dBdRR90]   Jacobus W. de Bakker, Willem-Paul de Roever, and Grzegorz Rozenberg, editors. *Stepwise Refinement of Distributed Systems: Models, Formalisms, Correctness (REX-Workshop)*. Number 430 in Lecture Notes in Computer Science. Springer, 1990.

[DDM86]   Carlos Delgado Kloos, Walter Dosch, and Bernhard Möller. On the algebraic specification of a language for describing communicating agents. In F. Radermacher and M. Wirsing, editors, *9. Jahrestagung der Österreichischen Gesellschaft für Informatik*, MIP-8604, pages 53–73. Universität Passau, Institut für Informatik und Mathematik, April 1986.

[Den85]   Jack B. Dennis. Data flow computation. In M. Broy, editor, *Control Flow and Data Flow: Concepts of Distributed Programming*, volume 14 of *NATO ASI Series F*, pages 345–398. Springer, 1985.

[Den96]   Claus Dendorfer. *Methodik funktionaler Systementwicklung*. Herbert Utz Verlag Wissenschaft, München, 1996.

[Dij75]   Edsger W. Dijkstra. Guarded commands, nondeterminacy and formal derivation of programs. *Communications of the ACM*, 18(8):453–457, August 1975.

[Dij76]   Edsger W. Dijkstra. *A Discipline of Programming*. Prentice-Hall Series in Automatic Computation. Prentice-Hall, 1976.

[DM01]   Walter Dosch and Sönke Magnussen. Computer aided fusion for algebraic program derivation. *Nordic Journal of Computing*, 8(3):279–297, 2001.

[DM02]   Walter Dosch and Sönke Magnussen. The Lübeck Transformation System: A transformation system for equational higher order algebraic specifications. In M. Cerioli and G. Reggio, editors, *Recent Trends in Algebraic Development Techniques (WADT 2001)*, number 2267 in Lecture Notes in Computer Science, pages 85–108. Springer, 2002.

[Dos00a]   Walter Dosch. Designing a single pulser. In N. Debnath, editor, *Proceedings of the 13th International Conference on Computer Applications in Industry and Engineering (CAINE-2000)*, pages

244–249. International Society for Computers and their Applications (ISCA), 2000.

[Dos00b] Walter Dosch. Refining infinite stream behaviours by bound functions. In M. Guizani and X. Shen, editors, *Proceedings of the International Conference on Parallel and Distributed Computing and Systems (PDCS 2000)*, volume II, pages 689–694. IASTED, Acta Press, November 2000.

[Dos01a] Walter Dosch. Curtailing infinite stream behaviours. In H.R. Arabnia, editor, *The 2001 International Conference on Parallel and Distributed Processing Techniques and Applications (PDPTA'01)*, volume II, pages 946–952. CSREA Press, 2001.

[Dos01b] Walter Dosch. Order-theoretic refinement of infinite stream behaviours. In E. Sha, editor, *14th International Conference on Parallel and Distributed Computing Systems (PDCS-2001)*, pages 68–74. International Society for Computers and their Applications (ISCA), 2001.

[Dos02] Walter Dosch. Scanning streams. In N. Debnath, D. Riesco, and G. Montejano, editors, *Proceedings of the International Conference on Computer Science, Software Engineering, Information Technology, e-Business, and Applications (CSITeA'02)*, pages 11–17. International Association for Computer and Information Science (ACIS), 2002.

[Dos03a] Walter Dosch. Deriving different views of an interactive double-ended bounded queue. In N. Debnath, editor, *Proceedings of the 18th International Conference on Computers and their Applications (CATA-2003)*, pages 397–403. International Society for Computers and their Applications (ISCA), 2003.

[Dos03b] Walter Dosch. Stream-based modelling of an interactive priority queue. In M.H. Hamza, editor, *Proceedings of the International Conference on Modelling and Simulation*, pages 559–565. Acta Press, 2003.

[DP90] B. A. Davey and H. A. Priestley. *Introduction to Lattices and Order*. Cambridge University Press, 1990.

[dRE98] Willem-Paul de Roever and Kai Engelhardt. *Data Refinement: Model-Oriented Proof Methods and their Comparison*. Number 47 in Cambridge Tracts in Theoretical Computer Science. Cambridge University Press, 1998.

[DS99]   Walter Dosch and Annette Stümpel. Transformational design of a merge agent for ordered streams. In R.Y. Lee, editor, *1999 AoM/IAoM Proceedings of Computer Science: 17th Annual International Conference, Number 1, Part A*, volume 17, pages 171–176. Association of Management and the International Association of Management (AoM/IAoM), Maximilian Press Publishers, 1999.

[DS00]   Walter Dosch and Annette Stümpel. Merging ordered streams. In S.Y. Shin, editor, *Proceedings of the 15th International Conference on Computers and their Applications (CATA-2000)*, pages 377–382. International Society for Computers and their Applications (ISCA), 2000.

[DS01a]   Walter Dosch and Annette Stümpel. From stream transformers to state transition machines with input and output. In N. Ishii, T. Mizuno, and R. Lee, editors, *Proceedings of the 2nd International Conference on Software Engineering, Artificial Intelligence, Networking and Parallel/Distributed Computing (SNPD'01)*, pages 231–238. International Association for Computer and Information Science (ACIS), 2001.

[DS01b]   Walter Dosch and Annette Stümpel. Views of an unbounded buffer. In J. Hammer and R.Y. Lee, editors, *Proceedings of the 1st International Conference on Computer and Information Science (ICIS'01)*, pages 108–115. International Association for Computer and Information Science (ACIS), 2001.

[DS02]   Walter Dosch and Annette Stümpel. Refining a bounded buffer. In N. Callaos, M. Margenstern, and B. Sanchez, editors, *Proceedings of the 6th World Multiconference on Systemics, Cybernetics and Informatics (SCI 2002)*, volume XI, Computer Science II, pages 176–183. International Institute of Informatics and Systemics (IIIS), 2002.

[DW90]   Frank Dederichs and Rainer Weber. Safety and liveness from a methodological point of view. *Information Processing Letters*, 36:25–30, 1990.

[DW91]   Frank Dederichs and Rainer Weber. Reply to the comments by M. Abadi et al. *Information Processing Letters*, 40(3):143, 1991.

[DW98]   Walter Dosch and Bernd Wiedemann. Calculating list homomor-
          phisms for parallel bracket matching. In H.R. Arabnia, editor,
          *Proceedings of the International Conference on Parallel and Dis-
          tributed Processing Techniques and Applications (PDPTA '98)*,
          volume IV, pages 1710–1717. CSREA Press, 1998.

[DW00]   Walter Dosch and Bernd Wiedemann. List homomorphisms with
          accumulation and indexing. In G. Michaelson, P.W. Trinder, and
          H.-W. Loidl, editors, *Trends in Functional Programming*, pages
          134–142. Intellect, 2000.

[EHS97]   Jan Ellsberger, Dieter Hogrefe, and Amardeo Sarma. *SDL –
          Formal Object-oriented Language for Communicating Systems*.
          Prentice-Hall, 1997.

[Eil74]   Samuel Eilenberg. *Automata, Languages, and Machines*, vol-
          ume A. Academic Press, 1974.

[Eme90]   E. Allen Emerson. Temporal and modal logic. In van Leeuwen
          [vL90], chapter 16, pages 995–1072.

[FCO90]   John T. Feo, David C. Cann, and Rodney R. Oldehoeft. A
          report on the Sisal language project. *Journal of Parallel and
          Distributed Computing*, 10:349–366, 1990.

[Fea87]   Martin S. Feather. A survey and classification of some pro-
          gram transformation approaches and techniques. In L.G.L.T.
          Meertens, editor, *Program Specification and Transformation*,
          pages 165–195. IFIP, Elsevier Science Publishers, 1987.

[FPS01]   Hacène Fouchal, Eric Petitjean, and Sébastien Salva. An user-
          oriented testing of real time systems. In *Electronic Resource
          of IEEE/IEE Real-Time Embedded Systems Workshop (Satel-
          lite of the IEEE Real-Time Systems Symposium) London, 3rd
          December 2001*, 2001. http://rtds.cs.tamu.edu/.

[Fra86]   Nissim Francez. *Fairness*. Texts and Monographs in Computer
          Science. Springer, 1986.

[Gor80]   Michael J.C. Gordon. The denotational semantics of sequential
          machines. *Information Processing Letters*, 10(1):1–3, 1980.

[Gue81]   Irène Guessarian. *Algebraic Semantics*. Number 99 in Lecture
          Notes in Computer Science. Springer, 1981.

[Gum93]   H. Peter Gumm. Another glance at the Alpern–Schneider char-
           acterization of safety and liveness in concurrent executions. *In-
           formation Processing Letters*, 47:291–294, 1993.

[Gun93]   Carl A. Gunter. *Semantics of Programming Languages – Struc-
           tures and Techniques*. MIT Press, 1993.

[Har87]   David Harel. Statecharts: A visual formalism for complex sys-
           tems. *Science of Computer Programming*, 8:231–274, 1987.

[Hen82]   Peter Henderson. Purely functional operating systems. In
           J. Darlington, P. Henderson, and D.A. Turner, editors, *Func-
           tional Programming and its Applications: an Advanced Course*,
           pages 177–192. Cambridge University Press, 1982.

[Hoa72]   C.A.R. Hoare. Proof of correctness of data representations. *Acta
           Informatica*, 1:271–281, 1972.

[Hoa80]   C.A.R. Hoare. *Communicating Sequential Processes*. Interna-
           tional Series in Computer Science. Prentice-Hall, 1980.

[Hof01]   Björn Hoffmeister. Entwicklung eines Simulators zur Darstel-
           lung der Kommunikation in verteilten Systemen. Semesterarbeit
           am Institut für Softwaretechnik und Programmiersprachen der
           Medizinischen Universität zu Lübeck, 2001.

[HRS84]   Kevin Hammond and V.J. Rayward-Smyth. A survey on syn-
           tactic error recovery and repair. *Computer Languages*, 9:51–67,
           1984.

[HU79]   John E. Hopcroft and Jeffrey D. Ullman. *Introduction to Au-
           tomata Theory, Languages, and Computation*. Addison-Wesley,
           1979.

[Huh97]   Michaela Huhn. *On the Hierarchical Design of Distributed Sys-
           tems*. PhD thesis, Fachbereich IV (Mathematik, Informatik,
           Naturwissenschaften), Universität Hildesheim, Germany, 1997.

[Kah74]   Gilles Kahn. The semantics of a simple language for parallel
           programming. In J.L. Rosenfeld, editor, *Information Processing
           74*, pages 471–475. North–Holland, 1974.

[Kel76]   Robert M. Keller. Formal verification of parallel programs. *Com-
           munications of the ACM*, 19(7):371–384, July 1976.

[Kel78]   Robert M. Keller. Denotational models for parallel programs
            with indeterminate operators. In E.J. Neuhold, editor, *Formal
            Description of Programming Concepts, Proceedings of the IFIP
            Working Conference 1977*, pages 337–366. North–Holland, 1978.

[Kin94]   Ekkart Kindler. Safety and liveness properties: A survey. In
            Bulletin of the EATCS, volume 53, pages 268–272. EATCS, June
            1994.

[Kle52]   Stephen Cole Kleene. *Introduction to Metamathematics*.
            Wolters-Noordhoff Publishing and North-Holland Publishing
            Company, 1952.

[KM77]   Gilles Kahn and David B. MacQueen. Coroutines and networks
            of parallel processes. In B. Gilchrist, editor, *Information Pro-
            cessing 77*, pages 993–998. North–Holland, 1977.

[Lam78]   Leslie Lamport. Time, clocks, and the ordering of events in a
            distributed system. *Communications of the ACM*, 21(7):558–
            565, July 1978.

[Lan65]   Peter J. Landin. A correspondence between ALGOL 60 and
            Church's lambda-notation: Part I. *Communications of the
            ACM*, 8(2):89–101, February 1965.

[LL90]   Leslie Lamport and Nancy Lynch. Distributed computing: Mod-
            els and methods. In van Leeuwen [vL90], chapter 18, pages
            1157–1199.

[LS89]   Nancy A. Lynch and Eugene W. Stark. A proof of the Kahn
            principle for input/output automata. *Information and Compu-
            tation*, 82:81–92, 1989.

[LT89]   Nancy Lynch and Mark R. Tuttle. An introduction to in-
            put/output automata. *Centrum voor Wiskunde en Informatica,
            Amsterdam, CWI-Quarterly*, 2(3):219–246, September 1989.

[LY96]   David Lee and Mihalis Yannakakis. Principles and methods of
            testing finite state machines – a survey. *Proceedings of the IEEE*,
            84(8):1090–1123, August 1996.

[Mag03]   Sönke Johannes Magnussen. *Mechanizing the Transformation
            of Higher-Order Algebraic Specifications for the Development of
            Software Systems*. Logos Verlag, 2003.

[Mil89]   Robin Milner. *Communication and Concurrency*. International Series in Computer Science. Prentice-Hall, 1989.

[Möl94]   Bernhard Möller. Ideal streams. In E.-R. Olderog, editor, *Programming Concepts, Methods and Calculi*, IFIP Transactions A-56, pages 39–58. North–Holland, 1994.

[Möl98]   Bernhard Möller. Ideal stream algebra. In Möller and Tucker [MT98], pages 69–116.

[Möl99]   Bernhard Möller. Algebraic structures for program calculation. In M. Broy and R. Steinbrüggen, editors, *Calculational System Design*, volume 173 of *NATO ASI Series F*, pages 25–97. IOS Press, 1999.

[MT88]   Karl Meinke and J.V. Tucker. The scope and limits of synchronous concurrent computation. In F.H. Vogt, editor, *Concurrency '88*, number 335 in Lecture Notes in Computer Science, pages 163–180. Springer, 1988.

[MT92]   Karl Meinke and J.V. Tucker. Universal algebra. In S. Abramsky, D.M. Gabbay, and T.S.E. Maibaum, editors, *Background: Mathematical Structures*, volume 1 of *Handbook of Logic in Computer Science*, pages 189–411. Oxford University Press, 1992.

[MT98]   Bernhard Möller and John V. Tucker, editors. *Prospects for Hardware Foundations*. Number 1546 in Lecture Notes in Computer Science. Springer, 1998.

[Nai97]   Kshirasagar Naik. Efficient computation of unique input/output sequences in finite-state machines. *IEEE/ACM Transactions on Networking*, 5(4):585–599, August 1997.

[NV95]   Rocco De Nicola and Frits Vaandrager. Three logics for branching bisimulation. *Journal of the ACM*, 42(2):458–487, March 1995.

[Par83]   D. Park. The "fairness" problem and nondeterministic computing networks. In *Foundations of Computer Science IV*, pages 133–161. Mathematisch Centrum, Amsterdam, 1983.

[Par90]   Helmut A. Partsch. *Specification and Transformation of Programs: a Formal Approach to Software Development*. Springer, 1990.

[PF99a]   Eric Petitjean and Hacène Fouchal. From timed automata to testable untimed automata. In H. Frigeri, W.A. Halang, and S.H. Son, editors, *Real Time Programming 1999 (WRTP'99)*. Pergamom, 1999.

[PF99b]   Eric Petitjean and Hacène Fouchal. A realistic architecture for timed testing. In *Fifth IEEE International Conference on Engineering of Complex Computer Systems*, pages 109–118. IEEE Computer Society Press, 1999.

[PK82]   Robert Paige and Shaye Koenig. Finite differencing of computable expressions. *ACM Transactions on Programming Languages and Systems*, 4(3):402–454, 1982.

[Plo81]   Gordon D. Plotkin. A structural approach to operational semantics. Technical Report DAIMI FN-19, Computer Science Department, Aarhus University, September 1981.

[PR98]   Michael Prasser and Peter Rittgen. Bemerkungen zu Peter Wegners Ausführungen über Interaktion und Berechenbarkeit. *Informatik Spektrum*, 21(3):141–146, 1998.

[PS97]   Jan Philipps and Peter Scholz. Compositional specification of embedded systems with statecharts. In *Theory and Practice of Software Development (TAPSOFT'97)*, number 1214 in Lecture Notes in Computer Science. Springer, 1997.

[PTH98]   M.J. Poole, John V. Tucker, and A.V. Holden. Hierarchies of spatially extended systems and synchronous concurrent algorithms. In Möller and Tucker [MT98], pages 184–235.

[Rei98]   Wolfgang Reisig. *Elements of Distributed Algorithms: Modeling and Analysis with Petri Nets*. Springer, 1998.

[RJB98]   James Rumbaugh, Ivar Jacobson, and Grady Booch. *The Unified Modeling Language Reference Manual*. Addison-Wesley Object Technology Series. Addison-Wesley, 1998.

[RS96]   Michel Raynal and Mukesh Singhal. Logical time: Capturing causality in distributed systems. *Computer: Innovative Technology for Computer Professionals, IEEE Computer Society*, 29(2):49–56, February 1996.

[Rum96]   Bernhard Rumpe. *Formale Methodik des Entwurfs verteilter objektorientierter Systeme.* Herbert Utz Verlag Wissenschaft, München, 1996.

[Rut01]   Jan J.M.M. Rutten. Elements of stream calculus (an extensive exercise in coinduction). *Electronic Notes in Theoretical Computer Science: MFPS 2001: Seventeenth Conference on the Mathematical Foundations of Programming Semantics*, 45, 2001.

[Sch93]   Fred B. Schneider. What good are models and what models are good? In S. Mullender, editor, *Distributed Systems*, chapter 2, pages 17–26. Addison-Wesley, 1993.

[Sch98a] Peter Scholz. Design of reactive systems and their distributed implementation with statecharts. PhD Thesis, TUM-I9821, Technische Universität München, August 1998.

[Sch98b] Peter Scholz. A refinement calculus for statecharts. In E. Astesiano, editor, *First International Conference on Fundamental Approaches to Software Engineering (FASE'98)*, number 1382 in Lecture Notes in Computer Science, pages 285–301. Springer, 1998.

[SDW96]   Ketil Stølen, Frank Dederichs, and Rainer Weber. Specification and refinement of networks of asynchronously communicating agents using the assumption/commitment paradigm. *Formal Aspects of Computing*, 8(2):127–161, 1996.

[SHLG94] Viggo Stoltenberg-Hansen, Ingrid Lindström, and Edward R. Griffor. *Mathematical Theory of Domains.* Number 22 in Cambridge Tracts in Theoretical Computer Science. Cambridge University Press, 1994.

[SL90]   A. Udaya Shankar and Simon S. Lam. Construction of network protocols by stepwise refinement. In de Bakker et al. [dBdRR90], pages 669–695.

[SM94]   Reinhard Schwarz and Friedemann Mattern. Detecting causal relationships in distributed computations: In search of the holy grail. *Distributed Computing*, 7:149–174, 1994.

[SNR96]   Peter Scholz, Dieter Nazareth, and Franz Regensburger. Ministatecharts: A compositional way to model parallel systems. In K. Yetongnon and S. Hariri, editors, *9th International*

              *Conference on Parallel and Distributed Computing Systems
              (PDCS'96)*. International Society for Computers and their Ap-
              plications (ISCA), 1996.

[SNW93]   Vladimiro Sassone, Mogens Nielsen, and Glynn Winskel. A clas-
              sification of models for concurrency. In E. Best, editor, *Concur-
              rency Theory (CONCUR'93)*, number 715 in Lecture Notes in
              Computer Science, pages 82–96. Springer, 1993.

[Şte94]   Gheorghe Ştefănescu. Algebra of flownomials. Technical Report
              TUM-I9437, Technische Universität München, October 1994.

[Ste97]   Robert Stephens. A survey of stream processing. *Acta Infor-
              matica*, 34(7):491–541, 1997.

[Şte00]   Gheorghe Ştefănescu. *Network Algebra*. Discrete Mathematics
              and Theoretical Computer Science. Springer, 2000.

[Stø96]   Ketil Stølen. Refinement principles supporting the transition
              from asynchronous to synchronous communication. *Science of
              Computer Programming*, 26:255–272, 1996.

[Tho90]   Wolfgang Thomas. Automata on infinite objects. In van
              Leeuwen [vL90], chapter 4, pages 133–191.

[Tho97]   Wolfgang Thomas. Languages, automata, and logic. In
              G. Rozenberg and A. Salomaa, editors, *Handbook of Formal
              Languages*, volume 3: Beyond Words, pages 389–455. Springer,
              1997.

[Tre96a]   Jan Tretmans. Test generation with inputs, outputs, and
              quiescence. In T. Margaria and B. Steffen, editors, *Tools
              and Algorithms for the Construction and Analysis of Systems
              (TACAS'96)*, number 1055 in Lecture Notes in Computer Sci-
              ence, pages 127–146. Springer, 1996.

[Tre96b]   Jan Tretmans. Test generation with inputs, outputs and repet-
              itive quiescence. *Software — Concepts & Tools*, 17:103–120,
              1996.

[vL90]   Jan van Leeuwen, editor. *Formal Models and Semantics*, vol-
              ume B of *Handbook of Theoretical Computer Science*. Elsevier
              Science Publishers, 1990.

[WA85]   William W. Wadge and Edward A. Ashcroft. *Lucid, the Dataflow Programming Language*. Number 22 in APIC Studies in Data Processing. Academic Press, 1985.

[Wec92]   Wolfgang Wechler. *Universal Algebra for Computer Scientists*. Number 25 in EATCS Monographs on Theoretical Computer Science. Springer, 1992.

[Weg97]   Peter Wegner. Why interaction is more powerful than algorithms. *Communications of the ACM*, 40(5):80–91, May 1997.

[Weg98]   Peter Wegner. Interactive foundations of computing. *Theoretical Computer Science*, 192:315–351, 1998.

[WN95]   Glynn Winskel and Mogens Nielsen. Models for concurrency. In S. Abramsky, D.M. Gabbay, and T.S.E. Maibaum, editors, *Semantic Modelling*, volume 4 of *Handbook of Logic in Computer Science*, pages 1–148. Oxford University Press, 1995.

Appendix A

Basic Order Theory

Definition A.1 (partial order)

A pair $(M, \leq)$ is called a *partially ordered set*, or *partial order* for short, iff $\leq$ is a reflexive, transitive, and antisymmetric relation on the non-empty set M. □

The symbol of the order relation can be omitted if it is clear from the context.

Definition A.2 (directed set)

A subset N of a partially ordered set M is called a *directed set*, iff it is not empty and every two elements in N have an upper bound in N. □

Equivalently, N is a directed set, iff every finite subset of N has an upper bound in N.

Definition A.3 (complete partial order, consistently complete)

A partial order $(M, \leq)$ is called a (pointed) *complete partial order*, or *cpo* for short, if every directed subset has a least upper bound in M and if the least element of M, denoted $\perp$, exists.

A cpo $(M, \leq)$ is called *consistently complete* if every subset of M which has an upper bound in M also has a least upper bound in M. □

The results involving cpo's in Section 2.1 can be transferred to cpo's without a least element, called pre-cpo's. Nevertheless the cpo's we use indeed have a $\perp$-element.

Definition A.4 (downward closed set, downward closure)

A subset N of a partially ordered set M is called *downward closed*, iff for each $b \in N$ and $a \in M$ we have: $a \leq b \implies a \in N$.

$\downarrow N = \{x \in M \mid \exists y \in N : x \leq y\}$ denotes the *downward closure* of a subset N of a partially ordered set M. □

217

Definition A.5 (chain)
A *chain* K is a totally ordered subset of a partial order $(M, \leq)$, that is any two elements of a chain are comparable: $x \leq y$ or $y \leq x$ for all $x, y \in K$. □

We summarize some properties of functions on partial orders which play an important role in stream processing.

Definition A.6 (strict function)
A function $f : C \to D$ between two partial orders $(C, \leq_C)$ and $(D, \leq_D)$ with least elements $\bot_C$ and $\bot_D$, respectively, is called *strict*, iff it preserves the bottom element:

$$f(\bot_C) \ = \ \bot_D \qquad\qquad\qquad □$$

Definition A.7 (monotonic function)
A function $f : C \to D$ between two partial orders $(C, \leq_C)$ and $(D, \leq_D)$ is called *monotonic*, iff for all $x, y \in C$:

$$x \leq_C y \quad\Longrightarrow\quad f(x) \leq_D f(y) \qquad\qquad □$$

Definition A.8 (continuous function)
A monotonic function $f : C \to D$ between two cpo's $(C, \leq_C)$ and $(D, \leq_D)$ is called *continuous*, iff for each directed set $E \subseteq C$:

$$f\left(\bigsqcup\nolimits_C E\right) \ = \ \bigsqcup\nolimits_D f(E) \qquad\qquad □$$

Lemma A.9
The composition $g \circ f : A \to C$ of strict / monotonic / continuous functions $f : A \to B$ and $g : B \to C$ yields again a strict / monotonic / continuous function. □

Lemma A.10
Let B be a cpo. The function space $[A \to B]$ ordered by

$$f \leq g \quad\Longleftrightarrow\quad \forall x \in A : f(x) \leq g(x)$$

forms a cpo. Also, the subsets of strict, monotonic and continuous functions each form a cpo. □